The New Greek Cuisine

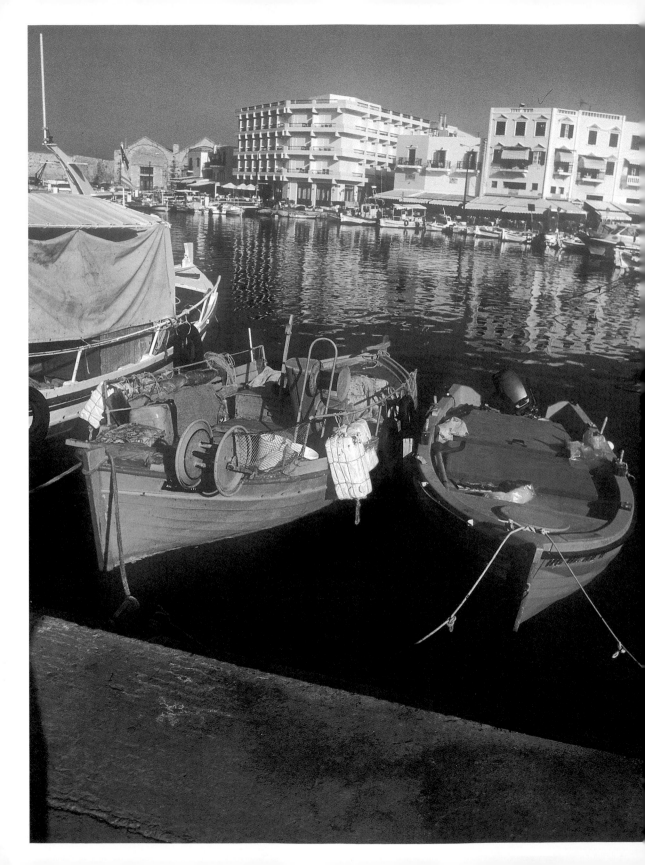

The New Greek Cuisine

Jim Botsacos
with Judith Choate

Photographs by Shimon and Tammar
Photographs of Greece by Laurie Smith
and Jim Botsacos

BROADWAY BOOKS   NEW YORK

PRINTED IN THE UNITED STATES OF AMERICA

BROADWAY BOOKS and its logo, a letter B bisected on the diagonal, are trademarks of Random House, Inc.

Visit our Web site at www.broadwaybooks.com

Book design by Nancy Campana/Campana Design
Instructional illustrations by Laura Hartman Maestro

Library of Congress Cataloging-in-Publication Data
Botsacos, Jim.
    The new Greek cuisine / Jim Botsacos with Judith Choate.
       p. cm.
    1. Cookery, Greek.   2. Molyvos (Restaurant) I. Title.
  TX723.5.G8B6856 2006
  641.59495—dc22   2005058207

ISBN-13: 978-0-7679-1875-6
ISBN-10: 0-7679-1875-4

10 9 8 7 6 5 4 3 2 1

FIRST EDITION

To Maria, my wife, my guardian angel, my soul mate

To Sofia, my daughter, my #1 taster, and my savior

To James (Dimitri), my son, my inspiration, my future

You are my breath, my love, my life

Contents

Foreword

For my family, and me, the creation of Molyvos represents not only a lifetime of work but also the joy of growing up in a small fishing village on the island of Lesvos in Greece. The memory of the village of Molyvos is kept alive through my children, who have spent many summers in what is always remembered as a very magical, almost mythical setting: how everyone knows each other and greets one another when passing through the streets; the early morning song of the local farmers walking the streets with their donkeys, selling the day's produce; the happiness the whole village feels when a fishing boat comes back with a successful catch; the aroma from the village bakery, known as the *fourno*; delicious smells that permeate the streets on your way home.

What I remember most about Molyvos is the daily afternoon family meal, where every bite turns into a celebration of life. These vivid memories are the foundation of my family. They are the bond and the joy that we share together. We are proud to bring a little of Molyvos to New York, where these precious moments from the past will live on through you. Welcome to Molyvos, join us at our table, and share in our celebration.

John Livanos, owner
Molyvos Restaurant, New York City

Preface

One sunny Saturday in February 1997, I surrendered the kitchen of my Athens apartment to Jim Botsacos. This may not sound like a big deal, especially to those people who today take cooking classes and make wonderful, delicious messes in my kitchen in Kea. But back then I wouldn't let anybody, and certainly not a professional chef, prepare food in my tiny kitchen. After all, I had seen chefs in action and knew there wouldn't be nearly enough room in my confined space for a professional to work, especially one who wasn't familiar with the whereabouts of my pots and pans, knives and spoons, spices and ingredients. But Jim was surprisingly and delightfully different from the other chefs I'd met and worked with since the publication of my first book in the U.S.; he was neat, clean, and well organized. Even in this kitchen he had never seen before, he effortlessly prepared a wonderfully authentic home-cooked Greek meal. The buffet lunch Jim served that day was a tour-de-force celebration to wrap up our various trips around Greece. It came after countless meals in tavernas and restaurants on the mainland and the islands and a fair amount of time spent in the kitchens of friends and relatives, including my mother's. I don't remember every one of the delicious dishes he cooked for our friends that day, but I do recall wonderful fresh sardines marinated with lemon, olive oil, and garlic; leek pie wrapped in homemade phyllo; and a salad with paximadia, the savory barley rusks that later became so popular at Molyvos.

Before this trip, Jim had experienced only Greek food in resorts where the recipes had been altered to appeal to American clientele. At home, he had only had not-so-great family moussaka. Traveling with me in Greece as a native rather than as a tourist gave him an entirely different point of view. He was extremely wary of native Greek recipes, which, as an experienced chef, he considered far too simple to work in a restaurant. But as soon as he had firsthand experience of our cooking, he instinctively understood how the secret of Greek cuisine lay in simplicity and its clever combinations of fresh and flavorful ingredients and how the elaborate reductions, special sauces, and other tricks used in classical cooking had no place. Jim, being talented and open-minded, immediately understood this fundamental difference, which we Greeks take for granted.

Today almost every restaurant claims to base its dishes on fresh seasonal produce, but back then, when we started to try out recipes in the semifinished kitchen of Molyvos amid the steady hammering of construction work, we realized that our biggest challenge would be locating these necessary basic, fresh ingredients. Some, like Greek oregano, thyme-scented honey, and creamy sheep's milk feta, could be imported. But for others, like horta—the ubiquitous mixed greens used for salads, stews, or as filling for pies—Jim had to find growers who agreed to cultivate them. And whenever possible, he found quality local ingredients—excellent fish from the Atlantic, for example, or locally grown lamb that helped him re-create in the restaurant the taste of the home-cooked dishes he had loved during our trip. Miraculously, Jim even found a way to add flavor to almost flavorless American winter tomatoes!

Grasping the spirit of authentic foods, Jim worked both methodically and intuitively to come up with inspired dishes that, while respecting classical recipes, were brilliant new creations. This volume is abundant with exciting dishes that successfully bring together tradition and innovation. Jim's recipes are in essence, not just in name, *The New Greek Cuisine*.

Aglaia Kremezi

Acknowledgments

My dad, James T. Botsacos Sr., for allowing me to reclaim the house I grew up in and giving us full range for four full days of photo shoots. Also for his love, support, and his love of good food.

My mother, Laraine Botsacos, for her love and constant interest in my career.

I would like to thank the following people for their hard work, determination, and contributions to this book:

John Livanos, for sharing his dream that has become Molyvos.

Nick Livanos, for giving me the opportunity to be a part of a family enterprise.

Chef John Piliouras, whose passion for food helps keep Molyvos evolving. His quick wit, offering a joke at just the right time, and his precise measuring and conversion of recipes keeps us all on our toes.

Sous-chefs Carlos Carreto and Adolfo Vega (great recipe testers), for their loyalty and dedication over the years.

The present Molyvos management team: Zeki Yesilyurt, Kamal Kouri, and Angelo Spilios, for their attention to detail and dedication to the restaurant.

The entire Molyvos staff, for their hard work and commitment.

Judith Choate, whose talent and skill have made this book possible.

Aglaia Kremezi, for sharing her love of Greek food and culture, for her correct translation of Greek terminology, and for being a great friend.

Jennifer Josephy, my editor, for believing in my instincts and for being a great sounding board to help me make this book a reality. Kristen Green for keeping us organized and on deadline.

Jee Levin, John Fontana, and Maria Carella, for their teamwork, keen eye, and design talent.

Shimon and Tammar Photography, for feeling my vision and making it come alive in the photographs.

Alain Sailhac, my mentor, for taking me under his wing and teaching me the fundamentals of classic French cooking.

Michael Lomonaco, for giving me my first sous-chef position.

INTRODUCTION

I come from a family of cooks, some truly great home cooks and a few seasoned professionals. In the early 1900s, both of my dad's grandfathers were in the restaurant business. One, Peter Migliucci, began his culinary career cooking in the window (apparently the kitchen was too tiny to accommodate him) of a small restaurant on West 47th Street.

The other, my namesake, James Botsacos, and his brother, Nicholas, owned a liquor store and restaurant in the area of New York City now known as Washington Heights. In fact, my great-grandfather was known far and wide as "The Lobster King." My cousin Jimmy Mariolis was a chef on international cruise ships who eventually passed his pots, pans, and knives on to me. So, you see, the love of good food and fine dining is part of my DNA. I always knew that I was also going to be a cook too, but I never, for a moment, even with a name like Botsacos, thought that I would be the chef of a three-star Greek restaurant.

My dad's mother is Italian American, and his father is of Greek descent. My grandparents usually dined on Italian cuisine, but my grandmother has always been counted on to make spanakopita and Greek cookies for every family event. My mom is also of Italian descent, so her cooking style reflects that heritage, although it is highlighted by many traditional American standards. Through the years, the origins of our home-style cooking were homogenized, but the flavors of the Mediterranean reigned in the kitchen. Cooking was and continues to be a way of life for my family. My earliest memories are of cooking with my dad on Sundays, first in the borough of the Bronx in New York City and then in suburban Westchester County in a house right on Long Island Sound. Even at three, I had chores to do that helped complete the meal. Every Sunday, no matter the time of year or weather, we had a really big family meal that was engineered by my dad. It wasn't just our immediate family—Mom, Dad, my two sisters, and I—but also grandparents, aunts, uncles, cousins, and extended family and friends. The meal always began with a huge antipasto—cheeses and olives, Italian and Greek, salads, cured meats and fish, grilled vegetables, and lots of crusty breads—that we feasted on as we cooked and ended with fruit and more cheese with many courses in between. ✸ My dad is an automobile dealer by trade, but in his heart he is a fisherman and a gardener, so we have always had plenty of fresh, right-from-the-earth-and-sea ingredients. I remember one summer, when my dad got a lobster permit, we ate lobster every weekend. We did a lot of grilling, and Dad even hooked up an electric fryer outside so he could make fried eggplant in the summertime. There was always pasta, sauced with whatever inspired Dad on a given weekend. My mom

also contributed her "gravy," the traditional Sunday Italian red sauce for pasta that is filled with meats and meatballs. ✸ As I matured, so did Dad. He got more inventive as he ventured away from his Greek and Italian heritage and began experimenting with all kinds of flavors and ingredients. Seeing what he might put on the table was always interesting, and by my teenage years, with Dad introducing the family to all kinds of new ingredients, I got interested in food as a career. I went from making One-Eyed Suzies (a slice of white bread with a hole cut in the center to hold an egg, with the whole thing fried in butter) in my home-ec class to taking courses at Johnson & Wales (the renowned culinary school in Rhode Island) while still in high school. I thought that taking these extra courses would ensure my acceptance at Johnson & Wales, since I had no other professional cooking experience to add to my résumé. And, it did! ✸ When I was seventeen, I got my first "real" job at a local Italian restaurant. I was interviewed for the job while the owner and I picked over green beans, and, as I answered all of his questions in the affirmative, by the next day I had a full-time cook's job. Since the menu was pretty basic Italian that I was an old hand at helping my dad and mom prepare, I had no question that I was up to the job. I was more than ready to use the kitchen equipment I had inherited from my family, so I happily put myself in charge. After a couple of weeks, I had regular customers coming in asking for my dishes, especially my mussels in white wine and garlic. I was full of myself until I began having a hard time collecting the $25 a day I was supposed to be paid. Johnson & Wales seemed the better choice! ❂ I loved culinary school. I couldn't get enough! I loved learning the history of food and the science of food. I particularly loved learning to prepare the classic recipes of the French repertoire. Sauces were my forte, perhaps because I had absorbed my dad's enthusiasm for creating new sauces every Sunday. Little did I know that I would one day be making a standard béchamel sauce every day. ❂ While still in culinary school, my dad hooked me up with an interview at Manhattan's famed '21' Club. I started there as an extern, peeling grapes. When I finished culinary school, I asked the chef, Alain Sailhac, for a job. At first he said he had nothing available, but before I could look elsewhere Chef Sailhac called and offered me a job. I progressed up the ladder under the tutelage of four dif-ferent chefs, including the great Michael Lomonaco, and eventually worked my way up to executive sous-chef by the time I was twenty-four years old. After the '21' Club, I felt I was ready to be "the chef" and was fortu-nate to lead the kitchens at Park Avalon and Blue Water Grill for Steve Hanson, one of New York's top restaurateurs. I continued to learn during these years—not only about how to streamline a professional kitchen but also about how to run a profitable restaurant. ❂ I got married and took a break, thinking I would open my own spot when I returned from my honeymoon. Spending some of our time on Crete, we got an on-the-spot intro-duction to the expansiveness of the Mediter-ranean table. We became friendly with a local restaurant owner whose food was so extraor-dinary that we sometimes ate at his table three times a day. The meals never seemed to end, and you didn't only eat; you had to drink, talk about your life, your hopes and dreams—it was almost as though one meal quietly moved into the next. I thought that this was the way I would like to live. ❂ At some point during my career I had met Nick Livanos, a Greek restaurateur whose family owned Oceana, a three-star seafood restaurant in New York

City, and we had talked about working together one day. The opportunity came after working with Steve Hanson for another year. While on a week's break basking in the sun in Puerto Rico, I got a call from Nick asking me to become involved in the launch of a new concept in Greek dining. I immediately thought Greek diner and had little interest, but my curiosity was aroused once Nick explained that this was to be a "white tablecloth" restaurant called Molyvos, in honor of the village of his father's birth. I was a bit hesitant because I felt that it might be difficult to realize another person's aspirations and I could tell, even over the telephone, that a polished ideal was already set with the Livanos family. Yet I was intrigued by the idea of reaching into my own heritage for a new direction in my culinary career. I immediately returned to New York and within hours was on a plane to Greece with the Livanos family. ✸ Upon landing in Greece, we were met by Aglaia Kremezi, who, besides being a wonderful tour guide and fun to be around, is the leading authority on traditional Greek food. Her Athens apartment overlooks the Acropolis, so I also was immediately immersed in classical Greek architecture. Because of my heritage I was somewhat familiar with basic Greek foods, but I had never felt less Greek than when Aglaia led us through Greece and its islands, introducing us to ingredients and dishes that I had never heard of, much less tasted. Every day meant a new taverna, new mezedes, more ouzo, and wonderful talk of the ingredients that we were experiencing. ✸ Daily we visited all the markets, buying the fresh ingredients needed to make the dishes we would be cooking together. All the while, Aglaia insisted on using only the finest quality she could find. This was not what I was used to after years in restaurant kitchens—calling a purveyor, getting the raw ingredients delivered to the restaurant door, and then fighting over the phone when I wasn't happy with the quality delivered. It was almost as though I was back with my dad as he shopped—touching, feeling, discussing, bargaining for the best he could put on the table for his family. ✸ Because Greek food is so simple and direct, the raw ingredients must be pristine. Very little technique is applied to putting a recipe together; it is the individual flavors that must sing in the finished dish. This is a cuisine built on seasonal ingredients available to the home cook. Greek food is, for the most part, uncomplicated, but many dishes could now be considered contemporary and sophisticated with their use of unusual combinations, wild greens and herbs, and ingenious exploitation of modest ingredients. However, there is almost no ingredient in Greek cooking that is not available at the supermarket or greengrocer or, at the outside, a specialty food store (for specialty cheeses, particularly). Of course, many of the dishes that Aglaia introduced me to were "home-style" or peasant dishes that would require adjustments if they were to be featured on a fine-dining menu. So many dishes were, I found, one-dimensional, particularly the traditional braises or stews. Since all of the dishes tasted delicious, I had to approach innovation very carefully. I also had to take into consideration that many of the fresh-from-the-earth ingredients would not be the same even in the bounty of the New York City marketplace. The most memorable part of this trip was my first visit to Molyvos, a fishing village on Lesvos and the ancestral home of John Livanos. When we arrived, John and I, accompanied by our wives, Krista and Maria, went directly to the home of Dora Parisi, John's cousin. Molyvos is on a hill, where houses hang on the edges of cliffs and every house looks down on another white-washed abode. There are tiny, single lanes weaving through the community, allowing only one car to pass at a time. Dora's house is a landmark filled with ancient art where even the walls are stripped to reveal ancient frescoes. The welcoming table in this historical house was awesome. The entire tabletop was covered with food. There were so many *meze* (small) dishes that it was almost impossible to taste every one. We started with many different kinds of spreads and went on to an array of fish and vegetables. A perfectly braised calamari *stifado* (stew) cooked in red wine and seasoned with clove and cinnamon made me realize how the dish was supposed to taste. Stuffed baby eggplant with lamb was falling-apart tender. But perhaps the most extraordinary dish was a pumpkin/squash pie that was neither sweet nor savory that was served as a prelude to the desserts. It was made with grated pumpkin, *trahana* (a rustic Greek pasta), rice, fennel, a little sugar, scented with cinnamon, and baked in phyllo (see page 73). I had never tasted anything quite like it and vowed that I would learn to re-create such traditional dishes at the restaurant. After we had stuffed ourselves and drunk many toasts to our visit, we took a stroll through the village. John Livanos was like the mayor—he knew everyone, and everyone knew him! In fact, not only did he know everybody, but everyone seemed to be a cousin. The fishermen were coming in with the day's catch, and the townsfolk were down at the little port greeting the returning men. Each restaurateur was vying for the best of the catch. I felt as though we were on a movie set.

After Molyvos, we went on to a fifteen-day tour of the northeastern Greek islands of Chios and Lesvos sponsored by Oldways, a Boston-based organization devoted to preserving traditional foods around the world. In the small village of Chios, we had one of the best meals I had ever eaten. One dish was made with a rooster that had been braised slowly in a rich tomato-based sauce (almost like a cacciatora) and served with homemade pasta. A creamy yogurt was served, and the yogurt maker joined our group to talk about his product. To my amazement, he was from Brooklyn, where he owned a pizza parlor. He had returned to Chios to help his grandparents, and there were now three generations of his family in this village of about forty people.

When I returned to New York, I realized that I had a big job ahead. I had to develop a menu for Molyvos that would satisfy the Greek traditions of the Livanos family as well as delight the very tough New York restaurant critics. I did understand that, for John Livanos, Molyvos was to be the realization of a dream. And I have to say that he also understood that I needed to create a menu that would entice cosmopolitan diners. We had some rocky times as I applied some of my well-learned classic techniques to traditional Greek dishes, but our mutual respect won out, and we all worked together to bring a new style of Greek dining to the city. Even Mrs. Livanos worked with us, teaching us how to make her special baklava. It immediately found a place on the menu, where it remains to much acclaim.

From the beginning, I had to rethink ingredients. Like most of the cuisines of the Mediterranean, Greek cooking is market-driven and inspired by the seasons. The Molyvos menu had to be accessible and yet still authentic. So many Greek dishes feature wild greens and herbs that don't grow in the United States. Working with combinations of cultivated hearty greens and some of the more exotic salad greens, I found that I could recreate the fresh, slightly bitter taste of the traditional wild greens. I found local farmers who could supply us with herbs such as licorice-flavored Lesvos basil, which has a small tealike leaf that is thicker and more durable than Italian basil. Cheese purveyors had to be convinced to import some of the more obscure Greek cheeses. And John Pardalis, an extraordinary wine maven, introduced us to Greek wine and brandies that I had never known existed. (Kamal Kouiri, our current wine director, has taken the wine list to new heights.) An authentic Greek menu began to come together. ❊ Beyond ingredients, I had to rethink my approach to the finished dishes. Since Molyvos was to be a large restaurant located near Carnegie Hall and other theaters, the menu had to be filled with offerings that could be executed quickly to meet the needs of time-short pretheater diners. In my early years, the architecture of the finished dish was important. And, although I was no longer creating a monument to Frank Lloyd Wright on every plate, I still viewed the plate as a painting. It was very hard to translate home-style dishes into works of art that could be prepared and served in short order. I worked diligently to create dishes that could be put together *à la minute* (at the last minute) using an extensive *mise-en-place* (ingredients at the ready for final quick cooking or putting together). ❊ The lack of depth of flavor in many of the traditional recipes continued to haunt me. Slowly, I found that if I took some additional steps in putting them together, I could raise the intensity of the essence I sought. Greek cooks do not use stocks to make their stews and other braised dishes, so I decided to apply some of my training in classic culinary techniques to elevate these traditional dishes to new heights. One simple extension, to have a classically inspired rich meat, game, poultry, or fish stock at the base of the dish, immediately enhanced the final result. ❊ Another trouble spot was tomatoes. Many Greek dishes use fresh tomatoes, and I knew that we would always have to serve a traditional Greek Salad (page 136). The summer season for deliciously ripe, juicy tomatoes is very short. What to do? Through trial and error, we developed our own tomato-ripening system that carries us through the other months. All it takes is a little space and patience! ❊ From the minute Molyvos opened, I knew we had hit our mark. Greek diners loved our interpretations of traditional dishes, as did everyone else. Many of those original dishes remain on the menu, although they have been "tweaked" over the years. I continue to search for new ideas and recipes. We keep the traditional recipes that so delight our customers but add dishes that reflect the season or the availability of new ingredients. We go back to Greece as often as we can, and Aglaia Kremezi continues to offer support and inspiration in meetings and telephone conversations. The Livanos family are true Greeks, welcoming staff and diners alike with open arms and building friendships based on a love of tradition and a bountiful table. For me, I remain passionate about exploring the cuisine of Greece in the restaurant. And at home I keep the tradition of a great big family meal on Sunday with my wife, Maria, and our wonderful children, Sofia and James (aka Dimitri), at my side in the kitchen. ❀ Bringing the recipes that I have developed for Molyvos together in a cookbook has been a marvelous experience.

It has helped me realize how much my own Greek heritage has contributed to my passion in the kitchen. I hope that I have been able to express my enthusiasm in a way that makes this extraordinary cuisine easily accessible to all cooks. As we have been able to introduce heightened flavor to the traditional recipes of the Molyvos kitchen, it is my wish that you, the reader of my recipes, will be seduced by the richness of the Mediterranean table as I have experienced it. And that, along with the foods of Greece, the hospitality and generosity of the Greek people will add a new dimension to your life. I very much hope that the recipes that follow will tempt you to experience the warmth of the Greek table with your family and friends.

Kaliorexi,
Jim Botsacos
chef-partner, Molyvos

Pantry

Aleppo Pepper: Crushed, dark red, richly flavored pepper that is used throughout the Middle East. Made from dried, lightly salted Turkish chiles, it is available from Middle Eastern markets, spice shops, and some specialty food stores.

Barley Rusks (paximadia): A dry, crisp biscuit resembling zwieback made from barley flour, also known as *Cretan bread.* They are available from Greek and Middle Eastern markets. I particularly recommend the To Manna brand.

Beans: Many types of dried beans are used in Greek cooking, along with dried chickpeas, lentils, black-eyed peas, and other legumes. Both dried and fresh fava beans are used for salads and braises, as are white beans such as cannellini and kidney. Fresh green beans are also found in many summer salads.

Bulgur: Cracked wheat that has been steamed and dried comes in three grinds—coarse, medium (both used for pilafs and stuffings), and fine, used mainly for salads. It is a quick-cooking staple of Greek cooking. A variety of grinds can be found in health food stores and Middle Eastern markets. Fine bulgur is available from most supermarkets.

Caperberries: The whole berry rather than the more familiar buds of the Mediterranean caper bush. They are pickled and add a zesty accent to salads. They are available from Middle Eastern markets, specialty food stores, and some supermarkets.

Clarified Butter: Unsalted butter that has been melted so that the water and milk solids are separated out. It is frequently used for sautéing, as it can withstand higher heat than regular butter. In Greek cooking, it is often used to coat phyllo dough, so we always have it on hand. One pound of whole butter will generally yield about 1½ cups of clarified butter.

To make clarified butter, place the butter in a medium saucepan over extremely low heat. Cook for 25 minutes, constantly skimming off the white frothy matter that rises to the top as it melts. Raise the heat to medium-low and cook slowly, skimming off any white matter that rises to the top. The milk solids will congeal and sink to the bottom of the pan, and the remaining liquid butter will be clear yellow. Remove from the heat and let stand for 10 minutes. Carefully skim off any remaining white matter and then carefully pour the clear yellow liquid into a clean, nonreactive container—a glass jar works well. Do not allow any of the solid matter on the bottom of the pan to be poured off with the butter. Store, tightly covered and refrigerated, for up to 1 month.

Fava Beans: Used both fresh and dried in many Greek dishes. They are a large, slightly rounded, pale green bean found in a large, tough pod. In the United States, fresh beans are usually blanched so that their tough outer skin can be removed before the beans are cooked or eaten raw. In Greece, this skin is never removed. When cooked, dried fava beans have a rich, earthy flavor. The word *fava* is also used to describe a dish made from dried legumes (often yellow split peas), onions, and olive oil.

Fennel: An anise-flavored plant that has a thick bulb and feathery fronds, both of which are used in Mediterranean cooking. Wild fennel grows all over Greece and imparts a sweet, almost licoricelike flavor to many dishes. It is also cooked as a horta. Wild fennel is found in California but is not available commercially.

Gigantes: Dried giant Greek white beans that, when cooked, have a rich, creamy taste. Dried giant lima beans can be substituted, but they will not have the distinctive flavor and texture. Available from Middle Eastern and Greek markets and some specialty food stores.

Grape Leaves: In Greece, cooks buy fresh grape leaves in the spring and freeze them for use all year long. In America, for the most part, we have to be content with canned ones. California produces a very nice canned grape leaf that is preserved in a salt brine. If using these leaves, rinse them well to rid them of excess salt first.

Greek Oregano: A very aromatic dried herb that closely resembles marjoram in flavor. It is gathered in the spring after it has bloomed and dried in the sun. Available from Greek markets, spice markets, and some specialty food stores.

Greek Savory: A strongly flavored dried herb reminiscent of thyme and mint. Available from Greek markets.

Herbs: Greek cuisine uses primarily dried oregano and fresh mint, thyme, dill, parsley, and savory, along with some rosemary.

Honey: Greek honeys are renowned for their complexity and purity. Greek island honey is usually scented with thyme.

Horta: The Greek name for wild greens, most of which would be unknown in America. I substitute bitter greens such as mustard, chard, kale, escarole, orache, and amaranth in their place with, I believe, great success.

To blanch any tough green to be cooked further, bring a large pot of salted water to a boil over high heat. Add the greens, in batches if necessary, and return the water to a boil. Blanch for 1 to 2 minutes, depending on the toughness of the green, or until barely softened. Drain well and immediately place in an ice-water bath to stop the cooking. Do not soak the greens; just allow them to cool. Drain well and, using your hands, squeeze out all excess water.

Kalamata Vinegar: A deeply flavored Greek vinegar from Kalamata made from sun-dried grapes that tastes similar to Italian balsamic vinegar. Available from Greek markets and some specialty food stores.

Mastic: The piney-flavored resin of the mastic tree, used as a flavoring throughout the Mediterranean. Indigenous to Chios, it comes in crystallized form and must be crushed to a fine powder before being used. All over the island you will see women sifting resin remnants to get the clear, almost rock-candy-like nuggets of sap. Normally it is mixed with sugar before being ground to keep it from turning tacky. It is very expensive and is definitely an acquired taste. Available from Greek markets.

Mavrodaphne Wine: A dark, sweet Greek wine used mainly in cooking and baking. Sweet Marsala (from Sicily) and Commandaria (from Cyprus) are good substitutes.

Olive Oils: Full-bodied, beautifully flavored Greek olive oil is generally less expensive than Italian and French olive oil. Until recently most Greek olive oil was sold, in bulk, to Italian bottlers and sold as Italian olive oil throughout the world. This is no longer solely the case, with fine extra virgin Greek olive oils to be found at specialty food markets in the United States. I also use blended olive oil when a dish requires a lighter flavor. Blended oils are now available at most supermarkets.

Orzo: A small rice-shaped dried pasta used as a starch in many Greek dishes. Often used in braises, as it can be cooked for a long period of time without becoming mushy. In Greece, orzo is known as *kritharaki*. Available from most supermarkets.

Ouzo: The Greek national drink, ouzo is a clear, anise-flavored, quite sweet liqueur served throughout the country as an aperitif with mezedes. A variety of herbs are used to produce the drink, but the combinations and amounts are closely held secrets in each distillery. The main flavor comes from extract of anise. Ouzo is usually diluted with two parts of water for each part of liqueur. When diluted, it turns opaque and milky.

Paximadia (see barley rusks): Dry, hard, savory biscuits made with barley flour or a combination of barley and wheat flours that are eaten with mezedes or used in salads or sweets. Available from Greek markets.

Phyllo: Tissue-paper-thin sheets of pastry dough used in many savory and sweet Greek dishes. It is sold frozen in Middle Eastern markets, specialty food stores, and many supermarkets. The number sign (#) on a phyllo package indicates the weight of the dough. The thinner dough, #7, has fifteen sheets in a package. Phyllo #10 has ten sheets to a package, and is sometimes called "country" phyllo as it is heavier and easier to work with. Keep phyllo dough moist while working with it. To do this, place a sheet of parchment (or wax) paper on a baking sheet. Carefully unroll the entire package of phyllo dough (or the number of sheets required for your recipe) out on the parchment-lined baking sheet. Cover with another piece of parchment (or wax) paper and then cover the entire stack with a slightly damp, clean kitchen towel. Make sure that the towel is not too wet or it will render the dough soggy and unusable. When removing a sheet of dough, roll back the towel and top piece of parchment. Remove a sheet of phyllo dough, then reroll the towel and parchment back over the remaining sheets to keep them pliable until ready to use.

Quince: A fall fruit that is pale yellow in color with a strong floral scent and dry, astringent flesh that tastes somewhat like a cross between an apple and a Bosc pear. It is very high in pectin and is often used for its jelling properties. It is generally peeled and cooked before being prepared as spoon sweets or other confections.

Ras el Hanout: A basic but complex Moroccan spice mix (whose name means literally "head of the shop") for which every cook has a particular mix. However, commercial blends are now available at most specialty food stores as well as at spice shops and Middle Eastern markets.

Retsina: A traditional Greek wine that is strongly flavored with pine resin, yielding an almost turpentine-like taste. It is always served ice-cold.

Samos wine: A traditional Greek dessert wine that is syrupy sweet with stone fruit aromas. It is also used for cooking. A fine California Muscat is an excellent substitute.

Semolina flour: A coarsely ground durum wheat flour used to make pastas and, in Greece, some desserts. It comes in coarse and fine grinds with the fine more often used to make desserts. It is available from Italian and Middle Eastern markets, specialty food stores, and many supermarkets.

Sumac: A red berry that comes from a bush common throughout the Middle East. It can be purchased whole or ground and adds a slightly astringent, almost citruslike flavor and magenta color to dishes that cannot be duplicated with any other seasoning. It should be stored tightly covered and refrigerated so that it retains its flavor and color. Available from Middle Eastern markets, spice markets, and some specialty food stores.

Tahini: A thick paste made from ground sesame seeds used in Middle Eastern cooking. It is used to make traditional Greek hummus. Tahini is available from Middle Eastern markets, specialty food stores, and many supermarkets.

Tarama: Cured carp roe used as the base for a traditional Greek dish known as taramasalata (see page 31). It is often artificially tinted pink, but I prefer the more natural beige-colored roe. It is available from Greek markets and some specialty food stores.

Trahana: A traditional homemade Greek pasta similar to couscous. It is used in soups, stuffings, and stews. Also known as *ksionhondros,* it is made from ground whole wheat grains that have been soaked or cooked in soured or ordinary milk and then ground to resemble coarse bread crumbs. It is quite time consuming to prepare but a terrific addition to the pantry. You will find a recipe for it on page 75. Once made, it will keep forever like commercially prepared pasta. It is also available ready-made in Greek markets.

Yogurt: Greek yogurt is creamy, thick, and rich. It is available from Greek markets or specialty food stores. An excellent commercial brand, Total, is sold in fat-free, low-fat, and whole-milk versions in many supermarkets.

If you're using conventional yogurt, you will have to drain it. Line a colander with a double layer of cheesecloth and place it over a bowl deep enough to catch the draining liquid without the liquid's touching the bottom of the colander. Four cups of conventional yogurt will make 2 cups of drained thick yogurt. Place the conventional yogurt in the prepared colander and let it drain for 12 hours. Discard the liquid and measure out the desired amount of thick yogurt.

Greek Wines

Although the Greeks were among the earliest winemakers, centuries of oppression and devastating wars left winemaking very much a local craft. In recent years, however, the Greek wine industry has made tremendous strides toward international recognition, thanks to a serious investment in modern winemaking technology and the training of the native winemakers at the best viticulture schools around the globe.

Both of these advances are helping to bring the unique quality of Greek wines to the world's attention. This uniqueness starts with more than three hundred indigenous grape varieties, some of which have been cultivated since ancient times and each of which has a distinct flavor. But it's also a product of many microclimates that result from the lands' being surrounded by water. Greek vineyards are planted on widely diverse geological sites, and, because of broadly variable altitudes on vineyard orientations, the collective grape harvest has a long time to mature. In the end, the characteristics of any Greek wine depend—as they do anywhere else—on grape variety, growing environment, fermenting and aging conditions, and the winemaker's skill. The possibilities are infinite.

Many of those possibilities are becoming realized through not only modern winemaking methods but also legislation, especially since the mid-1990s, that has left Greece with the wine renaissance marked by impressive growths in the production of top-quality wine. Modern legislation began when Greek wine laws were drawn up in the early 1970s using similar criteria as France and most European countries. The technical aspects of the legislation were established by the members of the wine institute, a department of the Ministry of Agriculture. The program is currently administered by the Central Committee for the Protection of the Wine Production (KEPO). A number of considerations played a role in the determination of qualifying areas and products. Some of these include the historical role of the grape varieties, soil composition, location and vineyard elevation, yield, fermentation, and aging.

Greek wine laws were refined and fully adapted in the early 1980s as Greece prepared to join the European Union. The implementation of the Greek Appellations Laws had several important results: the preservation of the traditional varieties, the development of a distinct ethnic wine industry, dramatic effect on the grape varieties because of vineyard elevation and orientation, and setting of high standards for viticulture and vinification.

Today all Greek wines are legally classified as appellations of high-quality origin, controlled origin, *vin du pays,* or table wines. To qualify for these appellations, the wines must be from choice grape varieties, the winery must use a specific system of cultivation, there must be a set maximum level of vine yield per region, and the grape has to have a certain minimal sugar level. Wine producers must also provide detailed reports on the percentage of varieties in the vineyard, new plantings, production quality, and stock balance.

Greek law uses special terminology to classify wines, and many winemakers print these terms on their labels. *Cava* is an aging term used solely for wines assigned the *vin du pays* and table wine appellations. It signifies that a white wine has been aged for two years and that a red wine has been aged for three years before release. For wines that have been assigned an appellation of origin, the terms *reserve* and *grand reserve* are used. Reserve white wines must be aged for two years and red wines for three years. Grand reserve white wines must be aged for three years and reds for four.

Climate and the physical characteristics of the land give each wine its own definable profile. Macedonia in northern Greece (the largest single wine-producing region in the country) has as its appellations of high-quality origin Naoussa, Goumenissa, Amyndeon, and Côtes de Meliton.

Naoussa and its surrounding regions are known for cold, northerly winds in the winter and, with the exception of the usual summer drought, frequent rainfall throughout the rest of the year. The soil in the mountainous parts of the region is sandy-clay loam, while the plateaus offer sandy-clay soil. This type of soil is responsible for producing well-structured red wine, rich in body, with a complex bouquet of red fruits and spices and nuances of mushrooms and black olives that wonderfully complement the local cuisine.

Naoussa, recognized in 1971, produces red wines made from the grape variety Xynomavro ("acid black"), which marry well with the local cuisine ranging from flour-thickened sauces to bean soups, cured meats to lamb stew. One of the most familiar marriages is an aged Xyno-mavro wine with rabbit stifado (see page 220).

Goumenissa, recognized in 1979, produces dry red, made from Xynomavro and Negoska grapes. The introduction of the Negoska into the blend produces a softer wine with deep color, fruity bouquet, and supple taste.

The region that produces the appellation Amyndeon was recognized in 1972. This region has an almost continental climate with low temperatures and heavy snowfall in the winter and frequent northern winds in the summer. The red wines produced are usually lighter than those from the other northern appellations with an emphasis given to dry rosés and naturally sparkling rosés.

Côtes de Meliton was recognized in 1982. This region produces fine white wines made from grape varieties such as Athiri and Rhoditis that are extremely reliable, lean, and crisp, as well as wines produced by the Malagouzia grape, which offer a mouthful of ripe apricots that is

BORA POLISHES GLASSES PRIOR TO OPENING
THE RESTAURANT FOR THE DAY.

rich, round, and exciting to the palate. The red wines produced under this appellation are usually a blend of Limnio, Cabernet Sauvignon, and Cabernet Franc. Aged in small oak barrels for at least one year before release, these wines are very vibrant, with a rich, fruity character.

Epirus, in the northwest of mainland Greece, carries the appellation of high-quality origin Zista. Recognized in 1972, the winegrowing area is at twenty-two hundred feet above sea level. It produces a very small quantity of quality wines known for their light-bodied citrus aroma and taste.

Since the food of the Greek islands is usually quite simple and pure, clean flavors relying on the freshness and the quality of the ingredients, the wines produced to match it are generally crisp. Nine of the twenty appellations of high-quality origin and five of the eight appellations of controlled origin are located in the Greek islands. From the beautiful green and mountainous vineyard of Cephalonia in the Ionian Sea, the noble Robola produces distinguished wines with citrus and peach aromas mixed with smoky, mineral hints and a long lemony aftertaste, which makes them suitable for serving with fish marinato (see page 45).

Southeast of the Cyclades sits the breathtaking island of Santorini. Its soil composition of volcanic ash, lava, and pumice stone gives the wines unique characters. The winemaking in Santorini focuses on Assyrtiko, arguably Greece's finest white grape variety, which offers lively acidity and a clean, fresh, crisp taste with a hint of minerals. Some red wines are also cultivated on the island and consist of Mandelaria and Mavrotraganno varieties, which produce light and fruity reds with bright acidity. The dessert wines from Santorini are called "Visanto," a derivative of the name Santorini.

Rhodes is part of the Dodecanese Islands. It was one of the first areas in ancient Greece known for wine production. The dominant grapes are the white Athiri and red Mandelaria. Rhodes also produces sweet dessert wine made from Muscat grapes.

Samos Island, not far north of Rhodes, is famous for its dessert wines throughout the world. The major grape variety is the aromatic white Muscat, which is made as a dry white wine or a sweet dessert wine with its superb velvety palate and aromas of nectar and honeysuckle.

Peloponnese, the large and dramatically formed southern peninsula, has the greatest number (six) of the Greek wine appellations, as well as some interesting *vins du pays* and table wines.

On the plateau of Mantinia (appellation of high-quality origin) in Arcadia, the Moschofilero grape produces a fresh, dry, aromatic, slightly spicy white wine, while the same grape variety can be vinified with extended maceration to produce fresh, fruity rosé.

Not far from the lovely town of Nafplion we find Nemea, the most important appellation of high-quality origin in southern Greece. The noble Aghiorghitiko grape produces dry red wines known for their deep red color, complex aromas, and intense flavor.

In the northern west of the Peloponnes the elegant Rhoditis grape is used to produce the appellation wines of Patras. As the name implies, Rhoditis is a rose-colored grape that produces light white wines with citrus flavors. Patras is also associated with the production of three other appellations: a dessert wine appellation including Muscat and Muscat Rion, as well as the red Mavrodaphne. The name *Mavrodaphne* translates to "black laurel." This lightly fortified wine is sweet, full-bodied, and aromatic.

In the years since Molyvos opened, we have been thrilled with the growth of interest in Greek wines. Where diners once asked for the wines of France and Spain, they are now familiar with and request those indigenous to Greece. Since the names are often hard for non-Greeks to pronounce, wines are often requested simply by their appellation. We, of course, are delighted to share our knowledge and our cellar with our discerning patrons.

KAMAL KOUIRI, MOLYVOS'S FOOD AND BEVERAGE DIRECTOR, MANAGES THE EXTENSIVE WINE LIST, THE EIGHTEEN OUZOS, AND THE INTERNATIONAL BEER LIST.

Olives

In every area of Greece, olives play a dominant role in the local cuisine, but they reach a pinnacle at the meze table. Even the simplest spread will feature a couple of different types of olives and always olive oil. Olives have been such an integral part of Greek life that it is often said that the fortunes of the land can be told by the state of the olive tree.

It was on my trip to Lesvos that I got my Greek olive indoctrination. Lesvos is an island of four million olive trees and, in fact, produces about twenty-five thousand tons of olive oil annually—ten times as much as all of France. Every cook has a way of curing olives, making olive oil, and incorporating olives into other dishes. I think you could stay on the island for years and still not learn all of the olive secrets. But those I did learn I have introduced into my menus at Molyvos.

It should be no surprise that Greek olives are some of the world's best, with the Kalamata being the reigning king. Raised in huge quantities around the town of Kalamata in the valley of Messina on the western end of the Peloponnesian Peninsula, they are deep purple, almost-black gems. Small Kalamatas are little ovals carrying potent flavor. Much of their distinction comes from their curing in a red wine vinegar–based brine that translates to almost winelike overtones when eaten. It is said that the cream of the crop are those that have been hand-picked and selectively cured. Unfortunately, most of us will not have the opportunity to experience this taste as so few olives are treated with such respect. However, if you purchase Kalamata olives from a quality Greek market or specialty food store, you can come very near to the smooth, rounded flavor of a select olive.

I use Kalamata olives in cold dishes as well as hot because I love the flavor they add to a dish. They are also the olives I grew up on and still eat when cooking or as a late-night snack with some feta and bread when I'm finishing up in the kitchen. Rather than the typically small Kalamatas, I always look for big fat ones that are almost black in color—I find them meatier and richer in taste.

After Kalamata, the most well-known Greek olive is the large black Volos or Pelion. The olives are rather chewy and nutlike in flavor and are usually marketed as "Greek olives."

I particularly love Thassos olives, which are quite wrinkled and shriveled from their salt cure. What they lack in looks is made up in their rich, deep flavor. They are dry-cured and then stored in olive oil. For serving as a meze, I often season them with a fruity green olive oil and fresh herbs.

Amfissa olives are round and juicy, deep purple-black in color like Kalamata olives, but unlike many olives, they are almost sugarlike in their sweetness. Since they are picked only when very ripe, Amfissa olives have a softer texture and less sharp flavor than green olives. I find them the perfect mate for the Greek triumvirate of ouzo, sharp cheese, and olives.

You can now get many types of Greek olives in the United States. We have brine-cured, oil-cured, and recently we have tasted marvelous salt-cured olives. Throughout Greece, each area produces a local favorite, most of which are not exported. Some are as small as a pine nut and some as large as a walnut, each carrying its own distinctive flavor. In Athens, the Olive Shop of Sabbas Psychogios specializes in olives from throughout the country, and it is the only place I know of where you can sample many of these local specialties. At Molyvos, we are constantly seeking to introduce them to our guests.

A DISPLAY OF OLIVES IN AN ATHENS MARKET.

Cheeses

The cheeses of Greece are many and varied. Most of them are unknown in other parts of the world because they are rarely exported. Throughout the islands most households make their own cheese, harvesting the milk and making their cheese just once or twice a year. Since goats and sheep are the most common herds, most of the cheeses of Greece are made from their milk, although a few cow's milk cheeses are produced on some of the less mountainous islands.

Perhaps the most famous of all Greek cheese is feta. Traditional feta, made primarily with 60 percent sheep's with the addition of a small amount of goat's milk, is creamy, deeply white, and slightly sour tasting. Although it is stored in a salty brine to keep it fresh, it is not stored for long periods of time as it is meant to be eaten young with no aging. It is used as a meze as well as in salads, stuffings, and grain dishes. It was always on our meze platters when I was a boy, and it remains one of my favorite cheeses.

There are many styles of traditional feta cheese, ranging from rich and creamy to very, very tart and firm. When eating with Aglaia Kremezi in Greece we were amused by the fact that she always had to have two types—her husband, Kostas, preferred a firmer, sharp-tasting cheese, while Aglaia liked hers to be creamy and rich in flavor. I can easily enjoy either type.

Following feta, perhaps the other best-known Greek cheese is kasseri, a malleable, resilient cheese that is somewhat like Italian cacciocavallo. It is a spun-curd cheese produced from either ewe's or cow's milk and is generally consumed as a table cheese. I sometimes use it in combination with vlahotyri cheese, a hard sheep's milk cheese from Epirus, when I make Tyrokeftedes (page 59).

Lesvos produces some great cheeses. I often use *lathotyri* of Mitilini, a sheep's milk cheese aged in olive oil. Many of the other islands also produce memorable artisanal cheeses. Chios and Mykonos, among other islands, produce a crumbly blue-style cheese called *kopanisti* that I mix with feta, yogurt, and mayonnaise to make a Greek-style blue cheese dressing. Kos offers an extraordinary semihard cheese known as *possias.* Sifnos has *gilomeni manoura,* which is also a strong, semihard cheese. One of the most interesting cheeses that I have eaten in Greece was a *touloumotyri,* which is a pungent cheese made even more aromatic by its goat hide wrapping. Many of these cheeses are made in villages and carry different names from village to village. Unfortunately, most of them never reach the United States.

One of my favorite cheeses often featured on the Molyvos cheese-tasting platter is a smoked cheese called *metsovone.* Made from cow's milk with a touch of goat's milk, it has the firmness of an aged, sharp provolone and the smokiness of a smoked Gouda. The smokiness is particularly flavorful with the taste of vine cuttings and herbs.

Haloumi is a semihard cheese from Cyprus that is quite similar to mozzarella. Traditionally made from sheep's milk, the cheese is usually made from cow's milk commercially, with a bit of sheep's milk added for flavor. Unlike feta, which crumbles when sliced, haloumi is firm enough to slice and hold its shape when fried (as for the traditional dish called *saganaki*) or grilled. Haloumi is usually sprinkled with dried mint and sold vacuum-packed in brine.

At Molyvos, I use fresh *myzithra* cheeses for desserts much as they are used in Greece. Myzithra is simply a general name for many types of sweet, creamy fresh cheeses. These cheeses are made throughout Greece, usually from the whey left from other cheesemaking. If you can't find a traditional fresh Greek myzithra, sheep's milk ricotta is a good substitute. When myzithra is allowed to sour, it is salted and packed in barrels, producing *xinomyzithra* (sour myzithra), which is used as an alternative to feta.

The two other traditional Greek cheeses most frequently available in America are *kefalotyri* and *manouri.* Originally all Greek hard cheeses were called *kefalotyri,* but now a hard cheese made from a combination of sheep's and cow's milk is known as *kefalotyri.* It varies widely in flavor from region to region. Strongly flavored with a lingering sharp taste, it is used as a grating cheese and in savory dishes. Manouri, a combination of goat's and sheep's milk, is a creamy dessert cheese that is sweet and high in fat and is usually eaten with honey or spoon sweets.

THE ENTIRE MOLYVOS STAFF.

Mezedes

Communal dining is practiced throughout the Mediterranean, but nowhere with more enthusiasm than Greece, where most meals begin with a selection of mezedes—bite-sized tidbits of hot and cold foods—and ouzo and/or retsina to open the palate and to raise a toast to life's fortunes. Even more overflowing than the family tables of my childhood, a Greek meze table is, albeit in a rustic setting, a lavish celebration of a way of life steeped in tradition. In a Greek restaurant, diners might be offered up to forty meze dishes, while home cooks do their best at combining prepared Greek staples such as olives, roasted or pickled vegetables, cheeses, or cured fish and those made at the last minute in the home kitchen.

When I was growing up, our meals always started with small plates—usually with some cheese, olives, marinated or grilled vegetables, and sausage—so I did have some indication of what a meze table would include. Because of my dad's Greek heritage and Italian mother, he passed on a good sense of the Mediterranean tradition in our home. A family vacation in Greece when I was sixteen had introduced me to the real thing, but nothing had prepared me for the introduction I got when planning the Molyvos menu. ✺ *Excitement* would be too placid a description for my feelings the first time I experienced a great meze table in Greece. It awakened so many of my senses. It was made all the more extraordinary because the foods were very simple, straightforward, honest dishes that became perfect by relying on the superb quality of the ingredients. There were dishes both hot and cold, spicy and mellow, garlicky and smoky, sweetly fragrant and savory, crunchy and creamy—a variety of different olives; cheeses of all textures; simply grilled sardines; zucchini fritters; vegetables that were pickled, grilled, or perfectly seasoned with lemon and garlic . . . I could go on and on. For me it was like being at home with my extended family for Sunday dinner. ✺ Almost anything can be made into a meze. Even many appetizers can be used as mezedes when divided into smaller portions. Traditionally, meat-based dishes are not featured as meat has never been plentiful in Greece and is usually saved for the main

course or special occasions. However, everything else, except soup, will be found on a meze display. At Molyvos, I include both meat and fish along with vegetables and other traditional Greek dishes. What is most important is to have a cross section of textures, flavors, and aromas. ✺ If only a few mezedes are going to be served, everything can be put out at once. At the restaurant, I like to start with a flight of a few cold mezedes, followed by an equally impressive flight of warm or hot dishes. This is much as it is done in a Greek home, when many, many different types of food are going to be served. And, in fact, when the display is large enough, it often takes the place of the main course. ✺ At least equal in importance to the foods prepared at a communal meze table are the spirits to be drunk with them. In the alleyways of small Greek villages, there will always be tables and chairs filled with men sharing a bottle of ouzo, eating, and welcoming any passerby to join them. Ouzo, a crystal-clear, sticky-sweet, potent (up to 90 percent alcohol) liqueur, is the drink of choice. Although ouzo is usually thought of as being anise-flavored, it can have many different characteristics depending on the spices and herbs used to make it. It can be served neat but is usually poured over ice with a splash of cool water, creating an opaque, slightly milky liquid that is a perfect match for the fragrant, deeply flavored mezedes. It also works as a palate cleanser, which makes it an especially welcome drink with mezedes. We have more than eighteen ouzos and quite an impressive list of Greek wines at Molyvos, and recently these light, fruity, resinated Greek wines have become quite popular with mezedes dishes. Whatever is served, Greeks never offer drink without offering food. A luxurious meze table can be quite time-consuming to prepare. However, since so many of the dishes can be prepared in advance and served at room temperature, even a home cook can take a stab at extravagance. In fact, almost all of the recipes that follow can be made in advance—some even up to a few days ahead—so that when your guests gather, you will, following Greek hospitality, have plenty of time to spend with them. None of the ingredients are difficult to obtain, so shopping should pose no problem either. The many wonderful cheeses, olives, and other prepared Greek products available at specialty food stores and even many supermarkets should make it eminently possible to create your own expansive meze experience using the recipes in this chapter. What brings the vibrant flavors of mezedes together is the freshly baked country bread eaten with the little tidbits. Pita is usually the bread of choice, but each village has a bakery that supplies the specialty of the area. Unbelievably, in Athens, there are very few bakeries currently baking the traditional breads of Greece. At Molyvos, we serve freshly baked pita and olive bread with every meal. Mezedes are served family style, and the meze table is all about sharing. You share not only the food and drink but your life experiences as well. To me, this table signifies the warmth and generosity of the people and the love of family and friends. For each person that I met in Greece, the sharing of mezedes was symbolic of their wish to welcome me into their homes and hearts. The recipes that follow will help you re-create this experience at your table.

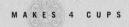

Taramasalata (Caviar Mousse)

Tarama, cured fish roe, usually that of carp, is the base of this dish, one of the great Greek mezedes. (Although one may think that tarama is imported to the U.S. from Greece, I have learned that most of it makes its way to Greece from Norway. The cheapest types are often tinted pink to enhance their appearance.) The combination of potatoes and almonds beaten into the roe creates a fluffy, gently flavored emulsion that can serve as a dip, a sauce, or a filling. This recipe came from a friend who got it from a store owner in Astoria, Queens, a New York Greek neighborhood.

Most people now use a food processor to blend the mixture, which tends to liquefy rather than emulsify. To achieve the best texture and flavor, you really should use a meat grinder as we do at Molyvos. If you don't have one, first grind the almonds in a food processor, finely dice the onions by hand, and then pulse the two together for only a second or two to combine. Put the cooked potatoes through a potato ricer or food mill and then combine them with the almond/onion mixture by hand. Then, and only then, should you proceed with finishing the recipe!

2 ounces whole almonds

2 cups plus 3 tablespoons corn oil

One $^1/_2$-pound Idaho potato, boiled in its skin, peeled, and chilled

$^1/_4$ medium yellow onion

$^1/_4$ pound tarama (carp roe)

2 tablespoons extra virgin olive oil

$^1/_3$ cup lemon juice concentrate

4 to 6 tablespoons seltzer water

Warm pita bread triangles for serving

1. Place the almonds in a heatproof bowl with boiling water to cover. Let stand until the water is tepid. Drain well and, using your fingertips, pop off and discard the skins.

2. Line a small tray or baking sheet with parchment or wax paper. Place the peeled almonds on the prepared tray and refrigerate for about 8 hours or overnight.

3. Preheat the oven to 200°F.

4. Remove the almonds from the refrigerator and place on a small baking pan. Transfer to the preheated oven and bake for about 15 minutes, just to dry slightly. Do not roast.

5. Pour about 1 teaspoon of the corn oil into a medium mixing bowl and, using your

fingertips, rub the oil around the interior of the bowl to coat lightly.

6. Combine the almonds with the potato and onion in the oiled bowl. Add 1 tablespoon of the oil and toss to coat, mashing the potato slightly and pulling the onion apart.

7. Working with about one third of the almond mixture at a time, pass it through an electric mixer fitted with the fine grinder attachment or through a stand-alone meat grinder into the oiled bowl, allowing the food to pass through the grinder completely before adding the next third. This will prevent clogging. The consistency should be of a coarse meal.

8. When all of the mixture has been ground, remove the grinder attachment from the mixer and fit the mixer with the bowl and paddle.

9. Place the tarama in the mixer bowl and, with the mixer on low speed, begin beating the tarama, adding the remaining corn oil in a slow, steady stream. Then add the extra virgin olive oil in a slow, steady stream. When well blended, remove the paddle attachment and change to the wire whip. Continuing to mix on medium speed, add the lemon juice in a slow, steady stream.

10. When well blended, stop the motor, scrape down the sides of the bowl, and add the almond mixture. With the mixer on low speed, slowly combine the mixtures.

11. When well combined, begin adding the seltzer, an ounce at a time, until the taramasalata is as light and airy as light, fluffy mashed potatoes.

12. Transfer to a nonreactive storage container, cover, and refrigerate for at least 1 hour before serving with warm pita triangles.

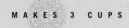

Melitzanosalata (Grilled Eggplant Salad with Tomato, Vinegar, and Parsley)

When we were eating our way through Greece, I tasted many, many versions of this meze. Too often they had little taste of eggplant because so many other ingredients had been added. I love the slightly smoky taste of eggplant, which I think is really brought out in this version of a classic Greek dish.

3 whole eggplants, about 4 pounds

2 garlic cloves, minced

³/₄ cup finely diced yellow onion

¹/₂ cup well-drained finely diced canned tomato

¹/₄ cup Greek yogurt (see page 13)

¹/₃ cup red wine vinegar

¹/₄ cup fresh lemon juice

¹/₂ cup extra virgin olive oil

About 3 tablespoons seltzer water

¹/₄ cup finely chopped fresh flat-leaf parsley

1 teaspoon dried oregano

Coarse salt and freshly ground pepper

Warm pita bread triangles for serving

1. Preheat and oil a grill. Place a wire rack on a baking pan. Set aside.

2. Pierce each eggplant in a few places with a dinner fork. Place the eggplants on the preheated grill and grill, turning occasionally to prevent burning, for about 15 minutes or until the eggplants are soft and the skin is black. Using a spatula, lift the eggplants from the grill and place on the wire rack in the baking pan to cool.

3. When the eggplants are cool, peel and discard the skin as well as any juices that have dripped into the baking pan.

4. Coarsely chop the eggplant flesh and place it in the bowl of a tabletop mixer fitted with the paddle. Add the garlic, onion, and tomato and mix on medium speed for 1 minute. Add the yogurt and mix for another minute.

5. With the mixer still on medium speed, slowly add the vinegar and lemon juice. When blended, with the mixer still running, add the oil in a slow, steady stream. Begin adding the seltzer, a tablespoon at a time, beating until the mixture is slightly thick yet light and relatively loose. Stir in the parsley and oregano and season with salt and pepper.

6. Transfer to a nonreactive container, cover, and refrigerate for 8 hours or overnight before serving with warm pita triangles.

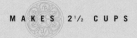

Tzatziki (Greek Yogurt with Cucumber, Garlic, and Mint)

One taste of tzatziki floods my palate with memories of Greece. It was part of the meze served at every meal. The texture of the grated cucumber against the thick, tangy Greek yogurt is a perfect contrast. Because of the recent interest in Mediterranean cooking and diet, Greek yogurt is now widely available. If you can't find it locally, try researching "Greek food" online, and you're sure to find a source that will deliver beautiful Greek yogurt right to your door.

1 large hothouse cucumber, peeled

Coarse salt and freshly ground white pepper

2 cups Greek yogurt (see page 13)

1 garlic clove, minced

2 tablespoons fresh lemon juice

1 tablespoon finely chopped fresh mint

1 tablespoon finely chopped fresh dill

Warm pita bread triangles for serving

1. Line a colander with a double layer of cheesecloth. Place the colander over a bowl deep enough to catch draining juices without the juices touching the bottom of the colander. Set aside.

2. Using a box grater, grate the cucumber through the medium holes into a mixing bowl. Add a pinch of salt and toss to combine. Transfer the cucumber to the colander and allow the juices to drain for 1 hour. Pull the cheesecloth up and twist the ends together to squeeze any remaining juice from the cucumber. Transfer the well-drained cucumber to a clean nonreactive container with a lid.

3. Add the yogurt, garlic, lemon juice, mint, and dill. Season with salt and pepper to taste and toss to combine. Cover and refrigerate for 8 hours or overnight before serving.

4. Serve chilled with warm pita bread triangles.

Vegetable Dolmades with Yogurt-Garlic Sauce

Dolmades are foods that are wrapped, usually in a leaf of some type. The most familiar are, of course, the classic grape-leaf dolmades, but chard, romaine lettuce, cabbage, and other firm green leaves can also be used. When the restaurant opened, I served these hot, but after I tasted them chilled in Greece, I changed my presentation.

Some variation on the accompanying yogurt sauce is seen in almost every taverna throughout Greece and Turkey. In mine, the drained cucumber juice used to thin the yogurt results in a subtly complex flavor.

$^1/_4$ cup dried currants

$^1/_4$ cup plus $^1/_2$ teaspoon olive oil

$1^1/_4$ cups finely diced white onion

Coarse salt and freshly ground pepper

1 garlic clove, minced

$^1/_4$ cup pine nuts

$^1/_4$ cup sliced almonds

$1^1/_2$ cups finely diced yellow bell pepper

$^1/_4$ teaspoon ground cinnamon

$1^1/_2$ cups short-grain white rice such as Arborio

5 cups Vegetable Stock (page 280)

$1^1/_4$ cups finely diced peeled, seeded plum tomato

$^1/_3$ cup chopped fresh mint

$^1/_3$ cup chopped fresh flat-leaf parsley leaves

5 tablespoons fresh lemon juice

32 brine-packed California grape leaves, stems removed, plus about 14 to line the baking dish, rinsed and well drained

Yogurt-Garlic Sauce (recipe follows)

I. Place the currants in a small heatproof bowl and cover with hot water. Set aside to plump for about 15 minutes while you proceed with the recipe.

2. Place a medium sauté pan over medium heat. When very hot but not smoking, add 2 tablespoons of the olive oil and swirl it around in the pan to just heat. Immediately

add the onion and a pinch of salt and cook, stirring occasionally, for about 6 minutes, or until translucent. Add the garlic and cook, stirring with a wooden spoon, for 2 minutes longer. Do not allow the aromatics to brown.

3. Stir in the pine nuts and almonds and cook, stirring constantly, for 3 minutes. Add the bell pepper and cook, stirring constantly,

for 2 minutes. Stir in the cinnamon and season with salt and pepper to taste.

4. Add the rice and stir for about 1 minute, or until the rice is glistening with oil. Add 1 cup of the stock and cook, stirring constantly, for about 7 minutes, or until the rice has absorbed the stock. Stir in another 2 cups of the stock and, when blended, fold in the tomato.

5. When the stock has reduced by two thirds and the rice is still very firm (a bit less than al dente), drain the currants and fold them into the rice. Remove the pan from the heat and fold in the mint, parsley, and 2 tablespoons of the remaining olive oil, tossing to incorporate. Taste and, if necessary, add salt and pepper.

6. Transfer the rice mixture to a baking sheet and, using a spatula, spread it out to an even layer to cool.

7. Preheat the oven to 350°F.

8. Fill a large bowl with ice and water. Set aside.

9. Fill a large pot with cold water. Add a tablespoon of salt along with 3 tablespoons of the lemon juice and place over high heat. Bring to a boil and then add the grape leaves, 3 or 4 at a time, and blanch for just 30 seconds. Using a slotted spoon, transfer the grape leaves to the ice-water bath to stop the cooking. Then transfer them to a double layer of paper towel to drain. Pat dry.

10. Line the bottom of a large baking dish with a single layer of grape leaves (about 7). Set aside.

11. Working with one grape leaf at a time, place the leaf rib side up on a flat surface. Neatly remove the stem if necessary. Place 1 teaspoon of the cooled rice mixture near the bottom, widest part of the leaf. Fold the bottom up over the rice filling and then fold each side in and over to cover. Begin rolling the leaf over the filling to make a tight, neat roll. Place the finished roll into the grape-leaf-lined dish, seam side down. Continue making dolmades until you have 32, packing them tightly into the baking dish so that the rolls will stay together.

12. Combine the remaining 2 cups stock with the remaining 2 tablespoons lemon juice and remaining ½ teaspoon olive oil in a medium saucepan over medium heat. Season with salt and pepper to taste and bring to a simmer. Remove from the heat and pour the hot stock over the dolmades in the baking dish.

13. Cover the dolmades with a single layer of grape leaves (another 7). Then place another, smaller baking pan inside the pan to hold the dolmades firmly in place. Place the pan in the preheated oven and bake for 30 to 40 minutes, or until the leaves are tender and the filling is cooked through. Remove from the oven and immediately drain off all of the liquid.

14. When cool, remove the layer of grape leaves and place the dolmades on a serving platter if serving immediately. Alternatively, place in a container with a cover and refrigerate until ready to use.

15. Serve at room temperature with Yogurt-Garlic Sauce.

Yogurt-Garlic Sauce

Makes about 1¼ cups

½ large hothouse cucumber, peeled
3 garlic cloves, minced
¾ cup Greek yogurt (see page 13)
1 tablespoon fresh lemon juice
Coarse salt and freshly ground pepper

1. Line a colander with a double layer of cheesecloth. Place the colander over a bowl deep enough to catch the draining liquid without the liquid touching the bottom of the colander.

2. Roughly chop the cucumber and then place it in a food processor fitted with the metal blade. Add the garlic and process just until finely chopped. Transfer the mixture to the colander and set aside to drain for about 30 minutes, or until all the juice has drained off.

3. Pull the cheesecloth up and tightly twist the ends together to force out any remaining juices into the bowl. Discard the cheesecloth and cucumber, remove the colander, and reserve the juice in the bowl.

4. Place the yogurt in a nonreactive mixing bowl. Whisk in the reserved cucumber-garlic juice along with the lemon juice. The sauce should be the consistency of a creamy vinaigrette. You may not need all of the juice. When blended, season with salt and pepper to taste.

5. Serve immediately or place in a nonreactive container, cover, and refrigerate for up to 1 day.

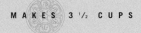

White Bean Hummus

Most hummus is made with chickpeas, but by using white beans we've come up with a lighter and creamier twist on the classic. Equally delicious—maybe even more so!

1 pound dried white beans, such as cannellini,
    soaked for 8 hours or overnight
2 garlic cloves, peeled
1 bay leaf
Coarse salt and freshly ground white pepper

3 tablespoons tahini
1½ teaspoons minced fresh garlic
¼ cup fresh lemon juice
¼ cup extra virgin olive oil
Warm pita bread triangles for serving

I. Drain the soaked beans well and transfer to a heavy saucepan. Add water to cover by 1 inch and place over medium-high heat. Bring to a boil, continually skimming off any foam or impurities that rise to the top. Lower the heat and add the whole garlic cloves and the bay leaf. Simmer, skimming frequently, for 30 minutes. Add salt to taste and continue simmering for about 15 minutes, or until the beans are tender. Remove from the heat and set aside to allow the beans to cool in the cooking liquid.

2. Drain the beans and measure out 4 cups, reserving any remaining beans for another use (such as in salads or a rice pilaf). Discard the whole garlic cloves and bay leaf.

3. Place the beans in a food processor fitted with the metal blade. Add the tahini and minced garlic and begin to process. With the motor running, add the lemon juice and then the olive oil, pouring in a slow, steady stream. Season with white pepper to taste and process to a smooth puree. Taste and, if necessary, add salt and pepper.

4. Transfer to a nonreactive container, cover, and refrigerate for about 1 hour, or until well chilled. Serve chilled with warm pita bread.

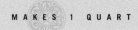

Greek Fava with Arugula, Spring Onions, and Capers

Greek fava is, rather than fava beans, cooked yellow split peas, which, with horta (wild greens), is a traditional accompaniment to fried fish. If you travel through Greece, you will find that the best yellow split peas are grown on the island of Santorini—just another great reason to plan a trip! They are usually simply smashed with a fork and seasoned, and I still make them in the traditional way from time to time. However, in this version I puree them with olive oil until they are quite fluffy and accent their sweetness with bitter arugula and salty capers. If you want to make individual meze portions, place about $^1/_2$ cup of the fava puree in the center of a small plate and top with $1^1/_2$ teaspoons extra virgin olive oil, $^1/_4$ teaspoon lemon juice, $^1/_2$ teaspoon capers, and about 1 tablespoon arugula leaves.

5 black peppercorns

4 garlic cloves, peeled and smashed

2 bay leaves

$^1/_4$ medium onion, peeled

$1^1/_2$ cups dried yellow split peas, well rinsed and picked clean of any debris

$^1/_2$ teaspoon ground turmeric

Coarse salt and freshly ground pepper

$^1/_4$ cup plus 2 tablespoons extra virgin olive oil, preferably Greek

$^1/_4$ cup fresh lemon juice

$^1/_4$ cup chopped scallion, including some of the green part

$^1/_4$ cup well-drained capers

1 cup chopped arugula

I. Combine the peppercorns, garlic, bay leaves, and onion in a piece of cheesecloth about 6 inches square. Gather up the ends and, using kitchen twine, tie the bag closed. Set the sachet aside.

2. Place the split peas and about $4^1/_4$ cups cold water in a medium saucepan over medium heat. Bring to a boil, skimming off

any impurities that rise to the top as the liquid heats. Add the turmeric along with the reserved sachet, lower the heat to a bare simmer, and cook, stirring occasionally, for 20 minutes. Add 1 teaspoon salt and continue cooking at a bare simmer for 10 minutes, or until the liquid has evaporated and the peas are porridgelike, adding water a couple of tablespoons at a time if necessary to prevent scorching. When ready, the peas should resemble thick polenta.

3. Remove the peas from the heat and allow to cool. Remove and discard the sachet. Transfer the peas to a food processor fitted with the metal blade and, with the motor running at its lowest speed, add 3 tablespoons of the oil along with 1 tablespoon of the lemon juice and process to a light, fluffy puree. Remove from the processor bowl and season with salt and pepper to taste.

4. When ready to serve, transfer the fava puree to a small serving platter. Sprinkle with the scallions and capers and drizzle the remaining 3 tablespoons of oil and 3 tablespoons of lemon juice over all. Scatter the arugula over the plate and serve.

NOTE: A sachet or bouquet garni is made up of several herbs and/or spices tied in a cheesecloth bag and added to stocks, soups, and stews for flavor. The cheesecloth bag facilitates the easy removal of the flavoring agent(s) from the cooking liquid and is always discarded once the dish is complete.

Pickled Cipollini Onions

Throughout Greece pickled foods are present on the meze table. Vegetables, fish, octopus—you name it, the Greeks pickle it. In Greece, traditionally, *volvi,* bitter wild hyacinth bulbs, are pickled and served during Lent. Because these wild bulbs are not available in the United States, I replace them with cipollini onions. Although assertive in flavor, cipollini are much sweeter than *volvi* but still make a terrific pickle. You could also substitute white or red pearl onions.

  You can pickle almost any crisp vegetable with the brine. Try a combination of 3 cups tiny pearl onions, 3 kirby cucumbers, cut crosswise into 1/4-inch-thick slices, and 1 bunch of scallions, trimmed to about half their length. Follow this recipe through the 1-minute boil, replacing the cipollini with the pearl onions. Then add the cucumber and scallions and allow them to cool in the hot brine before covering with olive oil and storing as directed.

2 cups white wine vinegar

2 cups sugar

5 whole cloves

2 bay leaves

2 cinnamon sticks

2 whole allspice

1 tablespoon coarse salt

1 teaspoon coriander seeds

1 teaspoon mustard seeds

Pinch of Aleppo pepper (see page 9)

2 1/2 pounds cipollini

2 tablespoons extra virgin olive oil

1. Combine the vinegar, 2 cups water, sugar, cloves, bay leaves, cinnamon sticks, allspice, salt, coriander seeds, mustard seeds, and Aleppo pepper in a large nonreactive saucepan. Place over low heat and bring to a simmer. Simmer for 2 to 3 minutes.

2. Raise the heat to high and add the cipollini. Bring to a boil and boil for 1 minute. Remove from the heat and transfer to a nonreactive container with a lid. Set aside to cool, uncovered.

(continued)

3. When cool, carefully pour the olive oil over the top to cover the cipollini. Cover the container and refrigerate for at least 8 hours or overnight before serving. May be stored, covered and refrigerated, for up to 6 weeks.

NOTE: Italian cipollini, also known as *wild onions,* are most easily found in the United States during the fall at Italian or Greek markets or specialty food stores.

WITH JOHN PILIOURAS, CHEF DE CUISINE, WHO HAS BEEN AT MOLYVOS SINCE IT OPENED.

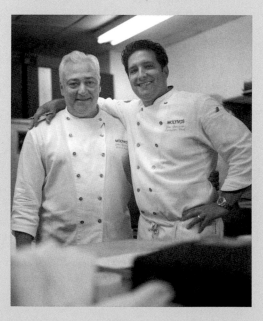

Ouzo-Cured Salmon with Fennel and Dill

Since the Greeks enjoy many different types of cured fish, I thought it would be a great idea to do a Greek spin on the traditional Scandinavian gravlax. I have to thank my chef de cuisine, John Piliouras, who is terrific at charcuterie and curing, for helping to devise what I think is a "killer" recipe—the sweet, fatty salmon is cured with the usual sugar, salt, and dill and then "Greekified" with a strong hit of ouzo and fennel seed and pollen. The pungent sweetness of the anise flavors is the perfect foil for the fatty, succulent salmon.

If you can't find the fennel pollen, don't worry; it's not essential to the perfect cure. I can tell you that this truly *is* "killer" served with warm pita and a glass of ouzo.

1 whole salmon, 10 to 12 pounds, tail and head removed, gutted, cut lengthwise in half, and boned to make 2 fillets with skin

3 cups packed light brown sugar

3 cups coarse salt

1/2 cup cracked black pepper

2 tablespoons fennel pollen

1 tablespoon fennel seeds, toasted and crushed (see Note)

6 cups chopped fresh dill, including stems

3 cups ouzo

1. Cut a piece of cheesecloth large enough to fold in half and then totally enfold the 2 fillets. Set aside.

2. Combine the brown sugar and salt with the pepper, fennel pollen, and toasted fennel seeds in a medium mixing bowl, stirring to combine well. Set aside.

3. Lay the salmon fillets out on a clean work surface, skin side down. Using tweezers or needle-nose pliers, carefully remove and discard any pinbones remaining in the flesh.

Using a sharp knife, trim off the thin belly meat, leaving an almost perfect rectangle of fish. (This is done because the belly meat is so thin it will cure quickly and then begin to dry out.)

4. Place the double layer of cheesecloth on a clean work surface. Generously sprinkle the sugar-salt mixture down the center, spreading it out slightly so that the fish will lie on a comfortable bed. Lay the fillets skin side down in the center of the sugar-salt

cure, with the interior edges touching. Generously coat the top of each fillet with a coating of the sugar-salt mixture. Cover with the dill and then sprinkle on the remaining sugar-salt mixture. Drizzle the fish with half of the ouzo. Place one fillet on top of the other to put the fish back together. Wrap the fish packet with the cheesecloth to enclose it. Drizzle the remaining ouzo on the cheesecloth to almost saturate it. Working carefully so that you don't lose too much of the curing mixture, tightly wrap the packet in plastic wrap.

5. Place the wrapped fish in a dish or on a platter large enough to hold it flat as well as to hold the liquid that may seep out as the fish cures. Place a heavy cutting board or other heavy object on top of the fish and refrigerate for 2 days, turning every 12 hours or so.

6. After 2 days, unwrap the fish and separate the fillets. Quickly rinse off any remaining curing mixture under cool water. Do not soak. Pat dry with paper towels. If not serving immediately, separately wrap each fillet in plastic wrap and refrigerate until ready to serve. The gravlax may be stored, refrigerated, for a week or so.

7. When ready to serve, using a slicing knife, cut each fillet, on the bias against the skin, into very thin, skinless slices. Serve with warm pita bread and thinly sliced lemon—and, of course, a glass of ouzo!

NOTE: To toast seeds, place them in a single layer in a skillet over medium-low heat or in a baking pan in a preheated 300°F oven. Turn frequently to keep them from burning and turning bitter. This should take no more than 5 minutes as seeds are quite oily and will brown quickly.

Fluke Marinato with Cucumbers, Capers, and Lesvos Basil

One summer out fishing off Long Island, I was lucky enough to catch a door-mat fluke. Since I knew just how fresh it was, I decided to try my hand at a Greek marinato. Many different styles of marinato are served all through Greece. Fresh anchovies and sardines are both marinated in lemon or vinegar and served raw. Another type of marinato is often made with small fish that are panfried and then marinated overnight in a sauce of extra virgin olive oil, garlic, and rosemary. I like to think that my version is a modern take on an Old World classic. Inspired by my buddy Doug Rodriguez, Nuevo-Latino chef extraordinaire, I came up with this dish based on his seviche. In the restaurant, I use sashimi-grade fluke and accent it with Lesvos basil (a special Greek herb), cucumbers, capers, and onions. The key to success is using pristine fish and serving it immediately, very, very cold, so the vibrant flavors dance right off the plate.

1 pound fluke fillet, all blood lines and dark flesh removed

1¼ cups fresh lemon juice

Coarse salt and freshly ground pepper

1 medium red onion, cut into julienne

6 thin slices jalapeño or Fresno chile

½ cup plus 2 tablespoons fresh orange juice

Pinch of sugar

½ cup finely diced seeded cucumber

2 tablespoons finely sliced scallion including some of the green part

1 tablespoon well-drained capers

1 tablespoon Lesvos or other fresh basil chiffonade (see Note)

2 tablespoons extra virgin olive oil

1. Place a medium stainless-steel bowl and 6 shallow serving bowls in the refrigerator for at least 30 minutes or until well chilled.

2. Make sure all the bones and skin are removed from the fish. Using a very sharp knife, cut the fillets crosswise into very thin slices. Place the slices in the chilled stainless-

steel bowl. Add the lemon juice and a pinch of salt. Then add the onion and chile and toss gently to combine. Let stand for about 2 minutes, or just until the edges of the fish slices begin to turn opaque.

3. Add the orange juice and a pinch of sugar. Place an equal portion of the marinato in each of the serving bowls. Sprinkle each portion with an equal amount of cucumber, scallion, capers, and basil. Taste and, if necessary, season with salt and pepper.

4. Drizzle a small amount of olive oil over the top and serve immediately.

NOTE: To make a chiffonade, or thin strips of a vegetable or herb, simply stack a small number of leaves, roll them up like a cigar, and then cut the roll crosswise into thin pieces. Pull the roll apart and you will have a pile of finely shredded leaves that will make an attractive garnish.

BRIAN AND MIKE, TWO OF MOLYVOS'S BARTENDERS.

Vinegar-Cured Branzino with Tomatoes, Rosemary, and Potato Salad

A childhood reminiscence of John Livanos's was the inspiration for this dish. His mother's skill at preparing the small fish from the daily catch made him long for the tenderly fried fish marinated in garlic, rosemary, vinegar, and olive oil that was an everyday meze in his house. I call this a *cooked marinato*. I used to do it with mackerel but now use branzino, a wonderful Mediterranean fish. A version of this dish is called *escabèche* in Spain and southern France, where it is served cold as an appetizer. This dish is best if left to marinate overnight.

½ cup all-purpose flour

1½ teaspoons coarse salt plus more to taste

¾ teaspoon ras el hanout

¾ teaspoon garlic powder

¾ teaspoon ground cumin

½ teaspoon Aleppo pepper (see page 9) or cayenne

8 garlic cloves, peeled and crushed

2 fresh rosemary sprigs

Freshly ground pepper

Six 2-ounce pieces skin-on branzino or red snapper fillet, pinbones removed

¼ cup plus ⅓ cup olive oil

Hot Brining Liquid (recipe follows)

2 tablespoons sliced garlic

1½ cups chopped peeled and seeded tomato (see page 113)

1 tablespoon chopped fresh flat-leaf parsley

½ teaspoon chopped fresh rosemary

Patatosalata (recipe follows)

Extra virgin olive oil for drizzling

1. Combine the flour, 1½ teaspoons salt, the ras el hanout, garlic powder, cumin, and Aleppo pepper in a shallow bowl, stirring to blend well. Set aside.

2. Scatter the crushed garlic and rosemary sprigs over the bottom of a glass baking dish large enough to hold all the fish in one layer. Set aside.

3. Season the fish with salt and pepper to taste. Working with one fillet at a time, lightly coat the fish in the seasoned flour. Shake off the excess flour.

(continued)

4. Heat ¼ cup of the olive oil in a medium sauté pan over medium heat for about 3 minutes, or until very hot but not smoking. Without crowding the pan and in batches, if necessary, add the coated fish, skin side down, and cook until the edges of the fillets are opaque and the center is slightly pink, 2 to 3 minutes. Turn and then immediately remove from the pan.

5. Place the fish in the prepared baking dish. Pour the hot brine over the fish and set aside to cool.

6. When cool, remove ¼ cup of the brine for use in the sauce. The brine should just barely cover the fish.

7. Cover the dish with plastic wrap and refrigerate for 24 hours.

8. Place the remaining ⅓ cup olive oil in a medium sauté pan over medium heat. Add the sliced garlic and sauté for 1 minute. Stir in the tomato and bring to a simmer. Add the reserved ¼ cup marinating liquid and again bring to a simmer. Simmer, stirring occasionally, for about 12 minutes, or until the tomato sauce is slightly thick.

9. Remove from the heat and set aside to cool.

10. When cool, stir in the chopped parsley and rosemary and set aside.

11. When ready to serve, place about 1 tablespoon of the Patatosalata in the center of each meze plate. Place a branzino fillet on top of the salad, along with a few pieces of tomato from the sauce. Drizzle the sauce over the top. Then drizzle with a bit of the brining liquid and extra virgin olive oil and serve.

Brining Liquid

Makes about 3 cups

1/2 cup white vinegar

3 garlic cloves, peeled and smashed

3 black peppercorns

1 fresh rosemary sprig

1 fresh thyme sprig

1 bay leaf

1 tablespoon coarse salt

2 teaspoons sugar

1 teaspoon coriander seeds

1 teaspoon mustard seeds

1. Combine 2½ cups cold water and the white vinegar in a medium nonreactive saucepan. Add the garlic, peppercorns, rosemary, thyme, bay leaf, salt, sugar, coriander seeds, and mustard seeds and place over high heat. Bring to a boil, then lower the heat and simmer for 5 minutes.

2. Place a strainer over a clean saucepan and strain the hot liquid through it into the clean pan. Pour over the top of the fish and marinate as directed.

Patatosalata

Serves 6

6 medium Yukon Gold (or other creamer) potatoes
Coarse salt and freshly ground pepper
Juice of 1 lemon
1 tablespoon extra virgin olive oil
1 tablespoon chopped fresh flat-leaf parsley
1 tablespoon chopped scallion, including some of the green part

1. Place the unpeeled potatoes in a medium saucepan with cold water to cover by 1 inch. Add a tablespoon of salt and place over high heat. Bring to a boil, then lower the heat and simmer for about 15 minutes, or until the potatoes are tender when pierced with a sharp knife. Remove from the heat and drain.

2. When the potatoes are cool enough to handle, peel and cut crosswise into thin slices. Place the sliced potatoes in a mixing bowl and add the lemon juice, olive oil, parsley, and scallion. Season with salt and pepper to taste and toss to combine. (The warmer the potatoes are when the seasoning is added, the more flavor they will absorb.)

3. Cover and set aside at room temperature until ready to serve.

Marinated Sardines with Fennel

It would be impossible to write a Greek cookbook and not include sardines, a national favorite. When I first began using this inexpensive and plentiful fish, I would use them whole in a salad. Then I got the idea to take them to a higher level with this sevichelike dish. I butterfly the fish, making sure there is not a bone left behind, then I marinate them and serve with some ouzo or a crisp white wine. A perfect snack—easy to do and even easier to eat, particularly with the ever-present glass of ouzo.

12 fresh 4- to 5-inch-long sardines, cleaned, scaled, heads removed, and butterflied (see Note)

Coarse salt

³/₄ cup white vinegar

2 cups plus 2 tablespoons extra virgin olive oil

Sea salt and cracked black pepper

Cracked fennel seeds

Pita bread for serving

1. Place a layer of sardines, skin side down, in a small baking dish or casserole. Lightly sprinkle with coarse salt and continue layering and salting until all of the sardines are in the pan. Cover with plastic wrap and refrigerate for 15 minutes.

2. Remove the sardines from the refrigerator and uncover. Pour the vinegar over the top and again cover with plastic wrap. Place the fish in the refrigerator to marinate for about 6 hours, or until it is almost milky white and opaque.

3. Remove the fish from the refrigerator, uncover, and drain off all the liquid.

4. Add 2 cups of olive oil to the dish, again cover with plastic wrap, and refrigerate for at least 6 hours or up to 3 days.

5. When ready to serve, remove the sardines from the oil and place 2 on each of 6 meze plates. Drizzle with a bit of the remaining 2 tablespoons of olive oil and sprinkle with sea salt, cracked black pepper, and cracked fennel seeds. Serve with pita bread and ouzo.

(continued)

Marinated Octopus
with Vinegar and Red Onions

Throughout Greece you will find some version of a vinegar-marinated octopus salad. This is my personal favorite. I slice the octopus paper-thin so that it absorbs the vinegar and then combine it with red onions marinated with a hint of sugar, vinegar, and sumac. At the last moment, a sprinkling of romaine chiffonade adds some additional color and texture.

Fresh octopus is available from fine fishmongers. The eight tentacles and the body are edible, but the eyes, mouth portion, and viscera are not. Although quite delicious, octopus can be very tough and must be blanched before finishing with other cooking methods.

5 tablespoons sherry vinegar

3 tablespoons red wine vinegar

1 tablespoon sugar

$^1/_2$ teaspoon ground sumac

Coarse salt and freshly ground pepper

$1^1/_2$ cups red onion julienne

1 whole $1^1/_2$-pound octopus, poached, head
    removed, and cut in half (recipe follows)

1 teaspoon dried Greek oregano

2 tablespoons extra virgin olive oil

6 romaine leaves, cut into chiffonade (see
    page 46)

1. Combine the vinegars with the sugar, sumac, and a pinch of salt in a nonreactive mixing bowl, whisking until the sugar has dissolved. Add the onion julienne and toss to coat. Sprinkle with a bit of salt to help pull the moisture from the onion. Cover and let stand at room temperature for 1 hour. Then refrigerate for at least 2 but preferably 6 hours.

2. Using a sharp knife, cut each tentacle from the poached octopus so that you have 8 pieces. Slice each tentacle crosswise into paper-thin pieces. Add the octopus slices to the marinated red onion. Cover and marinate for 1 hour. Add the oregano and drizzle with the olive oil. Season with salt and pepper to taste and fold in the romaine just before serving. Place on a serving platter or place equal portions on each small meze plate and serve immediately.

Poached Octopus

The poaching liquid is more than sufficient for up to ten baby octopus, so use whatever amount of octopus is called for in the recipe.

1 cup white wine vinegar

1 lemon

8 black peppercorns

4 bay leaves

2 tablespoons plus 2 teaspoons coarse salt

Whole or baby octopus, cleaned

1. Combine 1 gallon water and the vinegar in a large stockpot over high heat. Cut the lemon in half crosswise and squeeze each half into the water mixture, adding each squeezed half to the water. Add the peppercorns, bay leaves, and salt and stir to combine. Bring to a boil, lower the heat, and simmer for 10 minutes.

2. Using tongs or wearing thick rubber gloves and holding the octopus by the head, dunk the octopus body into the simmering water 3 times, leaving it submerged for about 5 seconds each time. This is called "scaring" the octopus, because the tentacles will curl up as you plunge the octopus into the water.

3. Drop the octopus into the simmering water after the final dunking and bring to a boil. Simmer for about 30 minutes, or until tender. Remove from the heat, drain well, and set aside to cool. If not using immediately, cover and refrigerate for up to 8 hours.

Keftedes in Red Sauce

Keftedes are Greek meatballs. Being Greek-Italian American, I really love my meatballs! My grandmother uses standard store-bought white bread soaked in milk to give her meatballs a light, almost fluffy texture, so since I have always loved her meatballs, I follow her recipe instead of using the rusks that are part of the traditional Greek recipe. This way, even in the restaurant kitchen, I am thinking about Sunday suppers with my family.

About 1 cup olive oil

1 cup finely diced yellow onion

Coarse salt

2 slices white bread

¹/₂ cup milk

¹/₂ pound 70-percent-lean ground beef

¹/₄ pound ground lamb

2 garlic cloves, minced

1 large egg, beaten

¹/₄ cup chopped fresh flat-leaf parsley

¹/₂ teaspoon dried oregano

¹/₂ teaspoon ground cumin, plus more for
    sprinkling

About ¹/₂ cup Fresh Bread Crumbs (recipe
    follows)

Red Sauce (recipe follows)

3 to 4 tablespoons extra virgin olive oil, or to
    taste

I. Heat 2 tablespoons of the olive oil in a large sauté pan over medium-low heat, swirling to coat the bottom of the pan with the oil. Add the onion along with a pinch of salt, cover, and lower the heat. Cook, stirring occasionally, for 10 to 12 minutes, or until the onion is translucent but has not taken on any color. Remove from the heat and set aside to cool.

2. Place the bread in a shallow bowl. Add milk to cover completely and soak, pressing on the bread to help it absorb the liquid until it is very soft. Break the soaked bread into small pieces.

3. Place the meats in a mixing bowl along with the reserved onion. Add the garlic, egg, 3 tablespoons of the parsley along with the oregano, cumin, and milk-soaked bread. Using your hands, work the mixture together until well combined, adding the Fresh Bread Crumbs, a tablespoon at a time, thoroughly mixing with your hands to make a moist but not wet mixture that no longer sticks to your hands. Cover with plastic wrap and refrigerate for about 30 minutes, or until chilled.

4. When chilled, form the mixture into balls about 1 inch in diameter (a 1-ounce ice cream scoop works well). If not frying immediately, place in a single layer on a baking pan or platter, cover with plastic wrap, and refrigerate.

5. Place the remaining olive oil in a large, heavy sauté pan over medium heat. When the oil is very hot but not smoking, add the meatballs in batches and fry, turning frequently, for about 5 minutes, or until the meatballs are browned evenly. Using a slotted spoon, transfer the meatballs to a double layer of paper towels to drain. This will have to be done in 2 batches.

6. Place the Red Sauce in a large saucepan over medium heat. Add the meatballs and bring to a simmer. Cook at a gentle simmer for about 1 hour, or until the meatballs are cooked through and the sauce is slightly thick.

7. Remove from the heat and fold in the remaining tablespoon of parsley. Place 4 meatballs along with a generous amount of sauce in each of 6 shallow bowls. Sprinkle with cumin to taste. Drizzle just a hint of extra virgin olive oil over the top and serve hot.

Fresh Bread Crumbs

Makes about 3 cups

Crumbs you don't use right away will keep in an airtight container stored in a cool, dry place for up to 1 month.

¹/₂ pound home-style white bread, cut into ¹/₄-inch cubes

1. Preheat the oven to 200°F.

2. Place the bread cubes in a single layer on a baking sheet and bake for about 25 minutes, or until golden. Remove from the oven and set aside to cool.

3. When cool, place the bread cubes in a food processor fitted with the metal blade. Process for about 2 minutes or until very fine.

Red Sauce

Makes about 2 quarts

2 tablespoons olive oil

1 cup diced yellow onion

Coarse salt and freshly ground pepper

8 garlic cloves, sliced

1 teaspoon ground cumin

1 teaspoon dried oregano

1 cup dry red wine, such as Aghiorghitiko, Cabernet Sauvignon, or Sangiovese

One 28-ounce can whole tomatoes with juice

2 teaspoons sugar

1 cup Chicken Stock (page 281) or low-sodium chicken broth

1. Heat the oil in a heavy saucepan over medium heat. Add the onion along with a pinch of salt, lower the heat, and cover. Cook, stirring occasionally, for 10 to 12 minutes, or until the onion is translucent but has not taken on any color. Raise the heat, add the garlic, and cook for 3 minutes, stirring occasionally. Stir in the cumin, oregano, and another pinch of salt and cook for 1 minute. Add the wine, raise the heat, and bring to a boil. Immediately lower the heat and simmer for about 15 minutes, or until the liquid has reduced by half.

2. Place the tomatoes in a mixing bowl and, using your hands, crush the tomatoes, taking care to remove any hard, tough pieces. Add the tomatoes and sugar to the saucepan and stir to combine. Raise the heat and bring to a boil, skimming off any impurities or excess fat that rises to the surface. Add the stock, season with salt and pepper to taste, and bring to a simmer. Use immediately or pour into a nonreactive container and cool to room temperature. Cover and refrigerate until ready to use or for up to 3 days.

Tyrokeftedes (Crispy Cheese Fritters)

Keftedes are everywhere in Greece, usually made from meat. These delectable little balls can, however, also be made from a base of cheese or even vegetables or seafood. I think this recipe, using three cheeses, is one of the best. In this version I lightly bind three different cheeses together to make a bite-sized treat. A couple of hints for perfect tyrokeftedes: (1) Freeze the base so that it is ice-cold and almost frozen in the center so that it will hold together when fried. (2) Use a combination of flour and cornstarch to prevent greasiness. (3) Use panko, Japanese bread crumbs, for a beautiful, crisp crust. I know, panko isn't Greek, but this is the new Greek cuisine that we're cooking!

7 ounces vlahotyri cheese, shredded

3¹/₂ ounces kasseri cheese, shredded

2¹/₂ ounces ricotta cheese

¹/₂ cup plus 1 tablespoon cornstarch

1¹/₂ tablespoons chopped fresh mint

Freshly ground white pepper

5 large eggs

1 cup all-purpose flour

1 tablespoon coarse salt

¹/₂ teaspoon freshly ground black pepper

3 cups panko bread crumbs (see Note)

3 cups extra virgin olive oil

1 cup peanut oil

Sliced lemons for serving (optional)

1. Line a baking pan with parchment. Set aside.

2. Combine the 3 cheeses in the bowl of a heavy-duty electric mixer fitted with the paddle attachment. Add 1 tablespoon of the cornstarch along with the mint and white pepper to taste and mix together on low speed. Add one egg, turn the mixer to medium speed, and mix to combine.

3. Using a ¹/₂-ounce ice cream scoop, scoop the cheese mixture into mounds and place on the prepared baking pan. Place in the freezer for about 20 minutes, or until well chilled but not frozen solid.

4. Remove the cheese mounds from the freezer and, working with one at a time, roll the mounds into little balls with your palms. Return the balls to the parchment-lined pan and again place in the freezer. Freeze until

almost solidly frozen in the center, probably about 20 minutes.

5. While the cheese balls are chilling, prepare the breading. Place 3 shallow bowls side by side on a counter. Place the remaining ½ cup cornstarch in the first bowl along with the flour, salt, and black pepper. Place the remaining 4 eggs in the second bowl and whisk to blend well. Place the panko in the third bowl.

6. Remove the cheese balls from the freezer and, working with one piece at a time, dip each one into the cornstarch mixture to coat lightly. Then dip into the beaten egg, shaking off any excess. Finally roll the ball in the panko, firmly pressing to ensure that the coating adheres but without damaging the round shape. Return the coated cheese balls to the parchment-lined pan until all balls are coated. Return to the freezer while the oil is heating.

7. Line a baking pan with a triple layer of paper towel. Set aside.

8. Preheat the oven to its lowest warming setting.

9. Combine the olive and peanut oils in a deep-fat fryer fitted with a basket over high heat. Bring to 325°F on an instant-read thermometer.

10. Using a slotted spoon, gently add the coated cheese balls to the hot oil. Do not crowd the pan. Fry for about 6 minutes, or until golden brown and crisp.

11. When brown, transfer the cooked tyrokeftedes to the paper towel–lined pan and continuing frying until all are done. Keep the cooked tyrokeftedes in the warm oven until ready to serve as a meze with sliced lemons if desired.

NOTE: Panko are coarse Japanese bread crumbs generally used to make a light, very crunchy coating on fried foods. They are available in Asian markets and some specialty food stores.

Grilled Greek Country Sausage

Analyzing my meze menu one day, I realized that we didn't offer any sausage. I thought it might be fun to follow the classic charcuterie techniques and make a Greek-flavored sausage that we could grill. Great sausage is easy to make if you follow a couple of rules. The ingredients and the equipment must be ice-cold—34°F is perfect—but not frozen. A bit of ice in the mix keeps the fat firm and the sausage from getting mushy.

The meat is cubed and then marinated so that it absorbs the maximum amount of flavor before being ground and stuffed.

1½ pounds boneless pork butt, cut into large dice

1 pound boneless lamb chuck, cut into large dice

1 bay leaf

6 tablespoons roughly chopped fresh flat-leaf parsley

2 tablespoons grated orange zest

2 tablespoons coarse salt

1½ tablespoons coarsely ground toasted fennel seeds (see page 44)

1 tablespoon coarsely ground toasted coriander seeds (see page 44)

1 tablespoon coarsely ground toasted black peppercorns (see page 44)

1 tablespoon roughly chopped garlic

1 tablespoon roughly chopped fresh mint leaves

2 teaspoons olive oil

½ teaspoon sugar

Pinch of Aleppo pepper or cayenne (see page 9)

3 ounces crushed ice (about ½ cup)

1. Combine the meats in a mixing bowl. Add the bay leaf, parsley, orange zest, salt, fennel, coriander, peppercorns, garlic, mint, olive oil, sugar, and Aleppo pepper and stir to combine. Cover with plastic wrap and refrigerate for 8 hours.

2. Set up either a meat grinder or a heavy-duty electric mixer fitted with the medium meat-grinding attachment.

3. Make an ice-water bath in a large bowl. Place a smaller bowl in the center of the ice-water bath. Place the bath under the meat grinder so that the ground meat mixture will fall into the bowl sitting in the center.

4. Remove the meat from the refrigerator. Remove the bay leaf and stir in the crushed ice. The ice, combined with the ice-water

bath, will keep the meat ice-cold, which will help bind the mixture. Immediately pass the meat mixture through the grinder into the bowl.

5. When all of the meat has been ground, stir it with a wooden spoon to ensure that it is evenly mixed.

6. Using the sausage-making attachment on the mixer, follow the manufacturer's instructions for making link sausage. If you have other sausage-making equipment, attach the casing to the tube, closing the end, and run the meat through the body so that it flows into the casing. The meat should be tightly packed into the casing, leaving at least 4 inches of empty casing at the end. (If you don't have sausage-making equipment, fill a pastry bag fitted with a standard large round tip and carefully fill the casing in the same manner.)

7. Starting at the closed end, seal off 5-inch links, twisting and pinching at each interval, until you have 10 links, each about 3½ inches long. Tie off the open ends with a firm knot. Wrap the links in plastic and refrigerate for at least 3 hours before grilling, broiling, or roasting.

NOTE: If all of this seems too difficult, you can always form the meat into patties, chill for at least 3 hours, and then grill, broil, or roast.

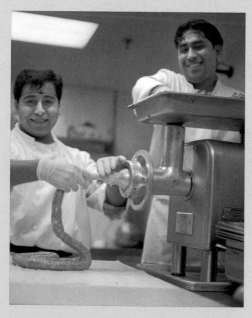

PORFIRIO (RIGHT), THE LINE COOK, WITH ADRIANE, THE BUTCHER, MAKING OUR GARLIC AND PORK SAUSAGE.

Pork Spareribs Marinated in Ouzo and Greek Spices

I love all kinds of ribs—Asian, barbecued, southern style, or backyard grilled. This is my "Greekified" version. I prefer to cook these on a charcoal grill where I can keep one side fairly cool to prevent quick cooking and even faster burning. They can also be prepared in a slow (about 225°F) oven. If you're using the oven, place the ribs on a rack on a baking sheet and bake as directed for about 2½ hours, or until cooked. When ready to serve, place the ribs, meat side up, under a preheated broiler and broil for a few minutes or until nicely caramelized. For a more authentic Greek dish, try using lamb spareribs.

3 racks (2½ to 3 pounds each) St. Louis–style pork spareribs, trimmed of thin skin and excess cartilage

1 cup ouzo

2 cups fresh orange juice

½ cup packed light brown sugar

2 tablespoons honey

3 tablespoons coarse salt

2 tablespoons coriander seeds

2 tablespoons cumin seeds

2 tablespoons anise seeds

2 tablespoons mustard seeds

2 tablespoons granulated garlic

1 tablespoon whole fenugreek

2 teaspoons ground cinnamon

1 teaspoon black peppercorns

1 teaspoon granulated sugar

¼ teaspoon ground cloves

1. Using the tip of a small, sharp knife, cut small slits in the thick part of the racks between rib joints to allow the meat to absorb the marinade and facilitate cutting after baking.

2. Place the ouzo in a medium nonreactive saucepan over medium heat. As the ouzo heats, it will ignite. The flame will burn for about 3 minutes, which will burn off the alcohol. If it does not flame by itself, shake the pan slightly, which will cause the vapors from the ouzo to ignite. Remove from the heat until the flame expires. Add the orange juice, brown sugar, and honey and return to medium heat. Cook, stirring frequently, for about 5 minutes, or until a glaze forms.

(continued)

About 1 cup of liquid should remain. Set aside to cool.

3. Combine the salt with the coriander, cumin, anise, mustard, garlic, fenugreek, cinnamon, peppercorns, granulated sugar, and cloves in a spice grinder and coarsely grind. Transfer to a small, shallow mixing bowl.

4. When ready to grill, working with one rack of ribs at a time, holding each by one end, slowly pull the meat through the spice mixture, taking care to coat both sides evenly. Transfer the coated ribs to a wire rack placed on a baking sheet large enough to hold them in a single layer.

5. Preheat and oil a gas grill or light a charcoal grill and burn the coals until covered in white ash, building the fire on one side of the grill to leave one cool side. Or, alternatively, preheat the oven to 225°F.

6. Place the racks, bone side down, on the hot grill, just above the cool side. Cover and cook for 1 hour. Uncover, turn, and grill for another hour. Again turn and, using a pastry brush, baste the meat side of the hot racks with the reserved ouzo glaze. Continue to grill for about 15 minutes, or until caramelized and slightly charred. Again turn and brush the remaining side with the glaze and grill for another 15 minutes, or until both sides are caramelized and the meat is very tender. Follow this procedure for oven baking. (If using the oven, place the racks under the broiler to char slightly before serving.)

7. Remove from the grill. Using a sharp knife, cut into individual ribs and serve.

JOHN PILIOURAS, CHEF DE CUISINE, CHECKS THE QUALITY OF THE FRESH OCTOPUS.

Pies

Pies or *pites* (the plural of *pita,* meaning "closed pie") are one of the mainstays of Greek cooking. Greeks enclose almost anything between thin layers of pastry, either phyllo dough or other homemade pastry, even bread dough. Most frequently, cooks use a combination of cheese and wild greens and herbs or garden-fresh vegetables when making pies. Sometimes a bit of meat or seafood is combined with rice for a richer filling. They can be made as one big pie or as individual pies, which I prefer (even at home) as I think diners enjoy having their own small serving and individual portions eliminate any waste. All of the following pies can be made in advance and frozen, before being cooked, for up to two weeks. Served warm or at room temperature, in the Greek tradition pies are served as a meze or an appetizer, but in America they are often used as a main course with the addition of a salad or mixed greens. Greek pies are the ultimate finger food!

Spanakopita (Spinach, Leeks, and Feta Wrapped in Crispy Phyllo)

This meze takes me straight back to my childhood. Any family celebration, large or small, would feature my grandmother's spinach pie. Now well into her eighties, my grandmother is still in charge of making the spanakopita. She uses pizza dough instead of phyllo, because she feels it is easier to handle, and, I have to admit, her pies taste great. As it was for me, spanakopita is now a favorite snack for my daughter, Sofia.

At Molyvos, I stick with tradition and use phyllo dough to make what is, after Greek salad, our best-selling traditional dish.

³/₄ cup plus **2** tablespoons olive oil

1¹/₂ pounds fresh spinach, stems removed

Coarse salt

1¹/₂ cups finely diced onion

1¹/₂ cups finely diced white part of leek

1 teaspoon minced garlic

1 large egg

³/₄ cup crumbled feta cheese

2 tablespoons grated kefalotyri cheese

1 tablespoon finely chopped fresh mint

1 tablespoon finely chopped fresh dill

1 pound frozen #10 phyllo dough, thawed as directed on package

1. Preheat the oven to 350°F.

2. Heat 2 tablespoons of the olive oil in a large sauté pan over medium heat. Add the spinach in handfuls, season with a pinch of salt, and sauté until all of the spinach has wilted, about 5 minutes. Remove from the heat and transfer to a colander placed in a bowl so that all liquid can be reserved. Press on the spinach to drain off any excess liquid.

3. Spread the spinach out on a baking pan. Transfer to the refrigerator for about 30 minutes or until cool.

4. When the spinach is cool, transfer to a clean cutting board. Using a sharp knife or cleaver, chop the spinach until very, very fine. Set aside.

5. Heat ¹/₄ cup of the remaining olive oil in a medium sauce pot over medium heat. Add the onion and another pinch of salt. Cover and cook, stirring occasionally, for about 10 minutes, or until the onion is soft and translucent but has not taken on any color. Stir in the leek, cover again, and cook for about 5 minutes. Uncover, add the garlic and another pinch of salt, and continue to sauté for 2 minutes, or until the leeks have softened but not taken on any color. Add the reserved chopped spinach, stirring until well blended. If the mixture is dry, add 1 to 2 tablespoons of the reserved spinach juice. Cook for 3 minutes longer, or until most of the liquid has evaporated.

6. Transfer the spinach mixture to a baking pan, spreading it out with a spatula to make an even layer. Refrigerate for about 1 hour, or until chilled.

7. Remove the chilled spinach mixture from the refrigerator and transfer it to a mixing bowl. Stir in the egg, cheeses, mint, and dill. Season with salt to taste and set aside.

8. Line at least 2 baking sheets with parchment paper. Set aside.

9. Hold the phyllo as directed on page 12.

10. Working with one sheet at a time, lay the phyllo out on a clean, dry surface. Using a pastry brush, lightly coat the phyllo with some of the remaining olive oil. Using a small, sharp knife, cut the oiled phyllo lengthwise into seven 2-inch-wide strips. Working with one strip at a time, place 1 tablespoon of the spinach mixture in the lower corner of the dough. Fold the bottom end of the dough over the spinach to meet the right edge of the dough, forming a triangle. Continue folding in the triangle shape until the entire strip has been folded.

11. Place the triangles on the prepared baking sheets as they are finished. (For very even browning, place the pies on wire racks on the cookie sheets before baking.) Continue making triangles until all the spinach mixture has been used.

12. When all of the pies have been made, place the baking sheets in the preheated oven and bake for about 20 minutes, or until golden brown and crisp. Remove from the oven and serve hot.

NOTE: Spanakopita can be made in advance and frozen, unbaked, for up to 3 weeks. Bake as directed above allowing about 5 extra minutes.

Hortopita (Wild Greens Pie)

Wrapping the hortopita in this fashion allows you to serve it as an appetizer or make it part of a meze table. For extra richness, fold in ½ cup crumbled feta cheese. You will need twelve 4-ounce soufflé dishes or other 4-ounce round molds for this recipe.

This pie calls for a homemade herb tea—vegetables, spices, and herbs that combine to create a light vegetable-herb broth essential to flavoring the greens.

About 1½ cups extra virgin olive oil

2 cups finely diced onion

Coarse salt and freshly ground pepper

1½ cups finely diced white part of leek

2 cups tightly packed blanched black kale (also called cavolo nero, or dinosaur kale), chard, or escarole, chopped

1½ cups tightly packed blanched fresh dandelion, mustard, or other bitter greens, chopped

Juice of 1 lemon

1 cup freshly brewed Herb Tea (page 289)

¼ cup sliced scallion

2 tablespoons chopped fresh dill

6 sheets frozen #10 phyllo dough, thawed as directed on package

I. Heat 3 tablespoons of the olive oil in a 4-quart saucepan over low heat. Add the onion and leek along with a pinch of salt. Cover and cook, stirring occasionally, for about 10 minutes, or until very soft and translucent.

2. Raise the heat to medium-high and add another tablespoon of the olive oil. Add the kale and cook for 2 minutes. Add the dandelion greens and season with salt and pepper to taste. Add the lemon juice, Herb Tea, and 2 tablespoons of the remaining olive oil. Lower the heat to medium and cook for 15 to 18 minutes, or until all of the liquid has evaporated. Remove from the heat and transfer to a baking sheet to cool.

3. When cool, stir in the scallion and dill and drizzle with 1 tablespoon of the remaining olive oil. Set aside.

4. Preheat the oven to 375°F.

(continued)

5. Line a baking sheet with parchment paper and place a wire rack large enough to hold the molds on it. Set aside.

6. Hold the phyllo as directed on page 12.

7. Lay one sheet of phyllo dough on a clean surface and, using a pastry brush, lightly coat it with a bit of the remaining olive oil. Using a sharp knife, cut the phyllo down the center lengthwise into 2 equal pieces. Then cut each piece lengthwise into 2 equal pieces so that you now have 4 pieces of equal size. Repeat the process to give you 8 strips, each approximately 1 inch wide. Work with just one piece of phyllo at a time because, if prepared in advance, the dough will dry out and be unusable.

8. Working with one mold at a time, lay one phyllo strip over the top of a mold. Gently press the phyllo down into the mold, letting the excess dough hang down over the outside of the mold. Lay a second strip of dough across the mold, slightly overlapping the first strip, and press it down into the mold as before. Using two more strips, continue to line the mold.

9. Taste the cooled greens mixture and, if necessary, season with additional salt and pepper. Spoon enough of the mixture into the mold to fill it about three-quarters full once packed down into the mold.

10. Fold the overhanging phyllo up and over the filling to enclose it completely. Using kitchen scissors, trim off any excess dough. Using a small, sharp knife, make 4 small slits in the top of the dough. Lightly brush with olive oil.

11. Continue making layered phyllo, lining and finishing the molds until you have completed twelve.

12. Place the filled molds on the prepared baking sheet. Place in the preheated oven and bake for 15 to 20 minutes, or until golden brown. Remove from the oven and set aside for 3 minutes.

13. Working with one at a time, invert the molds to remove the pies. Serve hot, as is or on top of a lightly dressed tossed green salad.

Kolokithopita (Squash Pie with Trahana, Rice, and Fennel)

I had versions of this pie on the island of Chios and in Molyvos, served either as a prelude to a sweet with grated cheese added to the filling or as a sweet minus the cheese. I loved the flavors. The slightly sweet overtones of kolokithopita make it a very intriguing pie. If you would like to add cheese to the mix, about 1 cup grated kasseri cheese would be perfect.

You will need twelve 4-ounce ramekins to execute the dish. To use this pie on the meze table, fill the ramekins only about one-quarter full and trim off the excess phyllo. You will have thin phyllo-covered disks that are easy finger food.

The trahana recipe makes much more than you will need. However, like commercial pasta, it will keep almost indefinitely.

6 cups tightly packed coarsely grated calabaza or
    butternut squash
1/2 cup long-grain rice, rinsed in cold water
1/2 cup Trahana (recipe follows)
Coarse salt and freshly ground white pepper

1/4 cup sugar
1 teaspoon ground cinnamon
6 sheets frozen #10 phyllo dough, thawed as
    directed on package
About 1 cup olive oil

1. Combine the squash, rice, trahana, and 1 teaspoon salt, mixing and breaking up the pasta with your hands. The salt will help bring out the moisture. Keep mixing with your hands until the rice begins to soften somewhat.

2. Transfer the mixture to a large baking dish, spreading it out in an even layer. Cover and refrigerate, mixing occasionally, for at least 12 hours, or until the rice has softened.

3. Remove the mixture from the refrigerator and let stand for 10 minutes. Transfer to a mixing bowl and add the sugar and cinnamon. When well blended, transfer the mixture to a clean kitchen towel and twist the liquid into a clean saucepan.

4. Place the liquid over low heat and cook for about 15 minutes, or until slightly thick and syrupy. Remove from the heat and set aside to cool.

(continued)

5. Return the squash mixture to the mixing bowl and stir in salt and white pepper to taste. Add the cooled cooking liquid.

6. Preheat the oven to 325°F.

7. Line a baking sheet with parchment paper and place a wire rack large enough to hold the ramekins on it. Set aside.

8. Hold the phyllo as directed on page 00.

9. Lay one sheet of phyllo dough on a clean surface and, using a pastry brush, lightly coat it with a bit of the olive oil. Using a sharp knife, cut the phyllo down the center lengthwise into 2 equal pieces. Then cut each piece lengthwise into 2 equal pieces so that you now have 4 pieces of equal size. Repeat the process to give you 8 strips, each approximately 1 inch wide. Work with just one piece of phyllo at a time because, if prepared in advance, the dough will dry out and be unusable.

10. Working with one mold at a time, lay one phyllo strip over the top of a mold. Gently press the phyllo down into the mold, letting the excess dough hang down over the outside of the mold. Lay a second strip of dough across the mold, slightly overlapping the first strip, and press it down into the mold as before. Using two more strips, continue to line the mold.

11. Spoon enough of the squash mixture into the ramekin, gently packing down, to fill the dish three-quarters full.

12. Working with one strip at a time, pull the overhanging phyllo dough up and over the center of the ramekin to completely enclose the filling. Using kitchen scissors, trim off excess dough. Using a paring knife, make small slits in the top of the dough. Using a pastry brush, lightly coat the top with a bit of olive oil.

13. Repeat this process for the remaining 11 ramekins, one at a time.

14. Place the ramekins on the prepared baking sheet. Place in the preheated oven and bake for 20 to 25 minutes, or until golden brown.

15. Remove from the oven and transfer to a wire rack to cool for 3 minutes.

16. When ready to serve, invert one mold onto each plate and unmold the pie. Serve hot.

Trahana

Makes about 1/2 pound

2 cups whole milk

1³/₄ cups Greek yogurt (see page 13)

Coarse salt and freshly ground pepper

1³/₄ cups medium bulgur

¹/₂ cup fine semolina flour

¹/₄ cup fresh lemon juice

I. Line a 15¹/₂'-inch × 10¹/₂-inch × 1-inch baking pan with parchment paper. Set aside.

2. Combine the milk, yogurt, and salt and pepper to taste in a heavy medium saucepan over medium heat, whisking to blend well. Cook for about 5 minutes, or until hot but not simmering.

3. Whisk in the bulgur and semolina flour. Add the lemon juice and bring to a simmer, whisking constantly. Lower the heat and cook at a bare simmer, occasionally mixing and cleaning the sides of the pan with a heatproof rubber spatula, for about 12 minutes, or until the mixture is the consistency of polenta and the grains are very soft.

4. Transfer the mixture to a nonstick jelly roll pan, spreading out to an even layer. Set aside to cool. The mixture will be very thick.

5. Using your hands and wearing rubber gloves, gently break the trahana into quarter-size pieces and place the pieces in a single layer on the prepared baking pan. Do not overcrowd the pan. Set aside to dry for 8 hours or overnight.

6. Preheat the oven to 200°F.

7. Place the dried trahana in the preheated oven and bake for about 3 hours, or until very hard. Remove from the oven and cool.

8. Transfer the cooled hard pasta to a container with a tight lid. Store in a cool dark place just as you would commercial pasta.

Eggplant Pie with Walnuts and Cumin

If the outdoor grill has been put away for the winter, don't despair, as I have often grilled egg-plant on the stovetop in a ridged stovetop grill pan or placed it under a broiler. This is a classic Greek combination of the smooth, slightly sweet eggplant with pungent cheese, a little spice, and the crunch of nuts.

3 medium eggplants

About 1¼ cups olive oil

5 leeks, white part only, well washed and diced

Coarse salt and freshly ground pepper

1 cup crumbled feta cheese

½ cup crumbled kefalotyri cheese

¾ cup coarsely chopped toasted walnuts (see Note)

2 tablespoons chopped fresh flat-leaf parsley

1 teaspoon ground cumin

About ¾ cup Fresh Bread Crumbs, as needed (page 57)

3 large egg yolks

1 teaspoon milk

18 sheets (2 packages) frozen #10 phyllo dough, thawed as directed on package

1 tablespoon sesame seeds

1. Preheat and oil a grill.

2. Place a wire rack on a baking pan. Set aside.

3. Pierce each eggplant in several places with a dinner fork. Place the eggplants on the preheated grill and grill, turning occa-sionally to prevent burning, for about 15 minutes, or until the eggplants are soft and the skin is black. (Or place the eggplants on a ridged stovetop grill pan over medium heat and grill, turning frequently, for about 25 minutes, or until soft and black. Cooking

under the broiler will take about the same time.)

4. Transfer the eggplants to a colander placed over a bowl and drain for about 30 minutes, or until most of the juice has drained off. Discard the juice.

5. When the eggplants are well drained and cool enough to handle, peel and discard the skin. Chop the flesh, place in a large mixing bowl, and set aside. You should have about 3 cups.

6. Heat 2 tablespoons of the oil in a large sauté pan over medium-low heat. Add the leeks along with a pinch of salt and cook, stirring occasionally, for 10 minutes. Adjust the heat if necessary to keep the leeks from browning.

7. Transfer the leeks to a bowl. Then place the bowl in an ice bath to cool the leeks quickly.

8. When the leeks are cool, combine them with the eggplant. Stir in the cheeses, walnuts, parsley, and cumin. Season with salt and pepper to taste. The mixture should be moist but not wet. If the mixture seems very moist, add just enough bread crumbs to tighten it. Cover and refrigerate for 12 hours.

9. Preheat the oven to 325°F.

10. Line a baking sheet with parchment paper and place a wire rack large enough to hold the pies on it. You may need 2 pans. Set aside.

11. Combine the egg yolks with the milk in a small bowl, whisking to combine.

12. Hold the phyllo as directed on page 12.

13. Lay one sheet of phyllo dough on a clean surface with the longest sides going from right to left. Using a pastry brush, lightly coat it with a bit of the remaining olive oil. Sprinkle with bread crumbs. Work with just one piece of phyllo at a time, because the dough quickly dries out and is rendered unusable.

14. Place about $1/3$ cup of the eggplant mixture in the center of the bottom of the phyllo sheet, spreading it out slightly. Fold in the ends and begin rolling up the dough, to make a long, thin cylinder. Keep brushing the dough with oil or it will begin to crack.

15. Beginning with one end, roll the cylinder up into a snail shape. Transfer the pie to the prepared baking sheet and, using a clean pastry brush, lightly coat with the egg wash and sprinkle with a few sesame seeds. Continue making pies until you have made 18.

16. When all of the pies have been prepared, place in the preheated oven and bake for 20 minutes, or until golden brown.

17. Remove from the oven and set aside to cool for 3 minutes before serving.

NOTE: To toast nuts, place them in a single layer in a skillet over medium-low heat or in a baking pan in a preheated 300°F oven. Turn frequently to keep them from burning and turning bitter. This should take no more than 5 minutes as nuts are quite oily and will brown quickly.

Leek and Cheese Pie

This crustless pie can be made quickly when unexpected guests arrive. It also makes a great light lunch served with a mixed green salad. Again, it can also be made in meze portions (see page 73).

¹/₄ cup extra virgin olive oil

1 large Spanish onion, finely diced

Coarse salt and freshly ground pepper

2 leeks, white part only, well washed and thinly sliced crosswise

2 tablespoons unsalted butter at room temperature

1 cup all-purpose flour, sifted

³/₄ teaspoon baking powder, sifted

3 large eggs at room temperature

7 ounces Greek yogurt (see page 13)

11 ounces feta cheese, finely diced (about 2¹/₄ cups)

¹/₄ cup chopped fresh dill

I. Heat the olive oil in a medium sauté pan over medium heat. Add the onion along with a pinch of salt and cook, stirring occasionally, for 6 to 8 minutes. Add the leeks, season with salt and pepper to taste, and continue to cook, stirring occasionally, for about 8 minutes, or until the vegetables are very soft and translucent. Remove the pan from the heat and place in an ice bath to cool.

2. Preheat the oven to 300°F.

3. Generously coat the inside of a 10-inch nonstick springform cake pan with the butter. Set aside.

4. Sift the flour and baking powder together. Set aside.

5. Combine the eggs and yogurt in a mixing bowl. Fold in the feta and dill. When well combined, whisk in the flour mixture. Fold in the cooled onion/leek mixture, folding until well blended. Season with salt and pepper to taste.

6. Pour the mixture into the prepared pan, gently tapping on the sides of the pan to level the top. Place in the preheated oven and bake for 30 minutes. Raise the heat to 350°F and bake for 10 minutes longer, or until the pie is set in the center.

7. Remove from the oven and set aside on a wire rack to cool for 10 minutes before un-molding. Cut into wedges and serve as is or, if desired, on a bed of lightly dressed mixed greens with a dollop of Greek yogurt on top.

VEGETABLES, HERBS, AND HORTA AT A GREEK MARKET.

Chicken Bourekia

This is a bit different from the chicken bourekia that I experienced in Greece—particularly with the addition of the chicken confit. In Greece, the chicken would simply be poached, which you can also do if you don't want to take the time to make the confit. However, since the confit can be made way in advance and the bourekia made early in the day and reheated, I urge you to give them a try.

$^1/_4$ cup duck fat (see Note) or unsalted butter

1 cup diced onion

1 cup diced white part of leek

Coarse salt and freshly ground pepper

1 cup Chicken Stock (page 281)

$^1/_4$ cup golden raisins

$^1/_4$ cup Samos wine, warmed

1 cup chopped fresh pea shoots (see Note)

$^3/_4$ cup toasted sliced almonds (see page 77)

1 tablespoon fresh mint chiffonade (see page 46)

1 tablespoon chopped fresh chives

1 tablespoon grated lemon zest

1 teaspoon ground fenugreek

$^1/_4$ teaspoon ground cinnamon

Pinch of freshly grated nutmeg

2 pounds Chicken Confit (recipe follows)

5 sheets frozen #10 phyllo dough, thawed as directed on package

About 1 cup extra virgin olive oil

I. Heat the duck fat in a large sauté pan over medium-low heat. Add the onion and leek along with a pinch of salt and cook, stirring occasionally, for 10 to 12 minutes. Add the stock, cover, and cook, stirring occasionally, for about 15 minutes, or until the onion and leek are very soft, adjusting the heat if necessary to keep them from browning. Remove the lid and cook for about 2 minutes, or just until the liquid has cooked off. Remove the pan from the heat and place in an ice bath to cool.

2. Meanwhile, combine the raisins with the warm wine in a small bowl. Set aside to allow the raisins to plump and cool. When cool, drain well, discarding the wine.

3. When the leek-onion mixture has cooled, transfer to a mixing bowl. Stir in the

cooled raisins, pea shoots, almonds, mint, chives, lemon zest, fenugreek, cinnamon, and nutmeg. When blended, fold in the confit. Season with salt and pepper to taste.

4. Preheat the oven to 300°F.

5. Line a baking sheet with parchment paper and place a wire rack large enough to hold the pies on it. Set aside.

6. Hold the phyllo as directed on page 12.

7. Working with one sheet of phyllo at a time and using a pastry brush, lightly coat a sheet with olive oil. Cut the phyllo lengthwise into 3 equal pieces.

8. Place about 2 tablespoons of the chicken filling about ½ inch from the bottom of each strip of phyllo. Fold the top over and the sides in to cover the filling and then roll the phyllo into an egg roll shape, brushing with olive oil as you go. Lightly brush the roll with olive oil and place the finished roll, seam side down, on the rack on the prepared baking sheet. Finish making the remaining rolls.

9. Place the pan in the preheated oven and bake for 20 minutes, or until golden. Remove from the oven, arrange pies on a platter, and serve family style.

NOTE: Duck fat, lard, or goose fat is available from specialty food stores or fine butchers. Pea shoots are available from specialty produce stores, farmers' markets, and some supermarkets.

Chicken Confit

Makes about 2 pounds

5 garlic cloves, unpeeled, smashed

5 fresh thyme sprigs

5 fresh oregano sprigs

3 fresh sage sprigs

12 whole allspice

6 whole cloves

4 cinnamon sticks

1 lemon, well washed and thinly sliced crosswise

About ¼ cup coarse salt

2 whole chicken breasts with skin and bone, halved

2 pounds lard or goose fat (see page 81)

1. Combine the garlic, thyme, oregano, and sage with the allspice, cloves, and cinnamon sticks in a small bowl. Stir in the lemon.

2. Place about 1 tablespoon of the salt in the bottom of an 11-inch-long rectangular glass baking dish. Sprinkle half of the herb/spice mixture over the salt. Lay the chicken breasts, skin side down, in a single layer on top of the seasoning. Sprinkle the remaining herb/spice mixture over the top, followed by a heavy rain of salt. Cover with plastic wrap and place a heavy pan on top of the dish to weight the chicken. Transfer to the refrigerator and let marinate for 2 days.

3. Unwrap the chicken, rinse under cool running water, and pat dry.

4. Place a wire rack on a baking pan. Place the chicken on the wire rack and refrigerate for at least 8 hours or overnight to dry the chicken out somewhat.

5. Preheat the oven to 375°F.

6. Place the lard in a heavy saucepan over low heat, heating just until melted.

7. Transfer the chicken to a baking pan. Pour the warm lard over the chicken to cover. Place in the preheated oven and bake for about 2½ hours, or until the chicken is falling off the bone. The fat should be at a bare simmer throughout the baking. If it bubbles rapidly, lower the heat as you don't want the chicken to cook too fast.

8. Remove the chicken from the oven and set aside to cool in the fat. When cool, refrigerate, covered with plastic wrap, until ready to use. The confit will keep, covered in the rich fat, for up to 2 weeks.

9. When ready to use, pull the meat from the skin and bones. Shred the meat and discard both the skin and bones.

MEZEDES AND PITAS, CLOCKWISE FROM TOP LEFT: TARAMASALATA, PAGE 31; GREEK FAVA WITH ARUGULA, SPRING ONIONS, AND CAPERS, PAGE 39; GREEK OLIVES; FLUKE MARINATO, PAGE 45; SPANAKOPITA, PAGE 69; OCTOPUS PIES, PAGE 85; KEFTEDES IN RED SAUCE, PAGE 56

MARINATED BEETS AND GIGANTES WITH SKORDALIA, PAGE 93

SHRIMP SAGANAKI WITH TOMATO
AND FETA, PAGE 112

GRILLED BABY OCTOPUS WITH FENNEL AND KALAMATA OLIVES, PAGE 116

KAKAVIA (GREEK-STYLE BOUILLABAISSE), PAGE 128

BARLEY RUSKS WITH TOMATOES
AND FETA, PAGE 141

GRILLED SWORDFISH WITH BABY CLAMS, WILD LEEKS, ASPARAGUS, AND
RETSINA-SCENTED LEMON-MINT BROTH, PAGE 173

Spicy Lamb Pie

I tasted many, many vegetable pies but very few meat-based ones in Greece. When I tasted a Moroccan lamb pie, however, I realized that I could introduce some of the flavors into a Greek dish. Originally I used meat from Lamb Youvetsi (page 198), and it was so delicious that I decided to create a recipe using ground lamb so we could make the pie even when we weren't making the youvetsi.

About 1 cup plus 6 tablespoons extra virgin
  olive oil

1¹/₂ pounds lean ground lamb

Coarse salt and freshly ground pepper

1¹/₂ cups finely diced onion

2 garlic cloves, minced

¹/₂ teaspoon ground cumin

¹/₂ teaspoon ground cinnamon

¹/₂ teaspoon dried Greek oregano

³/₄ cup dry red wine, such as Aghiorghitiko,
  Cabernet Sauvignon, or Sangiovese

1 cup chopped canned Italian plum tomatoes
  with juice

¹/₂ teaspoon Aleppo pepper or cayenne (see
  page 9)

¹/₂ cup Lamb Stock (page 284)

2 tablespoons chopped fresh flat-leaf parsley

6 sheets frozen #10 phyllo dough, thawed as
  directed on package

I. Heat 2 tablespoons of the olive oil in a large sauté pan over medium heat. Working in batches, season the lamb with a pinch of salt and add to the pan without crowding. Cook for about 5 minutes, or until well browned. Do not stir until the meat begins to brown. Remove from the heat and scrape into a colander placed in a bowl.

2. Heat 2 tablespoons of the remaining olive oil in the sauté pan. Add the onion along with another pinch of salt, cover, and cook, stirring occasionally, for about 10 minutes, or until very tender. Add the garlic and cook for another minute. Add the cumin, cinnamon, and oregano and cook for 1 minute. Add the wine and cook for about 5 minutes, or until slightly reduced. Stir in the tomatoes and bring to a simmer. Stir in the reserved drained lamb and season with the Aleppo pepper and salt and pepper to taste. Add the stock and cook, stirring occasionally, for 15 to 20 minutes, or until the pan is almost dry. Remove from the heat and stir in the parsley. Set aside to cool.

3. Preheat the oven to 350°F.

4. Line at least 2 baking sheets with parchment paper and place a wire rack on each one. Set aside.

5. Hold the phyllo as directed on page 12.

6. Lay one sheet of phyllo out on a clean surface. Using a pastry brush, lightly coat the phyllo with some of the remaining olive oil.

7. Using a small, sharp knife, cut the oiled phyllo lengthwise into 5 equal strips. Working with one strip at a time, place about 2 tablespoons of the lamb mixture in the upper corner of the dough. Fold the top end of the dough over the lamb to meet the right edge of the dough, forming a triangle. Continue folding in the triangle shape until the entire strip has been folded.

8. Place the triangles on the racks on the prepared baking sheets as they are finished.

9. When all of the pies have been made, place the baking sheets in the preheated oven and bake for about 20 minutes, or until golden brown and crisp. Remove from the oven and serve hot.

SERVES 6

Octopus Pie with Rice, Tomatoes, and Zucchini

Like many of the dishes at Molyvos, this dish evolved out of my experiences in Greece. Aglaia Kremezi, our consultant and mentor, had tasted an octopus pie in her search for island recipes, but she was not sure if Americans would like it. I found it so interesting that I decided to test the waters. I put my own twist on the basic traditional recipe and put it on the menu. It has become one of our customers' favorite dishes.

You will need six 4-ounce ramekins for this dish. If you would like to use this pie on the meze table, rather than as an appetizer, fill the ramekins only about one-quarter full and trim off the excess phyllo. You will need another 6 pieces of phyllo and an additional dozen ramekins, as you will have 18 meze-size portions. You will have thin phyllo-covered disks that are easy finger food.

About ³/₄ cup olive oil

2 cups diced onion

Coarse salt and freshly ground pepper

1 garlic clove, minced

¹/₂ teaspoon ground cinnamon

¹/₄ teaspoon dried Greek oregano

1 cup canned crushed tomatoes with juice

¹/₄ cup dry white wine

One 1-pound Poached Octopus (page 55), sliced crosswise ¹/₈ inch thick

¹/₄ cup short-grain rice such as Arborio

2 cups grated zucchini (grated on large holes of a box grater)

2 tablespoons chopped fresh flat-leaf parsley

3 sheets frozen #10 phyllo dough, thawed as directed on package

I. Place 2 tablespoons of the olive oil in a large, heavy saucepan over medium heat. Add the onion along with a pinch of salt. Cover and cook, stirring occasionally, for about 8 minutes, or just until the onion is translucent but not browned. Uncover and stir in the garlic. Cook for 1 minute. Add the cinnamon and oregano and then stir in the tomatoes. Cook,

stirring occasionally, for 2 minutes. Season with salt and pepper to taste. Add the wine, bring to a simmer, and simmer for about 3 minutes. Add the octopus, lower the heat, and cook, stirring occasionally, for about 8 minutes, or until the octopus is slightly tender. Finally, add the rice and ¹/₂ cup water and again bring to a simmer.

(continued)

Reduce the heat to very low and cook at a bare simmer for about 14 minutes, or until the rice is almost dry and cooked al dente. Stir in the zucchini and cook, stirring occasionally, for about 6 minutes, or until almost dry.

2. Remove from the heat and fold in the parsley. Taste and, if necessary, season with salt and pepper. Using a spatula, spread the mixture out on a baking pan to cool.

3. Preheat the oven to 350°F.

4. Hold the phyllo as directed on page 12.

5. Lay one sheet of phyllo dough on a clean surface and, using a pastry brush, lightly coat it with a bit of the remaining olive oil. Using a sharp knife, cut the phyllo down the center lengthwise into 2 equal pieces. Then cut each piece lengthwise into 2 equal pieces so that you now have 4 pieces of equal size. Repeat the process to give you 8 strips, each approximately 1 inch wide. Work with just one piece of phyllo at a time as the dough will dry out and be unusable if prepared in advance.

6. Working with one ramekin at a time, center one dough strip over the dish and press it down to line the ramekin, leaving the excess dough hanging over the side. Lay a second strip of phyllo into the dish, just slightly overlapping the first strip, and press it down as with the first strip. Repeat this procedure until each ramekin has a total of 4 strips lining it and completely covering the bottom of the dish.

7. Spoon an equal portion (about 3/4 cup) of the octopus mixture into each ramekin, gently packing down to fill the dish three-quarters full.

8. Working with one strip at a time, pull the overhanging phyllo dough up and over the center of the ramekin to completely enclose the filling. Using kitchen scissors, trim off excess dough. Using a paring knife, make small slits in the top of the dough. Using a pastry brush, lightly coat the top with a bit of olive oil.

9. Place the ramekins in a baking pan lined with parchment paper in the preheated oven and bake for 20 minutes, or until golden brown.

10. Remove from the oven and transfer to a wire rack to cool for 3 minutes.

11. When ready to serve, invert one ramekin onto each of 6 small plates and unmold the pie. Serve hot.

CRUZ, A SAUCIER IN CHARGE OF
ALL BRAISING AND STOCK-MAKING,
POACHING OCTOPUS.

Appetizers

In traditional Greek cooking, the meze table takes the place of a first course. In fact, the meze table can be so extensive and filling, featuring small portions of fish and meat dishes that would normally be entrees, that no main course is required at all. With the exception of the Papoutsakia, Cheese Saganaki, Pastitsio, and Grilled Lamb Pizza, which should be served as suggested in the recipes, the remaining appetizers in this chapter could, if prepared in smaller portions, serve as part of a meze table. At Molyvos, I, of course, offer a selection of appetizers on the menu. At home I may or may not serve an appetizer, depending on whether I have prepared a meze table or an antipasto platter. I feel that the latter works better for informal gatherings, while the classic soup or appetizer works better when doing more formal entertaining.

Chilled Baked Gigantes with Celery, Onions, and Tomatoes

Baked gigantes are terrific hot, but they also make a great starter when allowed to cool overnight so that the flavors meld. The sweet-and-sour taste that results from the honey and vinegar creates a marvelous balance of flavors. Baking the beans allows them to develop a creamy, buttery character that is the finishing touch to the dish.

¹/₂ pound Greek gigantes or dried giant lima
    beans, soaked for 8 hours or overnight

1 medium onion, peeled and halved

4 garlic cloves, peeled and smashed

4 fresh flat-leaf parsley sprigs

4 black peppercorns

1 bay leaf

Coarse salt and freshly ground pepper

2 tablespoons extra virgin olive oil

¹/₂ cup white onion in medium dice

¹/₄ cup fennel bulb in medium dice

¹/₄ cup celery in medium dice

¹/₄ cup carrot in medium dice

¹/₃ cup thyme honey

¹/₄ cup dry white wine

¹/₄ cup plus 1 teaspoon red wine vinegar

³/₄ cup diced peeled, seeded tomatoes (see
    page 113)

1¹/₂ cups Vegetable Stock (page 280)

2 tablespoons chopped fresh dill

Yogurt-Garlic Sauce (page 37)

I. Drain the soaked beans and place in a large saucepan.

2. Combine the halved onion, garlic, parsley, peppercorns, and bay leaf in a piece of cheesecloth about 6 inches square. Gather up the ends and, using kitchen twine, tie the bag closed. Add the sachet to the beans and fill the saucepan with enough cold water to cover the beans by 3 inches.

3. Place the saucepan over medium-high heat and bring to a boil. Lower the heat and simmer, stirring occasionally and skimming frequently with a metal spoon, for about 30 minutes. Add salt to taste and continue cooking for another 10 minutes, or until the beans are tender.

4. Remove from the heat and set aside. (The beans may be cooked up to this point, cooled, and stored, covered and refrigerated, for a day or two.)

5. Preheat the oven to 400°F.

6. Heat 1 tablespoon of the oil in a large sauté pan over medium heat. Add the chopped onion along with a pinch of salt and cook, stirring occasionally, for about 4 minutes, or until soft and translucent. Stir in the fennel, celery, and carrot and season with salt and pepper to taste. When well blended, add the honey, wine, and ¼ cup of the vinegar. Raise the heat and bring to a boil.

7. Lower the heat and simmer for about 6 minutes, or just until the vegetables are barely cooked. Stir in the tomatoes and skim with a metal spoon to remove any foam that rises to the top. Taste and, if necessary, season with salt and pepper.

8. Drain the beans. Add them to the mixture along with the stock. Bring to a simmer. Simmer for 5 minutes.

9. Cover with a tight-fitting lid and place in the preheated oven. Bake for about 1½ hours, or until the beans are very soft and creamy. Remove from the heat and set aside to cool.

10. When cool, transfer to a nonreactive container, cover, and refrigerate until chilled.

11. When ready to serve, remove from the refrigerator and stir in the dill, remaining tablespoon of olive oil, and remaining teaspoon of vinegar. Toss to combine.

12. Transfer to a serving bowl or platter, garnish with Yogurt-Garlic Sauce, and serve.

Marinated Beets and Gigantes with Skordalia

Throughout Greece, the combination of beets and skordalia is quite common, usually served during the many days of Lent. I have eaten some great dishes using the combination, but I think that there is none better than this, which uses skordalia to marry all of the flavors. Perhaps this version stands out because this skordalia is so, so good. I suggest using a meat grinder to achieve the perfect consistency for the potatoes, garlic, and almonds and just whipping (not pureeing) all of the ingredients together as you finish with the seltzer. The result will be light and airy, not heavy and tacky as is so often the case.

18 baby beets, stems removed
1 cup dry red wine, such as Aghiorghitiko,
    Cabernet Sauvignon, or Sangiovese
$1/4$ cup red wine vinegar
$1^1/2$ teaspoons coarse salt
Grated zest of 1 orange

2 tablespoons sherry vinegar
$1/2$ teaspoon sugar
$1/4$ teaspoon toasted anise seeds
Skordalia (recipe follows)
Marinated Gigantes (recipe follows)

1. Place the beets in a medium saucepan with cold water to cover by 1 inch. Add the wine, red wine vinegar, and salt and place over high heat. Bring to a boil, then lower the heat and simmer for about 1 hour, or until tender when pierced with the point of a sharp knife. Remove from the heat and set aside to cool in the cooking liquid.

2. When the beets are cool enough to handle, slip off the skins and trim off each end. Reserve $1/4$ cup of the cooking liquid.

3. Cut the beets into quarters. (If not using immediately, return the beets to the cooking liquid, cover, and refrigerate for up to 3 days.) Place the beets in a nonreactive bowl. Add the reserved $1/4$ cup cooking liquid along with the orange zest, sherry vinegar, sugar, and anise seeds, tossing to coat well.

4. Arrange 3 mounds of the beets at equidistant points around the edge of each of 6 luncheon plates. Mound about $1/4$ cup of the Skordalia in the center of each plate. Place three mounds of Marinated Gigantes at equidistant points between the beets and serve.

Skordalia

Makes about 4 cups

$^1/_2$ pound potato, boiled in its skin, then peeled

$1^1/_2$ cups corn oil

1 ounce (about 6) garlic cloves, peeled

2 ounces blanched whole almonds, skins removed

$^1/_3$ cup white vinegar

5 to 8 ounces seltzer water

1 tablespoon extra virgin olive oil

Coarse salt and freshly ground white pepper

1. Cut the potato into pieces. Set aside.

2. Place 2 tablespoons of the corn oil in the large bowl of a heavy-duty electric mixer fitted with the meat grinder attachment. Place the bowl under the grinder. (This can also be done with a mixing bowl and a freestanding grinder.) Place a small amount of the garlic and potato into the grinder and begin grinding, alternating adding the almonds and the remaining garlic and potato, a bit at a time. (Alternatively, you can use a potato ricer or box grater, but the consistency will not be as smooth.)

3. Remove the grinder attachment and fit the mixer with the paddle. Place the bowl in the mixer stand. Turn the speed to medium and slowly add one third of the remaining corn oil. With the motor running, drizzle in one third of the vinegar and then one third of the seltzer. Continue alternately adding the remaining two thirds of oil, vinegar, and seltzer, one third at a time, until all are incorporated. You should have a light, airy mixture. Stir in the olive oil and season with salt and white pepper to taste. Taste and, if necessary, add salt and vinegar. Transfer to a container, cover, and refrigerate for about 2 hours, or until chilled. (This will make more than required for this recipe. Serve the remaining Skordalia with toasted pita triangles or refrigerate it for another day's meze—it will keep for 3 days.)

Marinated Gigantes

1 pound Greek gigantes or dried giant lima beans, soaked for 8 hours or overnight

1 large white onion, peeled and quartered

$^1/_2$ head of garlic, sliced in half crosswise

$^1/_4$ bunch of fresh flat-leaf parsley stems

8 black peppercorns

2 bay leaves

Coarse salt and freshly ground pepper

1 small yellow bell pepper, finely diced

1 small red bell pepper, finely diced

$^3/_4$ cup finely chopped celery

$^1/_2$ cup finely chopped red onion

$^1/_4$ cup extra virgin olive oil

$3^1/_2$ tablespoons fresh lemon juice

1 tablespoon finely chopped fresh flat-leaf parsley

1 tablespoon finely chopped fresh dill

1. Drain the soaked beans and place in a large, heavy Dutch oven or saucepan. Add cold water to cover by about $2^1/_2$ inches.

2. Combine the onion, garlic, parsley stems, peppercorns, and bay leaves in a piece of cheesecloth about 6 inches square. Gather up the ends and, using kitchen twine, tie the bag closed. Add the sachet to the beans.

3. Place the beans over high heat and bring to a boil. Lower the heat to a gentle simmer. Simmer the beans, skimming off any foam that rises to the top and stirring from time to time, for 20 minutes. Add salt to taste and continue to simmer for 10 minutes, or until almost tender. Remove from the heat and set aside to cool at room temperature. (Cooling at room temperature helps the beans cool evenly. The beans may be prepared to this point and stored, covered and refrigerated, for up to 3 days before marinating.)

4. Drain the beans, reserving $^1/_4$ cup of the cooking liquid. Place them in a large nonreactive bowl. Add the yellow and red bell peppers, celery, and red onion and toss to combine. Stir in the reserved cooking liquid along with the olive oil and lemon juice and season with salt and pepper to taste. Cover and refrigerate for at least 3 and up to 8 hours.

5. When ready to serve, remove from the refrigerator and bring to room temperature. Fold in the parsley and dill and serve.

Papoutsakia (Stuffed Baby Eggplant)

Almost every Mediterranean country has a stuffed eggplant that is served as either an appetizer or a main course. This is my Greek version. I love to use the slightly sweet baby eggplant for individual portions, but feel free to use a large eggplant cut in half if you would like to make entree servings. The garnish of tomato sauce is tasty but is not necessary to enjoy the eggplant.

6 baby eggplants

6 tablespoons extra virgin olive oil, plus oil for
    drizzling

Coarse salt and freshly ground pepper

3 cups chopped onion

3 garlic cloves, minced

1 teaspoon dried Greek oregano

Pinch of Aleppo pepper (see page 9)

2 cups diced peeled eggplant (1 large eggplant)

One 28-ounce can plum tomatoes

Up to ¼ cup Fresh Bread Crumbs (page 57) if
    needed

½ cup coarsely chopped fresh flat-leaf parsley,
    plus parsley for garnish (optional)

1 teaspoon chopped fresh oregano

½ cup grated kefalotyri cheese, plus cheese for
    sprinkling

About 1 cup hot Tomato Sauce (page 102)

I. Preheat the oven to 375°F.

2. Line a baking pan with parchment paper. Set aside.

3. Using a sharp knife, cut an oval out of one side of each baby eggplant. Place the baby eggplants in a bowl. Sprinkle with 2 tablespoons of the olive oil and salt to taste.

4. Place the baby eggplants, cut side up, in the prepared baking pan. Bake in the preheated oven for about 25 minutes, until soft but not mushy. Remove from the oven and set aside to cool.

5. When cool, scoop out the pulp, leaving a shell about ⅛ inch thick. Chop the pulp and separately reserve it and the shells.

6. Place 3 tablespoons of the remaining olive oil in a large sauté pan over medium heat. Add the onion along with a pinch of salt. Cover and cook, stirring occasionally, for about 12 minutes, or until the onion is soft and translucent. Add the garlic and cook, stirring occasionally, for 2 minutes longer. Stir in the dried oregano, Aleppo pepper, and salt and pepper to taste. When

blended, stir in the diced eggplant and cook for 12 minutes. Then stir in the reserved eggplant pulp and cook for another 6 minutes.

7. Drain the tomatoes, reserving ¼ cup of the juice. Remove the seeds and finely chop the tomatoes. Add the chopped tomatoes to the eggplant mixture and cook for 3 minutes. Stir in the reserved tomato juice and cook for another 8 minutes, or until slightly thick. If the mixture seems too moist to be a stuffing, add fresh bread crumbs about a tablespoon at a time until the correct consistency has been reached. Do not add more than ¼ cup or the mixture will be bready.

8. Remove from the heat and set aside to cool.

9. When cool, fold in the parsley and fresh oregano. Taste and, if necessary, season with more salt and pepper.

10. Divide the mixture among the eggplant shells, mounding it slightly. Transfer to the prepared baking pan. Sprinkle with the cheese, drizzle with the remaining tablespoon of olive oil, and bake in the preheated oven for about 20 minutes, or until the eggplants are very hot and the cheese has melted.

11. Serve hot or at room temperature, on top of Tomato Sauce spread on a plate. Sprinkle with grated kefalotyri cheese, chopped parsley if desired, and extra virgin olive oil.

Cheese Saganaki

To be authentic, saganaki must be served in the traditional metal bowl-shaped pan with a flat bottom and two handles that can take the intense heat of the liqueur flame. If you enjoy this dish, I recommend purchasing the traditional servers for the complete Greek experience.

Three 18-ounce pieces haloumi cheese
1 cup cornstarch
About $^3/_4$ cup extra virgin olive oil

About $^3/_4$ cup blended olive oil
6 tablespoons ouzo
Lemon Sauce (recipe follows)

1. Using a serrated knife, cut each piece of cheese into 6 equal slices, allowing 3 per person.

2. Place the cornstarch in a shallow dish. Lightly coat each side of the cheese slices in cornstarch. Set aside.

3. Place the oils to a depth of $^1/_4$ inch in a large skillet and heat over very high heat until very hot but not smoking.

4. Add the coated cheese slices, without crowding the pan (you may have to do this in batches), and fry for about 2 minutes, or until golden. Turn and fry the other side for another minute or two, or until golden.

5. Using a slotted spatula, transfer the cheese to a double layer of paper towel to drain.

6. Place 3 pieces of cheese in each of 6 hot saganaki (or other heatproof) dishes. Take the dishes to the table and spoon a tablespoon of ouzo over each one. Using a fireplace match or a long butane lighter, ignite the ouzo, allowing it to burn out.

7. Pour the hot sauce over the top and enjoy the spectacle.

Lemon Sauce

Makes about 2 cups

2 cups Chicken Stock (page 281)
Juice of 2 lemons
Coarse salt and freshly ground white pepper
$1/2$ pound (2 sticks) unsalted butter, cut into pieces
1 tablespoon chopped fresh flat-leaf parsley

1. Place the stock in a heavy saucepan over medium-high heat and bring to a boil. Lower the heat and simmer for about 15 minutes, or until reduced by half.

2. Add the lemon juice along with a pinch of salt. When hot, begin whisking in the butter, a few pieces at a time.

3. When the butter has been completely incorporated and the sauce is emulsified cover, reserve, and keep warm.

4. When ready to serve, fold in the parsley and season with salt and white pepper to taste.

Pastitsio

Traditional pastitsio is made with a noodle that is long like spaghetti but round and hollow in the middle like the Italian bucatini. I find that penne holds up to the baking and prefer it when making this classic dish. Although this is an ingredient-heavy recipe, the tomato sauce and béchamel can be made in advance and the pastitsio can be put together early in the day (or even the day before) and baked just before serving.

¹/₄ cup dried currants

¹/₂ cup olive oil

1 pound 90-percent-lean ground beef

1 pound lean ground lamb

About 2¹/₂ tablespoons ras el hanout

About 1 teaspoon Aleppo pepper or cayenne (see page 9)

About 1¹/₂ tablespoons ground cinnamon

Coarse salt and freshly ground pepper

3 cups finely diced onion

6 garlic cloves, sliced

2 cups dry red wine, such as Aghiorghitiko, Cabernet Sauvignon, or Sangiovese

2¹/₂ cups canned crushed tomatoes, with their juices

1 pound dried penne pasta

Tomato Sauce (recipe follows)

Yogurt Béchamel Sauce (recipe follows)

¹/₄ cup grated kefalotyri cheese

1. Place the currants in hot water to cover and set aside to plump for 30 minutes. Drain well and set aside.

2. Place a large skillet over medium heat. When very hot, add 1 tablespoon of the olive oil and swirl to coat the bottom of the pan. Add ¹/₄ pound each of the beef and lamb, breaking it up into small pieces as you add it. Cook, stirring constantly to keep breaking up the meat, for about 3 minutes, or until lightly browned. Add ¹/₄ teaspoon each of the ras el hanout and the Aleppo pepper and a pinch of cinnamon along with salt and pepper to taste. Using a slotted spoon, transfer the browned meat mixture to a colander placed in a bowl to drain. When drained, transfer to a bowl and set aside. Continue browning, seasoning, and draining the meat in quarters until all of the meat has been browned.

3. Return the skillet to medium heat. Add 2 tablespoons of the remaining olive oil and,

when hot, stir in the onion along with a pinch of salt. Cover and cook for 10 minutes, or until soft and translucent. Add the garlic, stirring to just combine, and cook for another minute. Add the wine and cook, stirring occasionally, for about 25 minutes, or until the pan is almost dry. Add the tomatoes along with their juices, stirring to combine. Bring to a simmer and cook, stirring once, for 10 to 12 minutes. Add the reserved meat mixture and stir to combine. Take care—the pan will be quite full. Taste and season with salt, pepper, ras el hanout, cinnamon, and Aleppo pepper to make a very aromatic mixture. Add the reserved currants, stir gently to just combine, and cook for an additional 5 minutes. Taste again and, if necessary, adjust the seasonings. Transfer the mixture to a clean bowl to cool.

4. While the meat is cooking, prepare the pasta.

5. Bring a large pot of salted water to a boil over high heat. Add the pasta and return the water to a boil. Boil for 6 to 8 minutes, or until the pasta is al dente. Remove from the heat and drain well. Place the pasta in an ice-water bath to stop the cooking. Again, drain well.

6. Place the pasta in a large bowl. Add the remaining 2 tablespoons olive oil and toss to coat, to keep the pasta from sticking together.

7. Preheat the oven to 325°F.

8. Pour 1/4 cup of the Tomato Sauce into the reserved pasta, tossing to coat.

9. Pour 3/4 cup of the Tomato Sauce into the bottom of a deep 10-inch round casserole dish, spreading it out with a spatula to cover evenly.

10. Pour the pasta into the casserole, spreading it out in an even layer. Spoon the meat mixture over the pasta, making an even layer. Pour 3 cups of the Yogurt Béchamel Sauce over the meat, spreading it evenly over the top. Sprinkle with the kefalotyri cheese and bake in the center of the preheated oven for 25 minutes.

11. Turn the oven to broil and transfer the casserole to the broiler. Broil for about 5 minutes, or until the top is golden brown. Remove from the heat and allow to rest for 5 minutes before serving.

Tomato Sauce

Makes about 3 cups

$1/4$ cup olive oil

4 garlic cloves, sliced

1 teaspoon dried Greek oregano

Coarse salt and freshly ground pepper

One 28-ounce can crushed tomatoes with juice

I. Heat the oil in a medium saucepan over medium heat. Add the garlic and sauté for 2 minutes. Stir in the oregano along with a pinch of salt and sauté for another minute. Stir in the tomatoes and bring to a boil. Season with salt and pepper to taste, lower the heat, and simmer, skimming off any foam that rises to the top with a metal spoon, for 25 minutes.

2. Remove from the heat and set aside until ready to use.

Yogurt Béchamel Sauce

Makes about 4 cups

1 bay leaf
$1/2$ medium onion, peeled
2 whole cloves
$1^1/2$ cups whole milk
$1^1/2$ cups heavy cream
$1^1/2$ tablespoons unsalted butter
$1/2$ cup all-purpose flour
Coarse salt and freshly ground pepper
Freshly grated nutmeg
$1/2$ cup Greek yogurt (see page 13)

1. Attach the bay leaf to the onion half by piercing it with the 2 cloves. Set aside.

2. Combine the milk and cream in a medium heavy saucepan over medium heat. Cook without stirring for about 5 minutes, or just until the mixture begins to simmer. Remove from the heat and set aside.

3. Heat the butter in another medium heavy saucepan over medium heat. When melted and hot, add the flour and cook, stirring constantly, until the mixture is thick and smooth. Cook, stirring constantly, for 10 minutes. Remove from the heat and, whisking constantly to prevent lumps from forming, add the hot milk mixture in a slow, steady stream.

4. When well blended, return the mixture to medium heat. Add the onion half and bring to a simmer. Simmer for 10 minutes. Season with salt, pepper, and nutmeg to taste. Remove from the heat and set aside to cool.

5. When cool, fold in the yogurt and set aside until ready to use.

N O T E : In other recipes calling for plain béchamel sauce, prepare the above recipe without the final addition of the Greek yogurt.

Stuffed Rolled Sardines with Fennel and Tomatoes

This is a contemporary recipe based on a traditional Greek dish. Until recently, fresh sardines were difficult to find, but I have now seen them in the fish department of large supermarkets. They are a delicious, inexpensive fish that, in this dish, make a terrific starter—as either an appetizer or a meze.

About 6 tablespoons extra virgin olive oil, plus oil
 for drizzling

2¹/₂ cups finely diced onion

Coarse salt and freshly ground pepper

1 tablespoon minced garlic

1¹/₂ cups finely diced fennel bulb

Aleppo pepper (see page 9)

2¹/₂ cups diced peeled, seeded ripe tomatoes

¹/₄ cup dry white wine

¹/₄ cup sliced pitted Thassos olives

2 tablespoons chopped fennel fronds

1 tablespoon chopped fresh flat-leaf parsley

1 tablespoon fresh lemon juice

2 teaspoons fennel seeds, roasted and cracked

1¹/₂ cups Vegetable Stock (page 280)

12 fresh sardines, butterflied (see page 52)

1. Heat 3 tablespoons of the olive oil in a medium sauté pan over medium heat. Add the onion along with a pinch of salt, cover, and cook, stirring occasionally, for about 10 minutes, or until just cooked but not browned. Add the garlic and cook for another minute. Add the fennel and continue to cook, stirring occasionally, for about 5 minutes, or until the vegetables are soft. Season with Aleppo pepper and salt and pepper to taste. Add the tomatoes and, when blended, the wine. If necessary, add salt and

pepper to taste and cook for another 8 minutes, or until the mixture is quite thick.

2. Remove from the heat and fold in the olives, fennel fronds, parsley, lemon juice, and fennel seeds along with 1 tablespoon of the remaining olive oil. Set aside to cool.

3. Preheat the oven to 350°F.

4. Transfer about half of the filling to an 11 × 7-inch glass baking dish. Using a spatula, spread the filling out in a thin, even layer. You just want to barely cover the bottom of the dish.

5. Place the stock in a medium saucepan over medium heat. Season with salt and pepper to taste and bring to a boil. Remove from the heat and keep warm.

6. Place the butterflied sardines out on a clean surface. Working with one at a time, lay the fillet directly in front of you with the tail facing away. Season with salt and pepper to taste. Place 1 tablespoon of the filling across the fillet. Starting at the head end and rolling toward the tail, roll the sardine up and over the filling. Place the rolled sardine, tail facing up, in the prepared baking dish. Continue filling and rolling sardines until all have been completed.

7. Pour the hot stock into the dish to come halfway up the sides of the sardines. Drizzle with the remaining olive oil. Cover tightly with aluminum foil and bake in the pre-heated oven for about 20 minutes, or until heated through.

8. Remove from the oven and set aside to cool.

9. To serve, spoon about 2 tablespoons of the sauce onto each of 6 plates. Place 2 pieces of sardine on top and drizzle with extra virgin olive oil.

Poached Grouper Mayonesa

This is my contemporary version of athinaiki, a classic Greek dish. Traditionally, the fish is poached, boned, and molded into a fish shape, and decorated with thinly sliced carrots as scales and olives for eyes. Quite old-fashioned, but since the basic dish is so delicious, I thought it was worth reviving in this up-to-date version.

Juice of 1 lemon

$^1/_2$ cup dry white wine

2 tablespoons white vinegar

5 black peppercorns

2 celery ribs, thinly sliced

1 carrot, thinly sliced

1 onion, thinly sliced

Coarse salt and freshly ground white pepper

Three 7-ounce grouper fillets, skin on

Zest of 1 lemon

2 tablespoons finely chopped capers

1 tablespoon finely sliced fresh chives

1 tablespoon chopped fresh dill

1 cup Mayonnaise (recipe follows)

About 2 cups baby salad greens

Pickled vegetables (see page 41)

6 slices Lagana (recipe follows) or other crusty
   bread, toasted (optional)

1. Place 2 quarts cold water in a large saucepan. Add the lemon juice, wine, and vinegar along with the peppercorns, celery, carrot, and onion. Bring to a boil over medium heat. Immediately lower the heat and add enough salt to highly season the liquid—about 1 tablespoon. Simmer for 10 minutes.

2. Place the fish in the simmering liquid. Loosely cover and lower the heat to a bare simmer. Poach the fish for about 10 minutes, or until the flesh is white and very tender. Remove from the heat and allow the fish to cool in the poaching liquid. When cool, using a slotted spatula, carefully transfer the fish to a cutting board.

3. Gently pull off the skin using your fingertips.

4. Using a kitchen fork or 2 spoons, carefully pull the fish into flakes. Place the fish flakes in a mixing bowl, cover with plastic wrap, and refrigerate for about 30 minutes, or until chilled.

5. Fold the lemon zest, capers, chives, and dill into the Mayonnaise. Remove the fish from the

refrigerator and fold the Mayonnaise into the fish. Season with salt and white pepper to taste.

6. Place a small mound of baby greens in the center of each of 6 plates. Top with about 3/4 cup of the fish mixture. Place a small amount of pickled vegetables around the plate and serve with toasted Lagana or other crusty bread if desired.

Mayonnaise

Makes about 2 cups

3 large egg yolks at room temperature

1 large egg at room temperature

1 tablespoon plus 2 teaspoons fresh lemon juice

2 teaspoons Dijon mustard

1$\frac{1}{2}$ teaspoons coarse salt

$\frac{1}{2}$ teaspoon sugar

$\frac{1}{2}$ teaspoon freshly ground white pepper

1$\frac{1}{4}$ cups canola oil

$\frac{1}{4}$ cup extra virgin olive oil

1. Combine the egg yolks, egg, lemon juice, mustard, salt, sugar, and pepper in a food processor fitted with the metal blade. Process for 1 minute. With the motor running, add one third of the canola oil in a slow, steady stream, processing to emulsify. Add 1 tablespoon of water and then another third of the oil and another tablespoon of water, processing to emulsify. If necessary to achieve mayonnaise consistency, add another tablespoon of water. With the motor running, add all of the remaining oil in a slow, steady stream, processing to emulsify completely.

2. Store, covered and refrigerated, for up to 3 days.

Lagana

Makes 2 loaves

¼ cup sugar

3 tablespoons active dry yeast

7 to 8 cups all-purpose flour (see step 4)

Olive oil for coating, plus 5 tablespoons extra virgin olive oil

1 tablespoon fine sea salt

Sesame seeds for garnish

1. Place 2¼ cups warm (110–115°F) water in a medium mixing bowl. Add the sugar and yeast, stirring to blend. Add ¼ cup of the flour, stirring to combine. Cover with plastic wrap and set aside for 15 minutes.

2. Lightly coat the inside of a large mixing bowl with olive oil.

3. Sift the remaining flour and the salt into a large mixing bowl. Make a well in the center and pour the olive oil into it, followed by the yeast mixture. Stir the wet ingredients into the flour with a wooden spoon, mixing until the dough can no longer be moved with the spoon.

4. Lightly flour a clean surface. Scrape the dough out onto the surface and begin kneading by hand. Knead for about 10 minutes, adding flour as necessary, until the dough is satiny smooth and silky to the touch. (The amount of flour required depends on the amount of moisture in both the flour and the air. You may need more and you may need less.)

5. Shape the dough into a ball and place it in the oiled bowl. Using a pastry brush, lightly coat the dough with olive oil. Cover with a kitchen towel and set aside to rise in a warm, draft-free spot for about 2 hours, or until doubled in volume.

6. Line 2 baking sheets with parchment paper. Set aside.

7. Lightly flour a clean surface. Transfer the dough to the floured surface and begin kneading by hand. Knead for about 5 minutes, or until the dough is back to the original size. The dough should be soft but not sticky and warm.

8. Divide the dough into 2 equal pieces. Shape each piece into a loaf about 6 inches long.

9. Lightly flour a clean surface. Working with one loaf at a time and using a rolling pin, shape each loaf into a flat oval about 15 inches long and 6 inches wide. Place each oval on a prepared baking sheet.

10. Using a kitchen fork, prick the top of each piece of dough in several places. Using a pastry brush, lightly coat the top of each piece with olive oil and sprinkle sesame seeds over all. Cover with a clean kitchen towel and set aside in a warm, draft-free spot for about 1 hour, or until doubled in volume.

11. Preheat the oven to 400°F.

12. Transfer the breads to the preheated oven and bake for about 20 minutes, or until golden brown.

13. Remove from the oven and transfer to a wire rack to cool before slicing and serving.

14. Store, tightly wrapped and refrigerated, for up to 3 days. Reheat before serving.

Seared Dayboat Sea Scallops with Greek Fava and Red Onion, Tomato, and Caper Stew

In this dish, the stew could make a great meze on its own. The addition of the seared scallops takes the dish to a much higher level. In addition, the creaminess of the fava makes a terrific partner for sweet scallops. We are fortunate to get absolutely pristine dayboat scallops but large, fresh scallops (10 to the pound) may be used.

¹/₂ cup capers, well drained

¹/₃ cup plus ¹/₄ cup olive oil

6 cups red onion julienne

Coarse salt and freshly ground pepper

2 cups Mavrodaphne wine

1¹/₂ cups canned tomato puree or sauce

2 cinnamon sticks

1 tablespoon sugar

Pinch of Aleppo pepper (see page 9)

¹/₂ cup Oven-Dried Tomatoes (see page 168)

12 jumbo dayboat sea scallops, muscle removed

About ¹/₂ cup Greek Fava (yellow split peas, page 39) without the garnishes

2 scallions, including some of the green part, sliced

6 fresh flat-leaf parsley sprigs

1. Place the capers in a small bowl with cold water to cover. Soak for 20 minutes to remove excess salt. Drain well and set aside.

2. Place ¹/₃ cup of the olive oil in a large sauté pan over medium heat. Add the red onion along with a pinch of salt. Cover and cook, stirring occasionally, for about 15 minutes, or until the onion is soft but not browned. Uncover and stir in the wine, raise the heat, and simmer until the liquid has reduced by half.

3. Add the tomato puree, cinnamon sticks, sugar, Aleppo pepper, capers, and tomatoes. Season with salt and pepper to taste, lower the heat, and cook at a bare simmer for about 10 minutes, or until the sauce has thickened. Set aside and keep warm.

4. Heat the remaining ¹/₄ cup olive oil in a large sauté pan over high heat. When very hot but not smoking, season the scallops with salt and pepper to taste and carefully place them in the hot pan. Sear for 2 minutes, or until golden. Turn the scallops, lower the

heat to medium, and sear the remaining side for about 3 minutes, or until the scallops are slightly firm to the touch.

5. Spoon about 1 tablespoon of the Greek Fava in the center of each of 6 luncheon plates. Spoon a tablespoon of the caper stew over the fava. Carefully place scallops on either side of the fava and spoon another tablespoon of the stew over the top. Sprinkle with the scallions, garnish with a parsley sprig, and serve.

DAILY PRE-SERVICE STAFF MEETING IN THE RESTAURANT.

Shrimp Saganaki with Tomato and Feta

The term *saganaki* actually refers to the metal skillet-like pan with two handles in which various dishes, including the classic Greek fried cheese dish, are traditionally served. The term is also used to describe dishes incorporating tomatoes, onions, and feta cheese prepared in a baking pan. This dish is easy to prepare and makes a sensational presentation served in the traditional pan. If you don't have the traditional pan, use an attractive baking dish. I use both fresh and canned tomatoes for their difference in texture and acidity.

¹/₄ cup extra virgin olive oil, plus oil for drizzling

¹/₂ cup finely diced onion

Coarse salt and freshly ground pepper

3 garlic cloves, minced

1 teaspoon dried Greek oregano, plus oregano for sprinkling

1 cup diced peeled, seeded ripe tomatoes (see Note)

¹/₄ cup dry white wine

One 28-ounce can chopped tomatoes with juice

¹/₄ cup chopped fresh flat-leaf parsley

1¹/₂ pounds medium shrimp, peeled and deveined, tails left on

³/₄ cup diced feta cheese

1. Preheat the oven to 450°F.

2. Heat ¹/₄ cup oil in a large sauté pan over medium heat. Add the onion along with a pinch of salt. Cover and cook, stirring occasionally, for 8 minutes, or until soft and translucent. Add the garlic and sauté for another minute. Stir in the oregano along with a pinch of salt. Add the diced tomatoes and the wine and bring to a simmer. Simmer for 3 minutes.

3. Stir in the canned tomatoes with their juice, raise the heat to medium-high, and

again bring to a simmer. Simmer for about 6 minutes, or until the sauce has thickened slightly. Fold in the parsley and season with salt and pepper to taste, noting that the feta will add some saltiness.

4. Spoon just enough tomato sauce into the bottom of a saganaki pan (or a 9 × 14-inch glass baking dish) to cover. Working from the outside in, make 3 concentric circles of shrimp. (If using a baking pan, begin placing the shrimp, three at a time, tail-to-head, in neat rows across the dish, with the tails all

facing in the same direction and just barely touching. Add the remaining shrimp in overlapping rows of 3, shingle fashion, until the dish is filled. You should have 3 rows of 13 to 15 shrimp each.) Season the shrimp with salt and pepper to taste and then spoon the remaining tomato sauce over the top. Sprinkle the feta cheese over the top, drizzle with olive oil, and sprinkle with oregano.

5. Bake in the middle of the preheated oven for 20 minutes, or until very hot and bubbling with golden brown cheese.

NOTE: To peel tomatoes, bring a pot of water to a boil. Core and lightly score the tomato skin in quarters. Place the scored tomato in the boiling water for 30 seconds. Immediately remove and place the tomato in ice water to chill. Remove from the ice water and, using a paring knife, carefully pull off the skin. Once peeled, the tomato can be used in any recipe calling for cored, peeled tomatoes.

Mussels Krasata

This is a very straightforward, easy recipe that gets a wonderful aromatic hit of Greece from the fresh mint. Although this recipe calls for six pounds of mussels, it is actually very difficult to give an exact amount as they vary in size and a pound can vary from about eleven to fourteen mussels. To serve this dish as a hearty main course, allow about $1\frac{1}{2}$ pounds per person.

6 pounds small mussels, scrubbed and
    debearded (see Note)
Coarse salt and freshly ground pepper
1 cup cornmeal
3 tablespoons extra virgin olive oil
3 large garlic cloves, sliced

1 cup dry white wine
1 cup Clam Broth (page 287)
1 tablespoon Dijon mustard
1 tablespoon fresh mint chiffonade (see
    page 46)

1. Place the mussels in a large bowl of very cold water. Add a good handful of salt along with $\frac{1}{3}$ cup of the cornmeal and set aside for about 10 minutes. Drain well and then repeat the process two more times, draining well each time. This will purge any mud, sand, or debris from the mussels.

2. Heat 2 tablespoons of the oil in a large saucepan over medium heat. Add the garlic and cook, stirring constantly, for 1 minute. Add the mussels and then the wine. Cover and cook for about 4 minutes, or until the wine has begun to reduce. Add the broth,

raise the heat, uncover, and continue cooking, stirring and shaking the pan to cook the mussels evenly, for about 10 minutes, or until all of the mussels have opened. Discard any mussels that have not opened.

3. Using a slotted spoon, transfer the mussels to a serving platter. Stir the mustard along with salt and pepper to taste into the pan juices, then fold in the mint. Pour the juices over the mussels, drizzle with the remaining tablespoon of extra virgin olive oil, and serve.

NOTE: Fresh mussels can range anywhere from eleven to fourteen per pound for small, eight to eleven per pound for medium, and five to eight per pound for large. Occasionally, extremely large European mussels come to market that yield about three to five per pound. In the restaurant, we generally allow 1 pound of small mussels per person for an appetizer.

NOUHAD, A HOSTESS, SPEAKING WITH A CUSTOMER ON THE PHONE.

Grilled Baby Octopus with Fennel and Kalamata Olives

This is one of our signature dishes at Molyvos. I can't imagine ever taking it off the menu as it is a favorite all through the year. Even people who think they don't like octopus find themselves loving this simple dish.

About 1 cup extra virgin olive oil

¹/₄ cup white wine vinegar

3 lemons, halved

2 garlic cloves, chopped

3 teaspoons dried Greek oregano

9 baby Poached Octopus (page 55), heads removed, cut in half lengthwise

2 tablespoons olive oil

3 fennel bulbs, cut into julienne

Coarse salt and freshly ground pepper

1 garlic clove, sliced

¹/₂ cup dry white wine

1 cup Chicken Stock (page 281)

3 plum tomatoes, peeled, seeded, and cut into julienne (see page 113)

2 tablespoons sliced pitted Kalamata olives

2 tablespoons chopped fresh flat-leaf parsley

Tomato Salad (recipe follows)

6 caperberries

1 tablespoon chopped fresh chives

1. Combine ³/₄ cup of the extra virgin olive oil and the vinegar in a nonreactive container large enough to hold the octopus comfortably. Whisk in the juice of 2 of the lemons, the chopped garlic, and 1 teaspoon of the dried oregano. Add the octopus and toss to coat. Cover and refrigerate for 12 hours or overnight.

2. Heat the olive oil in a large sauté pan over medium heat. Add the fennel along with a pinch of salt and cook, stirring occasionally, for about 5 minutes, or just until the fennel is beginning to soften. Add the sliced garlic and cook for another minute. Stir in 1 teaspoon of the remaining dried oregano, followed by the wine, and cook, stirring occasionally, for

about 3 minutes, or until the pan is almost dry. Stir in the stock and the juice of the last lemon, raise the heat, and bring to a boil. Lower the heat and simmer for about 5 minutes, or until the liquid has reduced by half. Stir in the tomatoes and olives and season with salt and pepper to taste. Simmer for 1 minute.

3. Remove from the heat and fold in the parsley and 2 tablespoons of the remaining extra virgin olive oil. Set aside and keep warm.

4. Preheat and oil the grill.

5. Remove the octopus from the marinade and gently wipe off excess.

6. Place the octopus halves on the grill and grill, turning occasionally, for about 10 minutes, or until nicely browned.

7. Spoon equal portions of the fennel mixture into the center of each of 6 small plates. Spoon an equal portion of the Tomato Salad around the fennel on each plate. Top with an equal portion of octopus. Garnish with a caperberry and a sprinkle of chives and the remaining dried oregano. Drizzle with a bit of extra virgin olive oil and serve.

Tomato Salad

Makes about 3 cups

1 large red beefsteak tomato, peeled, seeded, and diced (see page 113)
1 large yellow beefsteak tomato, peeled, seeded, and diced (see page 113)
³/₈ cup finely diced red onion
2 tablespoons chopped fresh flat-leaf parsley
3 tablespoons extra virgin olive oil
Coarse salt and freshly ground pepper

Combine the tomatoes, red onion, and parsley in a nonreactive bowl, tossing to combine. Drizzle with the olive oil, season with salt and pepper to taste, and toss again to combine. Serve immediately.

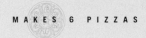
Grilled Lamb Pizza with Mint Pesto

This dish combines the best of my Greek and Italian heritage to create a very tasty pizza. The flavors are Greek, but the idea is certainly Italian. I love the smoky flavor of a grilled pizza shell. I also love the fact that the shells can be grilled early in the day and then the pizzas put together when you're ready to eat.

Although you can purchase roasted garlic, I prefer homemade for a cleaner flavor. Garlic is roasted in very low heat to draw out its sweet flavor. High heat will cause it to caramelize too quickly and turn bitter. It may be roasted with the top cut off for easy removal of the pulp, cut in half crosswise, or divided into cloves. I usually cut off the very top. You may roast as many heads of garlic as you will use in a week. I don't recommend longer storage.

$^1/_2$ **pound boneless lamb loin (or boneless rack of lamb) trimmed of all fat and silver skin**

2 tablespoons extra virgin olive oil

Coarse salt and freshly ground pepper

1$^1/_2$ cups Mint Pesto (recipe follows)

6 Grilled Pizza Shells (recipe follows)

24 Roasted Garlic cloves (recipe follows)

20 pitted Kalamata olives

20 cherry tomatoes, cut in half lengthwise

1 cup diced feta cheese

16 arugula leaves, torn into small pieces

1. Place the lamb in a bowl. Add the olive oil and season with salt and pepper to taste.

2. Heat a heavy sauté pan over medium-high heat. When very hot but not smoking, add the lamb. Sear, turning occasionally, for about 4 minutes, or until all sides are lightly browned and the lamb is still pink in the interior.

3. Remove from the pan and set aside to rest for at least 10 minutes.

4. Preheat the oven to 475°F, with a pizza stone in the oven if you have one.

5. Evenly spread 2 tablespoons of the Mint Pesto over each pizza shell. Distribute the Roasted Garlic among the pizzas, followed by the olives and cherry tomatoes. Sprinkle an equal portion of the cheese over each pizza. Place the pizza on the preheated pizza stone or on a heavy cookie sheet turned upside down in the oven and bake for 8 to 10

minutes, or until the cheese has melted and the crust is golden.

6. Slice the lamb crosswise into ⅛-inch-thick slices. Remove the pizzas from the oven and carefully lay an equal portion of lamb over the top of each pie. Sprinkle with arugula leaves, cut into wedges, and serve immediately.

Mint Pesto

Makes about 4 cups

2 cups arugula leaves
1 garlic clove, chopped
1 tablespoon pine nuts
2 cups fresh mint leaves
1 cup fresh basil leaves
1½ cups extra virgin olive oil
¼ cup grated kefalotyri cheese
Coarse salt and freshly ground pepper

1. Blanch the arugula for 1 minute in a small saucepan of salted boiling water. Drain well and place in a bowl of ice water to stop the cooking. Drain well and, using your hands, squeeze excess water from the arugula. Set aside.

2. Combine the garlic and pine nuts in a food processor fitted with the metal blade. Process to just puree. Add the reserved arugula along with the mint and basil, processing until pureed.

3. Turn off the motor and add the oil and cheese and process to incorporate. Season with salt and pepper to taste.

4. Scrape from the processor bowl into a nonreactive container. Cover and set aside. If you're not going to use the pesto for a few hours, refrigerate it, but bring back to room temperature before using.

Grilled Pizza Shells

Makes six approximately 10-inch shells

1½ ounces fresh yeast or two ¼-ounce packages active dry yeast

1 teaspoon sugar

6 cups all-purpose flour, sifted, plus flour for the work surface and, if necessary, the dough

¾ cup semolina flour, sifted

2 teaspoons fine sea salt

2 tablespoons extra virgin olive oil, plus oil for coating

I. Combine the yeast and sugar in a heatproof mixing bowl. Stir in 2¼ to 2½ cups barely warm (90°F) water, mixing until the yeast is dissolved. Set aside for about 15 minutes, or until the mixture is foamy.

2. Combine the flours with the salt in a large mixing bowl. Make a well in the center and pour in the yeast mixture. Add 1 tablespoon of the olive oil. Using a wooden spoon, gradually stir the flour into the liquid, working until the mixture is a soft dough that can be gathered into a ball.

3. Lightly flour a clean work surface. Place the dough in the center and, using your hands, knead for about 10 minutes, or until the dough is smooth and elastic, adding additional all-purpose flour if necessary.

4. Lightly coat the inside of a large bowl with oil. Transfer the dough to the oiled bowl, cover with plastic wrap, and set aside in a warm, draft-free spot for about 2 hours, or until doubled in volume.

5. Lightly flour a clean work surface. Transfer the dough to the center and cut it into 6 equal pieces weighing about ½ pound each. Using your hands, shape each piece into a ball that will fit into your palm.

6. Using a pastry brush, lightly coat the top of each ball of dough with the remaining oil. Place the dough balls on the floured surface, lightly cover with plastic wrap, and let rest for 20 minutes. (If not using immediately, lightly coat a baking dish with oil, place the dough balls in it, cover with plastic wrap, and refrigerate until ready to use, but not for more than 1 day. Reshape and bring to room temperature before using.)

7. When ready to use, preheat and oil a grill.

8. Lightly flour a clean work surface. Using your fingertips, vigorously press "dimples" into the dough, keeping the round shape. Using your hands, stretch each dough ball into a circle about 10 inches in diameter and ⅛ inch thick with an edge about ⅜ inch thick. This can be done by placing the dough over both of your fists held tight next to each other and gradually pulling outward with each fist while turning and stretching the dough. Keep moving your fists to the outside to avoid

tearing the dough in the center. If the dough becomes unmanageable, set aside to rest for 10 minutes before continuing to stretch it.

9. Lightly flour a pizza peel. Working with one circle of dough at a time, place the dough on the pizza peel and then transfer to the preheated grill. Grill for about 2 minutes, or until lightly browned on the bottom. Turn and grill for another minute.

10. Remove from the grill and set aside to cool.

Roasted Garlic

As many heads of garlic as you wish
$1/2$ teaspoon olive oil per head
Salt (optional)

1. Preheat the oven to 375°F.

2. Using a sharp knife, cut off the very top of each garlic head to just barely expose the flesh.

3. Place the garlic heads on a double sheet of aluminum foil large enough to tightly enclose them. Drizzle with just a bit of olive oil and, if desired, season with salt to taste. Seal tightly.

4. Place in a baking pan in the preheated oven. Bake for 40 to 50 minutes, or until very soft and golden brown.

5. Remove from the oven and set aside until still warm but cool enough to handle. Squeeze on the bottom of the cut head to force the pulp out of the skin or, if the head has cooled entirely, use a demitasse spoon to pry out the pulp. Discard the skins. If a recipe calls for roasted garlic puree, simply smash the flesh with a fork.

Soups and Salads

For the most part, Greek soups are hearty one-dish meals. Traditionally, many of them are made from grains, legumes, and vegetables since for centuries meat and poultry were scarce. Salads, too, are often hearty affairs made with cooked beans and bitter greens. One of the most interesting green salads that I have come across is from Lesvos, where a small head of romaine lettuce is sold with fennel fronds, wild cress, arugula, wild celery sprigs, and sprigs from a variety of herbs tied to it. The cook thinly slices the lettuce and other greens and tosses them with a simple vinaigrette. The salad has a peppery bite, quite unlike the standard American mild green salad.

SERVES 6

Chicken Magiritsa

This simple version of the classic Easter Magiritsa, which is similar to the traditional avgolemono soup, was given to me by Aglaia Kremezi. Chicken Magiritsa is always on the menu at Molyvos—I can't imagine that our customers would allow us to take it off! This is a terrific soup to make at home as the broth can be made way ahead of time and then the soup finished as needed. If you do this, pick the meat off the bones and cover it with broth so it doesn't dry out. I have taken a little creative license here as Greeks would always garnish with shredded romaine lettuce while I choose some pungent greens for more flavor.

10 black peppercorns

2 bay leaves

1 bunch of parsley stems

1 bunch of dill stems

1 head of garlic, loose skin removed and cut in
    half crosswise

2 tablespoons extra virgin olive oil

2 cups diced onion

Coarse salt and freshly ground pepper

3 quarts Chicken Stock (page 281) or fat-free,
    low-sodium canned chicken broth

One 3¹/₂-pound chicken, giblets removed

¹/₃ cup Avgolemono Sauce (recipe follows)

2 scallions, thinly sliced on a diagonal

Juice of 1 lemon

¹/₄ cup chopped fresh dill

1¹/₄ cups shredded baby greens

1. Combine the peppercorns, bay leaves, parsley stems, dill stems, and garlic in a piece of cheesecloth about 6 inches square. Gather up the ends and, using kitchen twine, tie the bag closed. Set the sachet aside.

2. Place a stockpot over medium heat. When just hot, add the olive oil. Then add the onion along with a pinch of salt. Cover and cook, stirring occasionally, for about 10 minutes, or until the onion is soft. Add the

stock, cover, and bring to a boil. Uncover and lower the heat to a simmer. Season both the cavity and the skin of the chicken with salt and pepper to taste and place it in the simmering stock along with the sachet. Return the stock to a boil and immediately lower the heat to maintain a gentle simmer. Simmer, skimming frequently with a metal spoon to remove any foam and impurities that rise to the top, for about 45 minutes, or until the chicken is very tender and the meat has begun to pull away from the leg bone.

3. Transfer the chicken to a platter and set aside until cool enough to handle.

4. Remove and discard the skin. Pull the meat from the bones and cut into bite-sized pieces. Set aside, discarding the bones.

5. Strain the chicken cooking liquid through a fine sieve, discarding the solids. Place the strained broth in a clean saucepan over medium-high heat and bring to a boil. Add the reserved chicken and reduce the heat to low.

6. Place the Avgolemono Sauce in a small heatproof bowl. Measure out 1 cup of the chicken broth and, whisking constantly, beat ½ cup of it into the sauce. When incorporated, whisk in the remaining ½ cup, beating to incorporate.

7. Whisking constantly, slowly pour the warm sauce into the simmering soup. When all of the sauce has been incorporated, fold in the scallions, lemon juice, and dill.

8. Place an equal portion of the shredded greens in each of 6 large shallow soup bowls. Ladle an equal portion of the soup into each bowl and serve.

Avgolemono Sauce

Makes about 2 cups

1¹/₂ cups Chicken Stock (page 281)
5 large eggs, separated
Coarse salt and freshly ground white pepper
¹/₄ cup fresh lemon juice
2 tablespoons all-purpose flour

1. Place the stock in a small saucepan over medium heat and bring to a bare simmer. Do not boil.

2. Place the egg yolks along with a pinch of salt in a small stainless-steel mixing bowl and, using a whisk or an electric mixer, whip until pale yellow.

3. Place the egg whites in another stainless-steel bowl large enough to fit firmly over hot water in a medium saucepan without touching the water. Add a pinch of salt and, using a whisk or mixer, beat until light and fluffy. Fold the beaten egg yolks into the whites, folding until well blended.

4. Combine the lemon juice and flour in a small bowl, whisking to blend well. Fold the lemon juice mixture into the egg mixture.

5. Bring a medium saucepan of water to a simmer over medium-high heat. Place the bowl holding the egg mixture over the simmering water, taking care that the bottom of the bowl does not touch the water. Whisking constantly, heat the egg mixture for about 4 minutes, or until it turns lighter in color and begins to thicken.

6. Continuing to whisk constantly, slowly begin to add the hot stock. As it is incorporated into the eggs, add all of the stock and cook, whisking constantly, for 2 to 3 minutes, or until very thick. Season with salt and pepper to taste. Remove from the heat and continue whisking for about 30 seconds; keep warm over hot water, taking care not to apply any additional heat or the sauce will curdle.

NOTE: Although not used in this instance, 1 tablespoon chopped fresh dill or sliced scallion can be added to avgolemono when it is being used as a sauce for vegetables or fish.

Kakavia (Greek-Style Bouillabaisse)

Traditionally this fisherman's soup is made with the smaller fish not suitable for market. The whole fish went into the pot along with any extra bones and the vegetables, peasant style. The fish was served alongside the broth and vegetables served as the soup. In Greece, scorpina, the Mediterranean varietal of sea robin or grunt, is most often used for this soup, but it is almost impossible to get here, so I use sea bass or snapper. For Molyvos, I have moved the recipe up a notch or two, using the bones for stock and the fillets in the soup.

Pinch of saffron threads

$^1/_4$ cup olive oil

2 cups finely diced yellow onion

Coarse salt and freshly ground pepper

2 garlic cloves, sliced

$^1/_2$ teaspoon dried Greek oregano

2 large beefsteak tomatoes, peeled, seeded, and
cut into $^1/_4$-inch dice (see page 113)

Kakavia Broth (recipe follows)

3 Idaho potatoes, peeled and cut into $^1/_4$-inch
dice

6 prawns with heads

18 mussels, scrubbed and debearded

6 sea scallops, halved crosswise

Six 3-ounce skin-on black sea bass or snapper
fillets

Juice of 1 lemon

1 tablespoon chopped fresh flat-leaf parsley

I. Combine the saffron with 1 tablespoon hot water in a small bowl. Set aside.

2. Heat the olive oil in a large saucepan over medium heat. Add the onion along with a pinch of salt. Cover and cook, stirring occasionally, for about 10 minutes, or until the onions have sweat their liquid and sweetened somewhat. Stir in the garlic and cook for 2 minutes. Add the oregano along with the saffron water.

3. Add half of the tomatoes and cook for 2 minutes. Pour in the Kakavia Broth and bring to a simmer. Simmer for 5 minutes. Add the potatoes and bring back to a simmer. Simmer for about 12 minutes, or until the potatoes are almost tender.

4. Add the remaining tomatoes and return to a simmer. Then add the prawns and cook for 1 minute. Stir in the mussels, followed by the scallops, and simmer for about 5 minutes,

or just until all of the seafood is tender. Remove from the heat.

5. Ladle the broth into a shallow saucepan and place over medium heat. Add the fish fillets and bring to a simmer. Simmer for about 5 minutes, or just until the fish is opaque and cooked through. Transfer a fillet to each of 6 shallow soup bowls along with an equal portion of the potatoes.

6. Return the broth to the saucepan with the other seafood. Place over medium heat and stir in the lemon juice and parsley. Taste and, if necessary, season with salt and pepper.

7. Ladle the hot broth over the fish and potatoes in the soup bowls, taking care that each bowl has an equal portion of the broth and seafood, and serve.

NOTE: This is the easy version of bouillabaisse. Cooking the fish fillets separately seems like make-work, but it is essential for them to keep their integrity and clear flavor. At home I often add a Lagana (page 108) crouton dipped in Skordalia (page 94) and garnished with fresh chives.

Kakavia Broth

Makes about 2 quarts

2¹/₂ pounds bones from white fish, heads split in half with no gills included

2 tablespoons olive oil

1 medium onion, coarsely chopped

1 leek, white part and some of the green, well washed and coarsely chopped

Coarse salt

1 fennel bulb, coarsely chopped

1¹/₂ cups dry white wine

Pinch of saffron threads

1 cup chopped canned plum tomatoes, drained

4 garlic cloves, smashed

3 parsley stems

2 bay leaves

1 fresh thyme sprig

1. Combine the saffron with 1 tablespoon hot water in a small bowl. Set aside.

2. Rinse the fish bones in cold salted water until the water is clear. This may take 3 or 4 rinses. Set the bones aside.

3. Place the olive oil in a large saucepan over medium heat. Add the onion and leek along with a pinch of salt, cover, and cook, stirring occasionally, for 10 minutes. Add the fennel and continue cooking for 8 to 10 minutes, or until the vegetables begin to soften.

4. Add the wine, raise the heat, and simmer for about 15 minutes, or until the liquid is reduced by half.

5. Add the fish bones and heads, cover, and cook for 10 minutes, or until the bones are opaque. Add the saffron water along with just enough water to cover by 2 inches (about 2 quarts) and again bring to a simmer, skimming frequently to remove any particles that rise to the top. Add the tomatoes, garlic, parsley stems, bay leaves, and thyme, along with salt to taste, and cook, stirring and skimming frequently, for about 25 minutes, or until a fragrant broth has formed.

6. Remove from the heat, cover, and let stand for 15 minutes, then strain through a fine sieve, reserving the liquid and discarding the solids.

7. Use the liquid as directed or as a base for any fish soup.

Vegetarian Lentil Soup

I grew up on one version or another of this soup. The Italian version added some small pasta and was topped with extra virgin olive oil and cheese. The Greek was seasoned with red wine vinegar and cracked black pepper. I often add my own touch—diced parsnips, which add a very deep, sweet flavor.

Any leftover soup can be stored, covered and refrigerated, for up to 3 days. You may need to add a bit of liquid when reheating.

$^1/_2$ pound dried lentils, rinsed

5 cups hot Vegetable Stock (page 280)

1 bay leaf

3 tablespoons olive oil

1 cup finely diced onion

Coarse salt and freshly ground pepper

1 garlic clove, minced

1 cup finely diced carrots

$^1/_2$ cup finely diced celery

$^1/_2$ teaspoon dried Greek oregano

$^1/_4$ teaspoon ground cumin

$^1/_2$ cup chopped canned Italian plum tomatoes
with juice

$^1/_2$ teaspoon Kalamata vinegar

$^1/_2$ cup grated kefalotyri or Parmesan cheese
(optional)

1. Combine the lentils with $2^1/_2$ cups of the stock in a medium saucepan over medium-high heat. Add the bay leaf and bring to a boil. Immediately lower the heat to a bare simmer and cook for 15 minutes, or until the liquid just barely covers the lentils. Remove from the heat and set aside.

2. Meanwhile, heat 2 tablespoons of the olive oil in a large saucepan over low heat. Add the onion along with a pinch of salt and cook, stirring occasionally, for 10 minutes. Add the garlic and cook for 1 minute. Raise the heat, stir in the carrots and celery and sauté for 2 minutes. Add the oregano and cumin along with salt and pepper to taste, stirring to combine. Stir in the tomatoes and cook for 1 minute. Add the lentils along with any liquid remaining in the pan. Add the remaining stock, cover, and bring to a boil, then lower the heat to a bare simmer and simmer, stirring occasionally, for 45 minutes, or until soft. Leave the cover slightly ajar while simmering.

(continued)

3. Remove the bay leaf and transfer 1 cup of the hot soup to a blender or food processor fitted with the metal blade and process to a smooth puree. Return the puree to the soup, stirring to blend well. Simmer for 5 minutes or so. Stir in the vinegar, and remove the bay leaf.

4. Ladle the soup into large shallow soup bowls. Using the remaining tablespoon of olive oil, drizzle the top of each bowl with oil. Top with a generous sprinkle of cheese if desired. Serve immediately.

Roasted Tomato Soup

Once the warm weather hits New York City, Molyvos customers begin asking for this soup. It has become our signature of summer as it can be made only when tomatoes are at their most luscious.

7 tablespoons olive oil, plus more for drizzling

6 large beefsteak tomatoes, cut in half lengthwise

2 small white onions, peeled and halved lengthwise

Coarse salt and coarsely ground pepper

2 teaspoons dried Greek oregano

2 garlic cloves, sliced

1 cup chopped canned plum tomatoes

1 quart Vegetable Stock (page 280)

1 to 2 teaspoons sugar

2 tablespoons Roasted Garlic (page 121), pureed

6 tablespoons warm cooked orzo

$1/4$ cup crumbled feta cheese

1. Preheat the oven to 350°F and line a baking sheet with parchment paper. Set a wire rack large enough to hold the tomatoes and onions on top of the parchment paper.

2. Using about 2 tablespoons of the olive oil, lightly coat the tomatoes and onions. Season with salt and pepper and 1 teaspoon of the oregano. Place them, cut side up, on the prepared baking sheet. Roast in the preheated oven for about 2½ hours, or until very soft and slightly shrunken, to concentrate the flavor. The onions may take a bit longer. Remove from the oven and set aside to cool.

3. Heat 2 tablespoons of the olive oil in a large saucepan over medium heat. Add the garlic along with a pinch of salt and cook, stirring frequently, for about 3 minutes, or just until the garlic begins to brown around the edges.

4. Immediately add the canned tomatoes and bring to a simmer. Stir in the cooled roasted tomatoes and onion, stirring to blend. Add the stock along with the sugar and salt and pepper to taste and bring to a simmer. Simmer for about 30 minutes, or until the vegetables are almost falling apart and the

soup is very fragrant. Whisk in the roasted garlic puree and remove from the heat.

5. Using a handheld immersion blender, process the soup to a smooth puree. Whisk in the 3 tablespoons of extra virgin olive oil and then pour the mixture through a sieve with large holes into a clean saucepan. Keep warm over very low heat.

6. Place a tablespoon of the orzo into each of 6 shallow soup bowls. Ladle equal portions of soup into each. Sprinkle with an equal amount of feta cheese and the remaining oregano. Drizzle extra virgin olive oil over the top and serve.

Shredded Romaine Salad

This is probably the simplest recipe that you will ever find in a cookbook. The first time I had this salad we were at Nick Livanos's uncle's house in Athens. I could see that much Greek pride was attached to its making—not only because of the quality of the garden-fresh lettuce but also because of the technique required to cut the romaine extremely thin. When he presented the salad, Nick's uncle said, "I'll bet you have never seen romaine sliced this thin, eh?" And I hadn't. At Molyvos, I often add some shredded red endive and baby arugula to give a hint of color and a little touch of spiciness.

1 large head of romaine

1 bunch (about 8) scallions, trimmed

1 bunch (about ¹/₄ pound) fresh dill, stems
   removed, chopped

¹/₄ cup plus 2 tablespoons extra virgin olive oil

Juice of 1 lemon

Coarse salt and freshly ground pepper

1. Separate the romaine leaves. Trim off any damaged parts and wash well under cold running water. Pat dry.

2. Lay 3 to 4 leaves on top of one another on a clean cutting board. Using a very sharp knife, cut the leaves crosswise into almost paper-thin strips. Place the romaine strips in a large bowl and continue stacking and cutting until all of the romaine has been sliced.

3. Slice the scallions crosswise on a diagonal and add them to the romaine. Add the dill and toss to combine.

4. Drizzle the lettuce mixture with the olive oil and lemon juice. Season with salt and pepper to taste and toss to combine. Serve immediately.

Greek Garden Salad

Greek vegetables come straight from the garden to the table. The ingredients are always room temperature so the maximum flavor can be reached. And, interestingly, other than in the traditional romaine salad, in Greece greens are not often used in summer salads—lettuce is added because tourists expect it. In America, Greek diners have to take the responsibility for adding so much lettuce to this classic home cook's summer salad. At Molyvos, I have taken the liberty of adding just a small amount of romaine to meet the American expectation.

3 beefsteak tomatoes

1 hothouse cucumber, scored, quartered
    lengthwise, and cut crosswise $1/4$ inch thick

1 small red onion

20 Kalamata olives, pitted and thinly sliced
    crosswise

1 cup diced feta cheese

1 tablespoon well-drained capers

Red Wine Vinaigrette (recipe follows)

1 teaspoon dried Greek oregano

Coarse salt and freshly ground pepper

2 cups shredded romaine

1. Core the tomatoes. Cut each tomato in half crosswise, then cut each half into 5 pieces. Place the pieces in a mixing bowl. Add the cucumber.

2. Cut the onion in half lengthwise and then slice each half lengthwise into thin julienne. Add the onion to the bowl.

3. Add the olives, cheese, and capers. Add the vinaigrette and toss to coat. Taste and season with oregano and salt and pepper to taste.

4. Place an equal portion of the lettuce on each of 6 salad plates or bowls. Top with an equal portion of the tomato mixture, sprinkle lightly with oregano, and serve immediately.

Red Wine Vinaigrette

Makes about ³⁄₄ cup

¹⁄₄ **cup red wine vinegar**
1 garlic clove, peeled and smashed
1 teaspoon dried Greek oregano
¹⁄₂ **cup extra virgin olive oil**
Coarse salt and freshly ground pepper

1. Combine the vinegar with the garlic and oregano in a small mixing bowl. Add the oil and, using a wire whisk, beat constantly until the mixture is emulsified. Season with salt and pepper to taste and set aside until ready to use.

2. Whisk briefly before using.

AN ATHENS VEGETABLE MARKET.

Sliced Tomatoes, Feta, Kalamata Olives, and Extra Virgin Olive Oil

This is a super-simple salad, but when tomatoes are perfectly ripe, there is nothing better. I usually cut 3 large slices from each juicy, meaty beefsteak tomato, but feel free to cut the tomatoes as you wish. Just make sure all the ingredients are at peak flavor.

18 thick slices ripe beefsteak tomato

¹/₄ cup plus 2 tablespoons basil chiffonade (see page 46)

About ¹/₄ cup plus 2 tablespoons extra virgin olive oil, or to taste

1 teaspoon dried Greek oregano

Sea salt and freshly ground pepper

³/₄ cup crumbled feta cheese

12 Kalamata olives, pitted and sliced

1. Chill 6 salad plates.

2. Place a slice of tomato in the center of each plate. Sprinkle a bit of basil on each slice. Shingle another slice of tomato over the first and add a sprinkle of basil. Shingle a final tomato slice over the other two. Drizzle with extra virgin olive oil. Season with a sprinkle of oregano, sea salt, and pepper to taste.

3. Make a generous mound of feta on top of the tomato. Sprinkle with the sliced olives. Drizzle extra virgin olive oil over the tomatoes and around the plate. Add a light sprinkle of oregano and serve immediately.

Warm Manouri Salad with Baby Beets and Pickled Pearl Onions

This is a relatively simple salad that is raised to a higher level with the addition of the warm manouri cheese. The Kalamata Vinaigrette is one of our signatures—if you haven't tried Kalamata vinegar, this is a great introduction to its zesty flavor. Any leftover vinaigrette will keep, covered and refrigerated, for a few days.

12 baby beets, tops removed
¹/₂ cup red wine vinegar
¹/₂ cup dry red wine, such as Aghiorghitiko,
    Cabernet Sauvignon, or Sangiovese
Coarse salt
Three ¹/₂-inch-thick round slices manouri cheese,
    each cut into 6 equal triangles

2 tablespoons olive oil
¹/₂ pound baby greens
¹/₂ cup Kalamata Vinaigrette (recipe follows)
18 Pickled Pearl Onions (see Note)

1. Place the beets in a medium saucepan with cold water to cover by 1 inch. Add the vinegar, wine, and 1 tablespoon salt and place over high heat. Bring to a boil, lower the heat, and simmer for about 20 minutes, or until tender when pierced with the point of a small sharp knife.

2. Remove from the heat and set aside to cool in the cooking liquid.

3. When the beets are cool, drain well, separately reserving the beets and the cooking liquid. Peel and quarter the beets lengthwise.

(If not using immediately, store the beets in the cooking liquid until ready to use.)

4. Preheat and oil a stovetop grill pan.

5. Using a pastry brush, lightly coat both sides of each piece of cheese with olive oil. Place the cheese on the preheated grill pan and cook for 30 seconds on each side, or until the cheese is just warm but not melted. Remove from the heat and set aside.

6. Place the greens in a large mixing bowl. Drizzle with 2 tablespoons of the vinaigrette, tossing to coat. Place an equal portion of the

dressed greens in the center of each of 6 salad plates. Place 8 pieces of beet on one side of the plate and 3 pickled onions on the opposite side. Place 3 pieces of cheese on top of the greens on each plate. Drizzle 1 tablespoon of the vinaigrette over each plate and serve.

Kalamata Vinaigrette

Makes about 1½ cups

2 tablespoons red wine vinegar

¼ cup Kalamata vinegar

3 tablespoons thyme honey

½ teaspoon dried Greek oregano

½ teaspoon coarse salt, or to taste

Pinch of freshly ground pepper

1 cup extra virgin olive oil

I. Combine the vinegars, honey, oregano, salt, and pepper in a small mixing bowl. Whisking constantly, add the oil in a slow, steady stream, beating until the mixture is emulsified. Taste and, if necessary, season with additional salt and pepper.

2. Store, covered, at room temperature until ready to use. Whisk briefly before using.

NOTE: Use the recipe for Pickled Cipollini Onions (page 41) to make Pickled Pearl Onions, replacing the cipollini with tiny pearl onions.

Barley Rusks with Tomatoes and Feta

This is one of the best ways to celebrate tomatoes at the height of the season. We had this dish on the menu when we opened in 1997, and it was an instant hit. Although the menu has changed, I still think this is a terrific dish—but only in the summer!

5 medium beefsteak tomatoes, peeled (see page 113)

Grated zest of 1 lemon

About ¼ cup plus 2 tablespoons extra virgin olive oil

Coarse salt and freshly ground pepper

Juice of 3 lemons

6 barley rusks

½ pound crumbled feta cheese

2 cups sliced pitted Kalamata olives

3 tablespoons chopped fresh flat-leaf parsley

1½ teaspoons dried Greek oregano

1. Place the tomatoes on a cutting board stem side down. Cut into quarters. Using a small, sharp knife, remove and reserve the membrane and seeds. Cut the tomato quarters into a medium dice and place in a mixing bowl. Set aside.

2. Pass the tomato membrane and seeds through a food mill or colander, pressing to extract as much liquid as possible. Discard the solids and combine the liquid with the diced tomatoes. Stir in the lemon zest along with 2 tablespoons of the olive oil. Season with salt and pepper to taste and set aside.

3. Combine the juice of 2 lemons with 3 cups water in a nonreactive bowl. Lay the barley rusks in a shallow dish and pour the lemon water over them. Soak for about 30 seconds, or until the rusks have softened slightly. Remove the rusks from the liquid, shaking off any excess moisture.

4. Place one rusk on each of 6 plates. Drizzle with the juice of the remaining lemon and a bit of olive oil (to help soften the rusk as well as add flavor).

5. Spoon an equal portion of the tomato mixture over the rusks. Top with an equal portion of feta and sliced olives. Using the remaining 3 tablespoons olive oil, drizzle oil over each serving. Sprinkle with parsley, dried oregano, and more pepper to taste. Serve immediately.

Seafood–Cretan Bread Salad

This recipe comes from John Piliouras, the chef de cuisine at Molyvos. One evening, after service, we had some leftover frutti di mare (or seafood salad) in which we were dipping some crusty bread. We were all commenting on how delicious it was. The next day John surprised us with this salad—his take on our late-night snack. It went right on the menu and has become one of our most popular dishes.

1 cup plus 3 tablespoons extra virgin olive oil

2 shallots, minced

2 garlic cloves, minced

2 pounds fresh mussels, scrubbed and
　debearded

2¹/₂ cups dry white wine

1 pound calamari, cleaned and cut into ¹/₄-inch
　rounds, tentacles cut in half

12 medium shrimp, peeled, deveined, and
　halved lengthwise

¹/₂ pound sea scallops, quartered

¹/₂ pound lump crabmeat, cartilage removed

¹/₂ cup fresh lemon juice

1 cup thinly sliced celery heart

¹/₂ cup diagonally sliced scallion, including some
　of the green part

¹/₄ cup sliced, pitted, cracked Greek green olives

2 tablespoons chopped fresh flat-leaf parsley

1 tablespoon chopped fresh mint

1 tablespoon chopped fresh dill

¹/₄ teaspoon sugar

Coarse salt and freshly ground pepper

6 barley rusks

I. Heat 1 tablespoon of the olive oil in a large skillet over medium heat. Add the shallots and garlic and sauté for 1 minute. Add the mussels and then the white wine, stirring with a wooden spoon to deglaze the pan. Raise the heat to high, cover, and bring to a boil. Lower the heat slightly and cook for about 5 minutes, or until the mussels have opened. Remove from the heat and uncover.

Remove and discard any mussels that did not open.

2. Using a slotted spoon, transfer the mussels to a baking pan. Set aside to cool.

3. Return the skillet to medium heat and bring the mussel-cooking liquid to a simmer. Add the calamari, stirring to mix. Add the shrimp and scallops and simmer for about 3 minutes, or just until the seafood is set.

Remove from the heat and, using a slotted spoon, transfer the seafood to the pan holding the mussels to cool. Measure out $1/4$ cup of the cooking liquid and set aside.

4. When the mussels are cool enough to handle, carefully remove the meat from the shells, discarding the shells. Place the meat in a large glass bowl. Add the cooled calamari, shrimp, and scallops along with the crabmeat, tossing to combine.

5. Combine the lemon juice, celery heart, scallion, olives, parsley, mint, dill, and sugar with the $1/4$ cup reserved cooking liquid in a medium nonreactive bowl. Whisking constantly, add 1 cup of the remaining olive oil and salt and pepper to taste. Pour the lemon juice mixture over the seafood and toss very gently to combine. Do not break up the crab. Cover with plastic wrap and refrigerate for 3 hours.

6. When ready to serve, working with one at a time, dip the rusks in cold water for about 30 seconds and shake gently to remove excess liquid.

7. Place one rusk in the center of each of 6 salad plates. Remove the seafood salad from the refrigerator and ladle an equal portion over the rusk on each plate, allowing the juices to baste the rusk and ooze out onto the plate. Drizzle a bit of the remaining 2 tablespoons of olive oil on the plates and serve immediately.

Octopus Salad with Grilled Peppers, Tomatoes, and Baby Greens

One day, after lunch at Molyvos, I went through the kitchen, pulling things together for a salad for myself. It was so delicious that I thought our diners would like it as much as I had. It is a simple mix, but the flavors seem to balance one another beautifully.

1 cup extra virgin olive oil

¹/₄ cup white wine vinegar

Juice of 2 lemons

2 garlic cloves, minced

1 teaspoon dried Greek oregano

3 Poached Octopus, halved (page 55)

6 packed cups mixed greens, chopped

1¹/₂ cups arugula, chopped

1 roasted red bell pepper, peeled and diced (see Note)

1 roasted yellow bell pepper, peeled and diced (see Note)

Lemon Vinaigrette (recipe follows)

18 caperberries, drained (optional)

1. Combine the oil and vinegar in a nonreactive container large enough to hold the octopus comfortably. Whisk in the lemon juice, garlic, and oregano. Add the octopus and toss to coat. Cover and refrigerate for 12 hours or overnight.

2. When ready to serve, combine the mixed greens, arugula, and bell peppers in a large mixing bowl. Set aside.

3. Preheat and oil the grill.

4. Remove the octopus from the marinade and gently wipe off excess.

5. Place the octopus halves on the grill and grill, turning occasionally, for about 10 minutes, or until nicely browned.

6. Remove the octopus from the grill and cut each half into 1-inch pieces.

7. Add the octopus pieces to the salad mix. Pour the vinaigrette over the top and toss to combine. Mound equal portions of the salad in the center of each of 6 salad plates. If using caperberries, garnish each plate with 3 of them and serve immediately.

Lemon Vinaigrette

Makes about 1 cup

Juice of 2 lemons
1 teaspoon dried Greek oregano
³/₄ cup extra virgin olive oil
Coarse salt and freshly ground pepper

Combine the lemon juice and oregano in a small mixing bowl. Add the oil in a slow, steady stream, whisking to emulsify. Season with salt and pepper to taste and set aside until ready to use. Whisk briefly before using.

NOTE: To roast bell peppers (or other peppers or chiles), place the whole pepper(s) over an open flame on top of the stove or under a preheated broiler. Use tongs to turn the pepper(s) frequently until all of the skin is blackened. Place the charred pepper(s) in an airtight plastic bag and allow to steam for about 15 minutes. Then remove the pepper(s) from the bag and, using your fingertips, gently push off the charred skin. Cut the peeled pepper(s) in half lengthwise and remove and discard the stem, seeds, and inner white membrane. Roasted peppers may be stored, tightly covered and refrigerated, for up to 3 days.

Black Pepper–Crusted Tuna with Marinated Cucumbers and Herb Salad

This is not your typical Greek recipe by a long shot! It is, however, based on ancient flavors. Early Mediterranean cooks fermented fish scraps and used the strong juices that resulted as a sauce in many dishes. Cilantro and coriander seeds were also used during the classic Greek period. This dish is one of my favorites as well as a favorite of Molyvos diners. The spices and cucumbers are familiar to the Greek palate, but the Asian fish sauce I use to mimic ancient Greek flavors adds a surprise note. You must have absolutely pristine tuna to make this salad, and preparation must begin one day prior to serving.

3 tablespoons coriander seeds

2 tablespoons black peppercorns

¹/₄ cup plus 3 tablespoons olive oil

Three 4-ounce sushi-grade bigeye tuna steaks

2 tablespoons sherry vinegar

2 tablespoons sugar

1 tablespoon nam pla, nuoc nam, or other Asian fish sauce (see Note)

1 hothouse cucumber, peeled, seeded, and finely diced

1 tablespoon chopped fresh cilantro

1 teaspoon sesame seeds, toasted (see page 44)

Coarse salt

1 cup mixed herb leaves, such as flat-leaf parsley, tarragon, basil, and dill

About ¹/₄ cup Kalamata Vinaigrette (page 140)

I. Combine the coriander seeds and peppercorns in a spice grinder and pulse for about 1 minute until coarsely ground. Pour the ground spices into a small shallow bowl. Add ¹/₄ cup of the olive oil and mix until a wet paste forms.

2. Working with one piece at a time, roll the edges of the tuna steaks in the spice paste, taking care that they are covered evenly. Individually wrap each coated tuna steak in plastic wrap and place in the freezer for 12 hours.

3. Combine the vinegar, sugar, and fish sauce in a small mixing bowl. Add the diced cucumber and toss to coat. Fold in the cilantro and sesame seeds, cover with plastic wrap, and refrigerate for at least 1 hour and up to 4 hours.

4. An hour before serving, remove the tuna from the freezer, unwrap, and season with salt to taste. Place a large sauté pan over medium-high heat. Add the remaining 3 tablespoons of olive oil and heat until smoking hot.

5. Place the tuna in the hot oil. Sear one side for about 2 minutes, or until nicely charred. Turn and sear the other side. The tuna should remain very rare in the center. Transfer the tuna to a baking sheet and refrigerate for 1 hour and up to 4 hours.

6. Place the herbs in a medium mixing bowl. Add about 2 tablespoons of the vinaigrette, tossing to coat. Set aside.

7. Remove the tuna from the refrigerator. Using a very sharp knife, cut each tuna steak into 6 strips. Place an equal portion of the marinated cucumbers in the center of each of 6 salad plates. Fan 3 slices of tuna over the cucumber on each plate. Spoon an equal portion of the herb salad at the side of each plate, drizzle a bit of the remaining vinaigrette over all, and serve immediately.

NOTE: Nam pla, nuoc nam, and other Asian fermented fish sauces add a pungent flavor to many dishes. They are available from Asian markets, specialty food stores, and many supermarkets.

Charred Lamb Salad with Pea Shoots, Lemon, and Capers

This salad makes a terrific main course. It is a great boon to the cook since the lamb can be prepared and placed on the plates early in the day. The plates can be covered with plastic wrap and stacked carefully in the fridge and then the finishing touches put on just before serving.

2 boneless racks of lamb

Coarse salt and freshly ground black pepper

1 tablespoon dried Greek oregano

2 teaspoons Aleppo pepper (see page 9)

2 teaspoons ground coriander

2 teaspoons ground cumin

2 teaspoons ground fenugreek

2 teaspoons dried mint

About ¼ cup extra virgin olive oil

1 tablespoon well-drained capers

1 cup mixed baby greens

2 tablespoons Kalamata Vinaigrette (page 140)

1. Using kitchen twine, carefully tie each piece of lamb at least once vertically and 4 times around the circumference to hold the meat firmly in place. Season with salt to taste.

2. Combine 1 teaspoon black pepper with the oregano, Aleppo pepper, coriander, cumin, fenugreek, and mint in a small bowl. When well combined, generously coat each piece of lamb with the spices.

3. Heat 2 tablespoons of the oil in a large heavy sauté pan over medium-high heat. When very hot but not smoking, add the lamb and sear for about 3 minutes, or until the meat is charred. Turn and continue searing until each piece of lamb is charred on all sides. You do not want to cook the lamb; it should remain red in the center. The charring process should take no more than 15 minutes. (If the oil in the pan gets too black, remove the lamb, wipe out the pan, and start fresh with more oil as the darkened oil will add an unpleasant flavor to the meat.)

4. As soon as the lamb is completely charred, using tongs, transfer it to a cookie sheet. Place in the freezer to quickly stop the cooking and to firm the meat. Allow to rest in the freezer for about 20 minutes, or until the lamb is very firm but not fully frozen.

5. Remove the lamb from the freezer and untie all of the string. Using a slicing knife, cut the lamb crosswise into almost-paper-thin slices.

6. Place an equal portion of lamb in a circle of slightly overlapping slices to completely cover each of 6 dinner plates. Drizzle the lamb with a bit of the remaining extra virgin olive oil and sprinkle with an equal amount of the capers.

7. Place the greens in a small bowl and drizzle with the vinaigrette. Season with salt and pepper to taste and place a small portion on top of the lamb on each plate. Serve immediately.

Seafood

Throughout Greece, but most particularly on the islands, fresh fish reigns supreme—that is, fish that has been out of the water no more than twelve hours and often much less. There are more boats in the Greek islands than there are cars—a statistic that should indicate the possibility of great fish on the table. Although fish is not plentiful in the waters of the Aegean Sea, and what is caught is generally quite small, each variety is deeply flavorful.

Greeks tend to cook fish very simply. Larger fish are usually grilled or baked, small ones are frequently dredged in flour and fried in olive oil to be eaten whole as a meze. Grouper and small fish are often poached in an aromatic white wine broth, with the broth served separately as a soup. Octopus, squid, and cuttlefish are extremely popular and are cooked in a variety of ways. Hearty one-dish meals are often built around them either as stews or in combination with pasta or grains and greens. Only a few varieties of Aegean fish are available in the United States. I have adapted many of the traditional ideas for our commonly available varieties. I believe that all of the recipes reflect their heritage and are equal in flavor to their Greek counterparts.

JOSÉ VEGA PREPARES BRANZINI, ROYAL DORADE, AND RED MULLET.

Grilled Whole Fish

Grilling fish with bones keeps the flesh moist and flavorful. Some people don't like looking at a whole fish, however, so you can also remove the head and tail, leave the fish intact, and lightly score the skin. You'll need an outdoor grill and wood chips to grill a fish successfully. A fish grilling basket is also helpful.

2 cups wood chips, preferably cherry or pecan

Olive oil for the grill

Six 1¼-pound whole red snapper, black sea bass, porgy, or other small whole fish, cleaned and gutted (scales, gills, and fins removed)

About ¼ cup extra virgin olive oil

Coarse salt and freshly ground pepper

3 lemons

1 teaspoon dried Greek oregano

6 plum tomatoes, peeled, seeded, membrane removed, and finely diced (optional; see page 113)

2 tablespoons chopped fresh chives (optional)

1. Place the wood chips in cold water to cover. Set aside.

2. Preheat the grill and lightly coat the rack with olive oil.

3. To prepare the fish, using a sharp boning knife, make a slight insertion at the top of the dorsal fin just below the head and continue making a slight incision, pressing the knife against the bones all the way down the spine stopping just above the tail. The head and tail should be intact. Turn the fish over and repeat the process on the other side. (See the illustration.) This will make it very easy to pull the flesh away from the bone once cooked. (We do this in the restaurant to make it easier for the guest to fillet the fish at the table, but it's not necessary to do this to enjoy the fish.)

4. Drain the wood chips and place them on top of the hot coals in the grill. The chips will ignite and emit a flavorful smoke.

5. Using a pastry brush, lightly coat the fish with some of the olive oil. Then season with salt and pepper to taste. Lay the fish directly on the grill and cover. Grill, covered, for 10 minutes. Turn, cover the grill again, and continue to grill for 10 minutes, or until the flesh is opaque and the skin is lightly charred.

Using a fish spatula, transfer the fish to a large serving platter. Brush the fish lightly with olive oil again. Cut each lemon in half crosswise, and squeeze one half over each fish. Sprinkle with oregano. If desired, garnish the platter with some diced tomatoes and chopped chives.

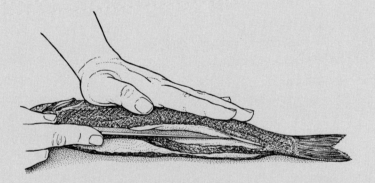

PARTIALLY FILLETING THE FISH BEFORE COOKING.

Crispy Cod with Skordalia and Marinated Beets

In Greece, this recipe is traditionally made with rehydrated salt cod. I find fresh cod very deli-cate and a great partner for skordalia and beets—a classic Greek combo! This is also a terrific preparation for skate wing; however, with skate I would recommend just a light Wondra flour coating in place of the cornstarch and flour mixture.

2 cups milk

1 cup all-purpose flour

1/2 cup cornstarch

1 tablespoon coarse salt

1/4 teaspoon freshly ground white pepper

4 large eggs

3 cups panko

1/4 cup chopped fresh flat-leaf parsley

1 teaspoon Aleppo pepper (see page 9)

Six 6-ounce pieces cod fillet

3 cups extra virgin olive oil

1 cup peanut oil

1 1/2 cups Skordalia (page 94)

Marinated Beets (recipe follows)

1 cup micro or baby greens

2 tablespoons chopped fresh chives

1. Preheat the oven to warm.

2. Place 4 shallow bowls, side by side, on a work surface. Place the milk in the first dish. Combine the flour, cornstarch, salt, and white pepper in the second dish. Place the eggs in the third dish and whisk until well blended. Combine the panko, parsley, and Aleppo pepper in the fourth dish.

3. Line a platter with parchment paper or plastic wrap. Set aside.

4. Place all the fish into the milk. Then, working with one piece at a time, dip the fish into the flour mixture, then the eggs, and

finally into the panko, pressing lightly so that the bread crumbs adhere. Place the coated fish on the prepared platter, cover, and re-frigerate for up to 6 hours until ready to cook.

5. Heat the oils to 325°F on an instant-read thermometer in a heavy skillet over high heat. Working with 2 pieces at a time, add the coated fish and fry for 6 to 8 minutes, or until golden brown and crisp on all sides. Using a slotted spatula, transfer the fish to a double layer of paper towel to drain and keep it warm in the oven. Fry the rest of the fish.

6. Place 2 tablespoons of the Skordalia in the center of each of 6 dinner plates. Make a semicircle of Marinated Beets around the Skordalia. Place a piece of fish, at a slight angle, into the Skordalia. Garnish with micro greens and chives and serve immediately.

Marinated Beets

5 medium beets, stems removed

1 cup dry red wine, such as Aghiorghitiko, Cabernet Sauvignon, or Sangiovese

$^1/_2$ cup red wine vinegar

1 tablespoon coarse salt

3 tablespoons sherry vinegar

2 tablespoons sugar

2 tablespoons chopped fresh dill

2 tablespoons sliced scallion, including some of the green part

1. Place the beets in a medium saucepan with cold water to cover by 1 inch. Add the wine, red wine vinegar, and salt and place over medium-high heat. Bring to a boil, lower the heat, and simmer for 25 to 30 minutes, or until the beets are tender when pierced with the point of a small sharp knife. Remove from the heat and allow the beets to cool in the cooking liquid. (They may be stored in the cooking liquid, covered and refrigerated, for up to 4 days.)

2. When cool, drain the beets, reserving 2 tablespoons of the cooking liquid. Peel the beets by pushing the skins off with your fingertips. Cut the beets into $^1/_8$-inch-thick slices and then into small dice.

3. Whisk the sherry vinegar and reserved beet-cooking liquid into the sugar in a small bowl. Add the diced beets and toss to coat. Cover and refrigerate until ready to serve or for up to 2 days.

4. Fold in the dill and scallion to serve.

SERVES 6

Pan-Seared Wild Striped Bass
with Mushroom Stifado

A stifado is a traditional Greek stew that is usually made with meat or seafood. It always has in its base tomatoes, pearl onions, and red wine seasoned with cinnamon, clove, and allspice. I have put a bit of a progressive twist on it with the addition of mushrooms, Mavrodaphne, a sweet wine, orzo, and rich veal stock. Replace the orzo with diced potato if you wish.

Note that the timing here is based on about 10 minutes per inch of thickness of the fish. This is such a simple dish that it's great for family dinners. You could first sear the fish on the stovetop and then transfer it to an attractive ovenproof baking dish to finish in the oven. You could then bring it to the table directly from the oven, serving the stifado as a side dish.

2 tablespoons olive oil
Six 6-ounce skin-on wild striped bass or other
    flaky white fish fillets, scored in a crosshatch
    pattern

Coarse salt and freshly ground pepper
Mushroom Stifado (recipe follows)
Chopped fresh chives for garnish

1. Preheat the oven to 375°F.

2. Place the olive oil in a large ovenproof sauté pan over medium-high heat, swirling the pan to make an even coating. (You may have to do this in batches or in 2 pans to avoid crowding the pan.)

3. Season the fish with salt and pepper to taste and place, skin side down, in the hot pan. Sear for about 3 minutes, or until the skin has taken on some color. Transfer to the preheated oven and roast for about 6 minutes, or

until the fish is opaque and the edges are quite brown but the fish is still raw in the center. Remove from the oven, turn the fish, and set aside to rest for about 3 minutes, or until the fish is just cooked in the center.

4. Spoon an equal portion of the Mushroom Stifado in the center of each of 6 dinner plates. Place a fish fillet on top. At the restaurant, we garnish the top with a tiny salad of micro greens, but a generous sprinkling of chopped chives works as well.

Mushroom Stifado

$^1/_2$ cup olive oil

$^3/_4$ pound cremini mushrooms, stems removed and caps quartered

$^3/_4$ pound shiitake mushrooms, stems removed and caps quartered

Coarse salt and freshly ground pepper

One 20-ounce can Italian plum tomatoes, with juice

5 peppercorns

4 garlic cloves, peeled

4 parsley stems

4 whole allspice

2 whole cloves

2 bay leaves

1 cinnamon stick

$1^1/_2$ cups Mavrodaphne wine

$^3/_4$ cup dry red wine, such as Aghiorghitiko, Cabernet or Sangiovese

3 red onions, cut into julienne

2 garlic cloves, sliced

Pinch of Aleppo pepper (see page 9)

1 cup Veal Stock (page 283)

Caramelized Pearl Onions (recipe follows)

$^1/_2$ cup orzo, cooked al dente

1 tablespoon chopped fresh flat-leaf parsley

1 teaspoon unsalted butter at room temperature

$^1/_2$ teaspoon balsamic vinegar

$^1/_2$ teaspoon red wine vinegar

1. Heat 2 tablespoons of the olive oil in a large sauté pan over medium-high heat. Add a single layer of the mushrooms and sauté for 3 to 4 minutes, or until well caramelized. In the last second, season with salt and pepper to taste. As the mushrooms are cooked, transfer to a baking pan in a single layer to cool. Continue heating fresh oil and sautéing the mushrooms until all of the mushrooms have been cooked.

2. Drain the tomatoes, reserving the juice. Using your hands, crush the tomatoes and set aside.

3. Combine the peppercorns, whole garlic cloves, parsley stems, allspice, cloves, bay leaves, and cinnamon stick in a piece of cheesecloth about 6 inches square to make a sachet. Gather up the ends and, using kitchen twine, tie the bag closed. Set aside.

(continued)

4. Combine the wines in a large saucepan over medium-high heat. Stir in 1½ cups of the reserved tomato juice and season with salt to taste. Bring to a boil and then lower the heat, add the sachet, and simmer, skimming frequently, for 10 to 12 minutes, or until reduced by half.

5. While the sauce is reducing, heat the remaining 2 tablespoons of oil in a medium sauté pan over medium heat. Add the onions along with a pinch of salt and toss to coat with oil and salt. Lower the heat, cover, and cook for about 15 minutes, or until the onions are soft and sweet. Uncover, raise the heat to medium-high, and cook for another minute or until golden. Add the sliced garlic and cook for another 2 minutes. Season with the Aleppo pepper and salt and pepper to taste. Stir in the reserved tomatoes and cook for 1 minute. Add the reduced tomato-wine sauce with the sachet and bring to a simmer.

6. Raise the heat and bring the mixture to a simmer. Add the stock, bring to a boil, lower to a simmer and add the reserved mushrooms. Lower the heat and cook for about 10 minutes, or until the mixture has thickened slightly. Fold in the Caramelized Pearl Onions and orzo.

7. Remove from the heat, taste, and, if necessary, season with salt and pepper. Remove and discard the sachet.

8. If not serving immediately, cool in an ice bath and store, covered and refrigerated, for up to 3 days. Reheat when ready to serve. Just before serving, stir in the parsley, butter, and vinegars.

Caramelized Pearl Onions

Makes about 1½ cups

1 tablespoon unsalted butter
1 tablespoon olive oil
1½ cups peeled blanched pearl onions
1½ teaspoons sugar

Heat the butter and olive oil in a medium sauté pan over medium heat. Add the onions and sprinkle with the sugar. Cook, continually shaking the pan to accelerate the glazing, for about 5 minutes, or until the onions are golden. Add ¼ cup water and cook, shaking the pan occasionally, for 10 minutes, or until the onions are nicely glazed. Remove from the heat and set aside until ready to use.

Pan-Roasted Black Sea Bass with Braised Horta, Melted Leeks, and Orzo

Horta is the Greek name for all wild greens. Many different varieties are picked all over Greece—from the roadsides around Athens to the hills of the islands. Braised with onions and finished with extra virgin olive oil, lemon, and dill, the horta in this recipe have a fresh, sweet taste that pairs beautifully with the sea bass. This dish has many traditional Greek ingredients, but I have put them together in a contemporary way to make an inviting meal.

¹/₂ cup extra virgin olive oil

3 cups diced onions

Coarse salt and freshly ground pepper

2 cups diced leeks, white part only

1 cup dry white wine

2 cups Chicken Stock (page 281)

¹/₄ cup fresh lemon juice

2 bunches of black kale, Swiss chard, dandelion
   greens, or mustard greens, blanched, and cut

crosswise into 2-inch pieces (see page 11)
   (about 3 cups)

¹/₂ cup orzo

2 tablespoons chopped fresh dill

Six 7-ounce skin-on black sea bass fillets

About 1¹/₂ cups micro greens (optional)

1. Heat 2 tablespoons of the olive oil in a large sauté pan over medium heat. Add the onions along with a pinch of salt. Cover and cook, stirring occasionally, for about 15 minutes, or until the onions are translucent but have not taken on any color. Add the leeks, cover, and cook for 6 minutes, or until soft and translucent. Season with salt and pepper to taste.

2. Add the wine, raise the heat, and bring to a boil. Boil for 6 minutes, or until the pan is almost dry. Add the stock, lemon juice, and 1 tablespoon of the olive oil along with the blanched greens, stirring to combine. Taste and, if necessary, season with salt and pepper. Bring to a simmer, lower the heat, and cook at a bare simmer for 10 to 12 minutes, or until the greens are very tender.

3. While the horta is cooking, cook and drain the orzo according to package directions. Fold the cooked orzo into the greens and simmer for 1 minute. Add the dill along

with 1 tablespoon of olive oil. Remove from the heat and keep warm.

4. Heat 2 tablespoons of the remaining olive oil in each of 2 large sauté pans over medium-high heat, swirling to coat the bottom of each pan with the oil. Season both sides of the fillets with salt and pepper to taste and place 3 each, skin side down, in each hot pan. Sear for 4 to 5 minutes, or just until the skin is brown and crispy and the edge of the fish is slightly opaque. Using a fish spatula, turn the fillets and cook for 1 to 2 minutes, or until the fish is opaque and easily pulls apart when touched with the point of a small sharp knife.

5. Place an equal portion of the warm horta-orzo mixture in the center of each of 6 shallow soup plates. Place a fillet on top of each and, if desired, place a small mound of baby greens on top. Serve immediately.

Blackfish Plaki with Potatoes and Tomatoes

Traditionally, most Greek cooks cook the whole fish in the sauce in the oven. In my method, the cook has more control over the final presentation, and the flavors of each component are kept intact. If you prefer the classic way, make the sauce ahead of time, sear the fish as I direct, and then place it in a baking pan. Cover with the sauce and bake in a preheated 375°F oven for about 20 minutes.

½ cup extra virgin olive oil, plus more for
    drizzling if desired

1 tablespoon unsalted butter

2 medium onions, cut into fine julienne

Coarse salt and freshly ground pepper

8 garlic cloves, sliced

1 teaspoon dried Greek oregano

1 cup dry red wine, such as Aghiorghitiko,
    Cabernet Sauvignon, or Sangiovese

2 cups diced canned Italian plum tomatoes with
    juice

2 cups Chicken Stock (page 281)

¼ cup Kalamata olives

6 medium Yukon Gold or new potatoes,
    blanched, peeled, and cut into ¼-inch-thick
    slices

3 tablespoons chopped fresh flat-leaf parsley,
    plus more for garnish

Six 7-ounce skinless blackfish fillets

1. Heat 2 tablespoons of the olive oil in a medium saucepan over medium-low heat. Add the butter and swirl to incorporate. When the butter begins to foam, add the onions along with a pinch of salt, stirring to coat well. Cook for 8 to 10 minutes. Raise the heat to medium and cook for 4 to 6 minutes longer, or until the onions are golden brown. Season with salt and pepper to taste. Add the garlic and sauté for 1 minute. Add the oregano and stir to combine. Add the red wine and bring to a boil. Boil for about 5 minutes, or until the pan is almost dry. Stir in the tomatoes, along with their juice, the stock, and a pinch of salt. Return to a boil. Add the olives and lower the heat to a simmer. Stir in the potatoes and bring to a simmer. Simmer for about 8 minutes, or until the sauce has thickened slightly and is very rich in texture and flavor. Stir in the parsley along with 2 tablespoons of the remaining olive oil. Taste and, if necessary, season with salt and pepper. Remove from the heat and set aside.

2. Preheat the oven to 375°F.

3. Place a large sauté pan over medium-high heat. When very warm, add 2 tablespoons of the remaining olive oil. Season half of the fish with salt and pepper to taste and place in the hot oil. Sear for 2 minutes. Turn and sear for another minute. Remove from the pan and set aside. Add the 2 remaining tablespoons oil to the pan and sear the remaining 3 pieces of fish.

4. Place about a third of the sauce in the bottom of a shallow 2-quart baking dish. Lay the potatoes over the sauce and then place the fish on top. Cover with the remaining sauce. Place in the preheated oven and bake for about 12 minutes, or until the fish is opaque and cooked through. Remove from the oven.

5. Place an equal portion of the potato slices in a circle of slightly overlapping slices on each of 6 dinner plates. Surround the potatoes with a healthy drizzle of the sauce and then place a piece of fish on top of the potatoes on each plate. Spoon some sauce over the fish and sprinkle each plate with some additional parsley and, if desired, a drizzle of olive oil. Serve immediately.

NOTE: You can use any flaky white fish, such as grouper, sea bass, or snapper, in this recipe, as long as you remove the skin. All of these fish will take longer to cook than the thinner blackfish.

Phyllo-Wrapped Red Snapper with Oven-Dried Tomatoes, Olives, and Capers

The basic idea for this dish comes from the classic French *en papillote*, by which foods are cooked in a parchment paper packet. I love this particular combination of ingredients because the aromas they release when you break into the crisp phyllo is stupendous. I prefer to keep the skin on the fish as I think that it adds wonderful flavor and a hint of color but you can also use skinless fillets.

5 tablespoons sliced Kalamata olives

3 tablespoons well-drained capers

18 pieces Garlic Confit (recipe follows)

1/4 cup minced fresh oregano

2 tablespoons minced fresh flat-leaf parsley

Six 7-ounce red snapper fillets

9 sheets frozen #10 phyllo dough, thawed as directed on package

Approximately 1 cup extra virgin olive oil

Coarse salt and freshly ground pepper to taste

3/4 cup sliced well-drained Oven-Dried Tomatoes (recipe follows)

2 large egg yolks

1 tablespoon milk

1 tablespoon sesame seeds

Ouzo Sauce (recipe follows)

1. Preheat the oven to 350°F.

2. Combine the olives and capers in a small bowl. Drizzle with a bit of the oil from the Garlic Confit and set aside.

3. Combine the oregano and parsley in a small bowl and set aside.

4. Using a small, sharp knife, lightly score the skin side of the fish to cross-hatch. Place the fish on a platter, cover with plastic wrap, and set aside.

5. Hold the phyllo as directed on page 12.

6. Line a baking pan with a piece of parchment or wax paper. Place a wire rack on top of the paper. Using a pastry brush and 1 tablespoon of the olive oil, coat the rack with oil. Set aside.

7. Stack 3 sheets of phyllo on top of each other and cut in half lengthwise down the center, so that you have six halves.

(continued)

8. Working with one at a time, place a full sheet of phyllo on a clean surface. Using a pastry brush, lightly coat it with a bit of the olive oil. Lay one of the half sheets of phyllo on the left side of the full piece and again lightly brush with olive oil. Season with salt and pepper to taste and sprinkle the left side with the herb mixture.

9. Season a fish fillet with salt and pepper and place, skin side up, in the center of the left side of the phyllo. Sprinkle with some of the herb mixture. Place about a teaspoon of the olive and caper mixture on top of the fillet. Cover with 3 pieces of Garlic Confit and an equal portion of the tomatoes. Drizzle lightly with some of the oil from the Garlic Confit.

10. Bring the right side of the phyllo up over the left side to completely cover the fish. Then, starting from the top right-hand corner, begin to fold the phyllo together to make a firm packet with a tight seal. Place the packet on the prepared rack. Continue making packets until you have completed all six.

11. Whisk the egg yolks and milk together in a small bowl. Using a clean pastry brush, lightly coat the edge of each packet with egg wash. Sprinkle the edges with sesame seeds. Brush the entire packets with the remaining oil. Place in the preheated oven and bake for 20 to 25 minutes, or until the fish is cooked through and the phyllo is golden brown. Remove from the oven.

12. Place the fish packets on a cutting board and bring the board to the table so that your guests can see the beautiful golden presentation. Using a knife, trim off the edges, exposing the aromatic fish. Transfer each packet to a plate, fully opening the phyllo packet. Spoon some of the Ouzo Sauce around the plate and serve.

Garlic Confit

Makes 24 pieces

1¼ cups extra virgin olive oil
24 large garlic cloves, peeled and root ends cut off

I. Place the oil in a shallow pan over medium heat and warm for 2 to 3 minutes, or just until a bit above room temperature. Add the garlic and when the cloves begin to sizzle, immediately lower the heat to a bare simmer. Cook for 6 to 8 minutes, or just until the garlic has softened and colored somewhat.

2. Remove from the heat, cover, and set aside to cool.

3. When cool, strain through a fine sieve, separately reserving the garlic cloves and the oil. The oil can be used for cooking or flavoring.

DELIVERY OF WHOLE BRANZINI FLOWN IN FROM GREECE.

Oven-Dried Tomatoes

Makes 24 pieces

12 ripe plum tomatoes, cut in half lengthwise

1/2 cup plus 3 tablespoons extra virgin olive oil

Pinch of dried Greek oregano

Coarse salt and freshly ground pepper

12 fresh rosemary branches, each broken into 3 pieces

4 fresh oregano sprigs

3 garlic cloves, peeled and smashed

1. Preheat the oven to 300°F. Line a baking pan with parchment paper. Place a wire rack on top of the paper and set aside.

2. Combine the tomatoes with 3 tablespoons of the olive oil in a medium mixing bowl. Add the dried oregano and season with salt and pepper to taste, tossing gently to coat.

3. Place the seasoned tomatoes, cut side up, on the rack in the prepared pan. Be certain to leave space between the tomatoes to let air circulate freely around them. Place in the preheated oven and roast, turning every hour, for about 3 hours, or until dry with the flesh slightly moist. Remove from the oven and set aside to cool.

4. Place the fresh rosemary and oregano along with the garlic in a container large enough to hold the tomatoes in a single layer. Place the tomatoes, cut side up, on top of the herbs and garlic. Drizzle the remaining 1/2 cup oil over the top and season lightly with salt and pepper. Cover with plastic wrap and refrigerate until ready to use or for up to 1 week.

NOTE: You can also store the tomatoes in a glass canning jar. If so, make layers, separated by the herbs and garlic, and cover with extra virgin olive oil. Cover and store, refrigerated.

Ouzo Sauce

5 black peppercorns

1 bay leaf

$^1/_2$ teaspoon anise seeds

3 shallots, peeled and thinly sliced

1 cup ouzo

$^1/_4$ cup dry white wine

Coarse salt and freshly ground pepper

1 cup Chicken Stock (see page 281)

$^1/_3$ cup Greek yogurt (see page 13)

1 tablespoon chopped fresh chives

1 tablespoon chopped fresh dill

1. Combine the peppercorns, bay leaf, anise seeds, shallots, ouzo, and wine in a medium saucepan over medium heat. Add a pinch of salt and bring to a boil. As soon as the liquid comes to a boil, it will flame slightly. Immediately remove from the heat. When the flames subside, return the saucepan to medium heat and bring to a simmer. Simmer for 10 to 12 minutes, or until the pan is almost dry. Add the stock and again bring to a simmer. Remove from the heat and set aside to cool to just about room temperature.

2. Whisk in the yogurt. The mixture should be the consistency of a creamy vinaigrette. If not, whisk in a bit more yogurt. Strain through a fine sieve into a clean container. Season with salt and pepper and fold in the chives and dill. Serve at room temperature.

Steamed Salmon Wrapped in Grape Leaves with Bulgur Salad

Dishes just like this one are found all through Greece, usually made with small whole fish like mackerel or sardines. Salmon is so good for you and so readily available that it is what I generally serve at Molyvos. In addition, the sweet full flavor of salmon balances the sharpness of grape leaves.

18 brine-packed California grape leaves, drained, blanched, stems removed (see page 36)

Six 6-ounce skinless salmon fillets

Coarse salt and freshly ground pepper

Grated zest of 1 lemon

1 tablespoon chopped fresh dill

Bulgur Salad (recipe follows)

Approximately ³/₄ cup Yogurt-Garlic Sauce (page 37)

1 tablespoon toasted pine nuts (see page 77)

2 tablespoons extra virgin olive oil

1. Prepare a steamer basket large enough to hold the fish in one layer or use a two-tiered Chinese-style steamer. Place over medium heat and bring to a simmer.

2. While the water is coming to a simmer, prepare the salmon. Place a grape leaf on a clean surface, vein side up. Place another grape leaf on top of it, slightly overlapping in the middle. Place another grape leaf, slightly overlapping at the top of the other two.

3. Season the fish with salt and pepper to taste. Place a piece of salmon in the center of the grape leaves. Place an equal portion of lemon zest and dill on the salmon. Fold the bottom up and over the salmon so that it covers the fish by about three quarters. Fold in the sides and then fold the packet over to enclose the fish completely. Repeat five more times.

4. Place the fish packets in a single layer in the steamer basket. Cover and steam for about 6 minutes for rare (up to 12 minutes for medium) or until the salmon is just cooked to desired degree of doneness.

5. Place equal portions of Bulgur Salad in the center of each of 6 dinner plates. Place a fish packet on top and drizzle Yogurt-Garlic Sauce over the packet and around the plate. Sprinkle the pine nuts around the edge of the plate and drizzle a bit of the extra virgin olive oil over all. Serve immediately.

PLACE A PIECE OF SALMON IN THE
CENTER OF THE GRAPE LEAVES.

FOLD THE BOTTOM UP AND OVER
THE SALMON. FOLD IN THE SIDES.

FOLD THE PACKET OVER TO
ENCLOSE THE FISH COMPLETELY.

171

Bulgur Salad

Serves 6

2¹/₂ tablespoons olive oil

1 medium white onion, finely diced

Coarse salt and freshly ground pepper

1 cup medium bulgur wheat

1 cup hot Herb Tea (page 289)

4 plum tomatoes, peeled, seeded, and cut into fine dice (see page 113)

1 hothouse cucumber, peeled, seeded, and cut into fine dice

1 garlic clove, minced

Juice and grated zest of 1 lemon

2 tablespoons toasted pine nuts (see page 77)

2 tablespoons chopped fresh mint

1 tablespoon chopped fresh flat-leaf parsley

2 tablespoons extra virgin olive oil

1. Heat the olive oil in a medium saucepan over medium heat. Add the onion along with a pinch of salt, cover, and cook, stirring occasionally, for about 8 minutes, or until the onion is very soft. Add the bulgur, stirring to blend. Add the hot Herb Tea and bring to a boil. Lower the heat and simmer for 3 to 4 minutes. Remove from the heat, cover, and set aside for 10 minutes, or until all of the moisture has been absorbed. Uncover and fluff the grains with a kitchen fork.

2. Transfer the cooked bulgur to a baking pan, spreading it out in an even layer. Set aside until cool and dry.

3. Place the cooled bulgur in a medium mixing bowl. Add the tomatoes, cucumber, garlic, lemon juice and zest, pine nuts, mint, and parsley, tossing to combine. Drizzle the extra virgin olive oil over all, season with salt and pepper to taste, and toss again to blend. Serve immediately or cover and refrigerate for up to 3 hours, until ready to serve. Bring to room temperature before serving to allow the flavors to shine.

Grilled Swordfish with Baby Clams, Wild Leeks, Asparagus, and Retsina-Scented Lemon-Mint Broth

I think this is one of spring's best dishes. It's light, aromatic, and easy to put together. It's best made in a saucepan called a *sauteuse*—a large shallow pan with handles that can serve as a saucepan, casserole, or Dutch oven.

Any flaky white fish such as snapper or wild striped bass can be used in place of the swordfish. You'll know the grill is hot enough to cook the fish perfectly when you can hold your palm about 2 inches above the grill for 3 seconds—any longer and the grill is too cold; any shorter and it is too hot.

12 ramps (wild leeks) (see Note)

18 pencil-thin unpeeled asparagus spears, trimmed and blanched

30 clams in the shell, such as Manila or Mahogany

About ¼ cup olive oil

Six 7-ounce, 1-inch-thick skin-on swordfish steaks

Coarse salt and freshly ground pepper

¼ cup retsina wine

3 cups Clam Broth (page 287)

Juice and grated zest of 1 lemon

¼ cup extra virgin olive oil

3 cups baby spinach leaves

1 tablespoon torn fresh mint leaves, plus 6 sprigs for garnish

1. Wash the ramps well and trim off the roots. Using a small sharp knife, cut the white part off on the bias and then cut crosswise into ½-inch-thick pieces. Cut the leaves into ¼-inch-wide strips. Set both aside, separately

2. Cut the top 1½ inches from each piece of asparagus. Cut the remaining spears crosswise into ⅛-inch pieces. Set aside.

3. Using a rough, green kitchen scrub pad, vigorously wipe the clams clean under cold running water. Place in a large bowl of cold salted water and swish to purge the clams of any sand. Drain and repeat twice more. Drain well and set aside.

4. Clean and lightly coat the grill with olive oil. Preheat to medium-high.

(continued)

5. Using a pastry brush, lightly coat both sides of the swordfish with some of the olive oil. Then season with salt and pepper to taste. Lay the fish directly on the grill and cover. Grill, covered, for 5 minutes. Turn, cover again, and continue to grill for 5 to 7 minutes, or until the flesh is opaque and the skin is lightly charred. Using a fish spatula, transfer the fish to a large serving platter. Tent lightly with aluminum foil to keep warm.

6. Heat 2 tablespoons of the olive oil in a sauteuse over medium heat. Add the white pieces of ramps along with a pinch of salt and cook, stirring frequently, for about 3 minutes, or until the ramps are quite fragrant and beginning to soften. Do not allow them to take on any color.

7. Remove the pan from the heat and add the wine, stirring to blend. Return the pan to medium-high heat and cook for about 3 minutes, or until the pan is almost dry.

8. Add the broth, followed by the clams. Add half of the lemon juice, cover, and bring to a bare simmer. As soon as the mixture comes to a simmer, begin checking the clams. As they open, transfer them to a sauté pan fitted with a lid using a slotted spoon. Continue removing clams as they open. This method speeds the cooking and keeps the clams from overcooking. Discard any clams that don't open within 8 minutes.

9. Add about $\frac{1}{4}$ cup of the cooking liquid to the clams and then drizzle with 2 tablespoons of the extra virgin olive oil. Cover and keep warm.

10. Taste the cooking liquid and season with salt and pepper to taste.

11. Add the asparagus and bring to a simmer over medium heat. Immediately fold in the reserved ramp leaf strips. Add the spinach, mint leaves, and remaining lemon juice along with the zest. Taste and, if necessary, adjust the seasoning. You should have a clear, vibrant broth with a perfect balance of light flavors. Drizzle with the remaining 2 tablespoons extra virgin olive oil.

12. Place 3 asparagus tips equidistant around the edge of each of 6 large shallow wide-rimmed soup bowls. Ladle an equal amount of the ramp-asparagus mixture in the center. Place 3 clams between the asparagus tops and a piece of swordfish in the center. Carefully ladle the broth around the edge without allowing it to splash on the fish. Place 2 clams on top, garnish with a mint sprig, and serve.

NOTE: Ramps, also called wild leeks, are a wild onion that grows along the eastern seaboard of the United States. They somewhat resemble a fat scallion with broad leaves that mimic lily of the valley. They are quite pungent when raw but mellow beautifully when cooked. They are available only in the spring, either from farmers' markets or from specialty produce purveyors.

Monkfish Youvetsi with Orzo and Tomatoes

Youvetsi is traditionally associated with lamb in the Greek kitchen. This is my progressive take on a classic, using monkfish, a hearty, almost meaty fish. Unfortunately, it doesn't work with other, lighter, flakier fish. Unlike many other Mediterranean cuisines, Greek cooking occasionally combine fish and cheese. In this recipe, I use just a little feta to give the final accent.

1³/₄ cups extra virgin olive oil

Juice of 1 lemon

3 tablespoons sliced garlic

2¹/₂ tablespoons dried savory

Freshly ground pepper and coarse salt

2 monkfish loins, each cut crosswise into three
    3-inch-thick pieces (see Note)

3 cups diced onions

¹/₄ teaspoon Aleppo pepper (see page 9)

2 cups dry red wine, such as Aghiorghitiko,
    Cabernet Sauvignon, or Sangiovese

One 32-ounce can whole tomatoes packed in
    puree, drained and crushed by hand

1 quart Chicken Stock (page 281)

2 bay leaves

2 cinnamon sticks

2¹/₂ cups orzo

¹/₄ cup coarsely grated feta cheese

2 tablespoons chopped fresh flat-leaf parsley

1. Combine 1 cup of the olive oil with the lemon juice, garlic, 2 tablespoons of the savory, and a pinch each of salt and pepper in a small mixing bowl.

2. Place the monkfish in a large resealable plastic bag. Add the marinade and press lightly on the bag to release all of the air. Seal and refrigerate for at least 3 hours or overnight.

3. When ready to cook, preheat the oven to 425°F. Line a platter with paper towels.

5. Remove the monkfish from the plastic bag. Using your hands, push all of the excess marinade off the fish. Place the fish on the prepared platter to drain off any remaining marinade. Set aside.

6. Strain the marinade through a fine sieve into a small bowl. Remove all the sliced garlic and discard the marinade. Place the garlic on a cutting board and, using a sharp knife, finely chop it. Set the garlic aside.

(continued)

7. Heat ½ cup of the remaining oil in a large straight-sided sauté pan over medium-high heat. Season the fish with salt and pepper to taste and place in the hot pan. Sear, turning frequently, for about 10 minutes, or until all sides are nicely browned. Set the fish aside. Discard the oil.

8. Return the pan to low heat and add the remaining ¼ cup oil. When hot, add the onions along with a pinch of salt. Cover and cook, stirring occasionally, for about 10 minutes, or until quite soft and lightly colored. Stir in the reserved chopped garlic and cook for 1 minute. Add the Aleppo pepper along with the remaining savory and stir to blend well. Add the wine and, using a wooden spoon, stir to loosen all the browned bits in the bottom of the pan. Raise the heat and bring to a boil. Immediately lower the heat and simmer, stirring occasionally, for about 20 minutes, or until the liquid has reduced by half. Stir in the tomatoes, bring to a boil, and cook for 5 minutes. Add the stock, bay leaves, and cinnamon sticks. When well combined, remove the pan from the heat.

9. Add the fish to the pan. Return to medium heat and bring to a simmer. Cover and transfer to the preheated oven. Braise, turning the fish occasionally, for about 30 to 35 minutes, or until the fish is almost tender.

10. While the fish is braising, place the orzo in a large saucepan of boiling salted water and blanch for 2 minutes. Drain well and rinse with cold running water. Drain well again and then set aside.

11. Remove the fish from the oven, leaving the oven on. Uncover and, using a slotted spoon, transfer the fish to a platter. Tent lightly with aluminum foil to keep warm. Measure out and reserve 1½ cups of the cooking liquid.

12. Bring the liquid remaining in the pan to a simmer over medium heat. Stir in the blanched orzo and return the pan to the oven. Cook, uncovered, for about 15 minutes, or until most of the liquid has been absorbed and the orzo is almost cooked through. Check from time to time to ensure that the liquid has not evaporated. If the pan seems to be getting too dry, add some of the reserved cooking liquid. However, you do not want the mixture to be soupy.

13. Remove the pan from the oven, leaving the oven on, and place the reserved monkfish on top of the orzo. Cover and return the pan to the oven. Cook for 10 to 12 minutes.

14. Remove the pan from the oven and either serve family style—straight from the braising pan—or place an equal portion of the orzo on each of 6 dinner plates, top with a piece of monkfish, and spoon a bit of the reserved sauce over all. Either way, sprinkle the top with the grated cheese and chopped parsley before serving.

NOTE: Monkfish loins are also known as monkfish *tails.* You will have to have a fishmonger clean the monkfish as well as remove the tough skin. I call this cut of monkfish an "osso buco," as the pieces of monkfish resemble the veal shanks used for that traditional Italian dish.

FISH IN CENTRAL ATHENS MARKET.

Grilled Prawns with Spinach-Rice Pilaf

The pilaf that I use in this dish is a very traditional Greek dish called *spanakorizo.* Although I have paired it with seafood, it's a sensational side dish with roasted chicken or grilled lamb chops. Rather than plate the dish, you could serve the prawns on a platter with the pilaf in a bowl on the side.

30 large prawns, peeled and deveined, tails
    intact (see Note)
1 cup extra virgin olive oil
3 garlic cloves, minced
Grated zest of 2 large lemons

2 tablespoons chopped fresh flat-leaf parsley
1 teaspoon dried Greek oregano
Coarse salt and freshly ground pepper
Spinach-Rice Pilaf (recipe follows)

1. Place the prawns in a single layer in a glass baking dish.

2. Combine the oil with the garlic, lemon zest, parsley, and oregano in a small bowl. When well blended, pour the marinade over the prawns. Cover with plastic wrap and refrigerate for 3 to 12 hours.

3. When ready to cook, preheat and oil a grill.

4. Remove the prawns from the refrigerator. Uncover and, using your fingers, scrape the marinade from the prawns back into the dish. Reserve the marinade.

5. Place the prawns on a baking sheet and season with salt and pepper to taste. Grill for 3 minutes, then use a pastry brush to baste the prawns with the reserved marinade. Turn and grill for another 3 minutes and then baste again. Grill for 2 minutes longer, or until the prawns are nicely marked and cooked through.

6. Remove the prawns from the grill. Place an equal portion of the Spinach-Rice Pilaf in the center of each of 6 dinner plates. Nestle 5 prawns into the pilaf on each plate and serve immediately.

Spinach-Rice Pilaf

Serves 6

3 cups Chicken Stock (page 281)

¼ cup plus 3 tablespoons olive oil

2 cups finely diced onion

Coarse salt and freshly ground pepper

1½ cups finely diced peeled, seeded very ripe tomatoes

1½ cups long-grain white rice

½ pound fresh spinach, stems removed and cut into 1-inch pieces

Grated zest of 2 lemons

2 tablespoons chopped fresh dill

2 tablespoons unsalted butter at room temperature

1. Preheat the oven to 400°F.

2. Place the stock in a saucepan over medium heat and bring to a boil. Lower the heat enough to just keep the stock very hot.

3. Heat 3 tablespoons of the oil in an ovenproof saucepan over medium-high heat. Add the onion along with a pinch of salt. Cover and cook, stirring frequently, for 10 to 12 minutes, or until the onions have sweated their liquid and not taken on any color. Add the tomatoes, season with just a little salt and pepper (more will come later), and cook for 5 minutes. Add the rice and stir to coat. Season with salt and pepper to taste.

4. While the onion mixture is cooking, heat the remaining ¼ cup olive oil in a large sauté pan. Add the spinach, a couple of handfuls at a time, and cook, lifting and tossing, for about 5 minutes, or until the spinach is just cooked. Season with salt and pepper to taste. Remove from the heat and place in a colander to drain. When cool enough to handle, using your hands, squeeze out all excess liquid. Set aside.

5. Add the hot stock to the rice, raise the heat, and bring to a boil. Immediately lower the heat to a bare simmer. Taste and, if necessary, add more salt and pepper. Cover and place in the preheated oven. After about 10 minutes, uncover and check the liquid level. When the liquid is at the same level as the rice, fold in the reserved spinach. Bake for about 20 minutes longer, or until all of the liquid has been absorbed and the rice is tender. You might want to check after 12 minutes to see how the process is progressing, but don't stir!

6. Remove the pan from the oven and let the rice rest, covered, for 10 minutes. Uncover and fluff with a dinner fork, then fold in the lemon zest, dill, and butter just before serving.

NOTE: Prawns and shrimp—which is which? Technically, prawns are those crustaceans that belong to the lobster group such as the French langoustines, but for the most part the names *shrimp* and *prawn* are used interchangeably in the United States. Often, however, the largest shrimp are called *prawns.* At the restaurant we use the huge shrimp with heads that have recently become available. If you can find them (usually only at fine fish markets), by all means use them—particularly when grilling.

Roasted Jumbo Prawns with
Hot Pepper and Spiced Tomato Saltsa

This dish is another one that originated from a conversation with Aglaia Kremezi. She was telling me of experiencing a traditional dish from the Greek islands that contained tomatoes and slow-cooked onions that had been mixed with shrimp. I took the general concept and modernized it a bit with salsa and succulent jumbo prawns. This dish can be served as either an appetizer or a main course. The Hot Pepper Mix makes a terrific seasoning for grilled meats. Any left over can be stored in an air-tight container as you would any spices.

Spiced Tomato Saltsa (recipe follows)

24 jumbo prawns or shrimp with heads, peeled and deveined, tails intact

1¹/₂ tablespoons Hot Pepper Mix (recipe follows)

Coarse salt

Hot Pepper–Bread Crumb Mix (recipe follows)

6 tablespoons extra virgin olive oil

1. Preheat the oven to 400°F.

2. Place just enough of the Spiced Tomato Saltsa in the bottom of a 16 × 10 × 2-inch baking dish to cover evenly.

3. Season the prawns with the Hot Pepper Mix and salt to taste. Place them slightly shingled in 2 side-by-side lines in a single layer over the tomato salsa in the baking dish. Sprinkle the Hot Pepper–Bread Crumb Mix over the top. Drizzle with the olive oil and place in the preheated oven.

4. Bake for 15 to 20 minutes, or until the prawns are pinkish white and the bread crumbs are golden brown. Remove from the oven, drizzle with the remaining olive oil, and serve immediately.

Spiced Tomato Saltsa

Makes about 6 cups

$^1/_2$ cup olive oil

4 medium onions, halved and cut into thin half-moon shapes

Coarse salt and freshly ground black pepper

$1^1/_2$ teaspoons ground cumin

$^1/_2$ cup sweet wine such as Mavrodaphne or sweet Marsala

One 32-ounce can diced tomatoes with juice

6 whole allspice

6 whole cloves

2 cinnamon sticks, chopped into small pieces

2 tablespoons coriander seeds, smashed

3 tablespoons finely chopped fresh flat-leaf parsley

I. Heat the oil in a large deep skillet with a lid over low heat. Add the onions along with a pinch of salt. Cover and cook, stirring frequently, for 20 to 25 minutes, or until very soft but not browned. Raise the heat to medium-high, uncover, and cook for 10 minutes, or until lightly colored. Add the cumin and then the wine and cook for 10 to 12 minutes, or until the pan is almost dry. Add the tomatoes and season with salt and pepper.

2. Combine the allspice, cloves, cinnamon sticks, and coriander seeds in a piece of cheesecloth about 6 inches square to make a sachet. Gather up the ends and, using kitchen twine, tie the bag closed. Add the sachet to the simmering onion/tomato mixture. Cover and simmer for 20 minutes, or until the sauce is quite thick. Uncover, stir in the parsley, and season with salt and pepper to taste. Remove from the heat and keep warm until ready to serve.

Hot Pepper Mix and Hot Pepper–Bread Crumb Mix

2 tablespoons Aleppo pepper (see page 9)

1¹/₂ tablespoons dried Greek oregano, crumbled

1 tablespoon fennel seeds, toasted and crushed (see page 44)

1 tablespoon dried grated orange zest

1¹/₂ teaspoons dried mint, crumbled

1¹/₂ teaspoons dried basil, crumbled

1 cup Fresh Bread Crumbs (page 57)

¹/₃ cup extra virgin olive oil

¹/₄ cup chopped fresh flat-leaf parsley

1 garlic clove, minced

1. Combine the Aleppo pepper, oregano, fennel seeds, orange zest, mint, and basil in a mortar and pestle. When well blended, measure out and reserve 3 tablespoons. This is the Hot Pepper Mix.

2. In a separate bowl, combine the bread crumbs with the olive oil, parsley, and garlic. Stir in the 3 tablespoons reserved Hot Pepper Mix. This mixture should resemble wet sand. If it doesn't, add olive oil, about ¹/₂ teaspoon at a time. This is my Hot Pepper–Bread Crumb Mix.

3. Set aside until ready to use.

Steamed Mediterranean Mussels with Cinnamon Basil, Ouzo, and Feta Cheese

If you can find them, use cultivated Mediterranean mussels that are grown in California or Washington State. They have a thin shell and plump, juicy meat. If you can't find them, try for Prince Edward Island mussels, which are almost as good. I love the scent of the cinnamon basil, but you can use absolutely any herb that pleases you. Whatever you do, however, have plenty of crusty bread to sop up the delicious broth.

To serve this dish as an appetizer you will need about ³⁄₄ pound mussels per person.

¹⁄₄ cup olive oil

2 garlic cloves, sliced

Pinch of Aleppo pepper (see page 9)

1 medium tomato, peeled, seeded, and chopped
(see page 113)

¹⁄₂ cup ouzo

2 cups Clam Broth (page 287)

2 tablespoons chopped fresh cinnamon basil

90 mussels, scrubbed and debearded

Grated zest of 1 lemon

¹⁄₂ cup diced feta cheese

Coarse salt and freshly ground pepper

2 tablespoons extra virgin olive oil

1. Preheat the broiler

2. Heat the olive oil in a sauteuse (see page 173) or large shallow pan over medium-high heat. Add the garlic and cook for about 2 minutes, or just until fragrant. Add the Aleppo pepper, stirring to blend. Stir in the tomato and cook for 1 minute. Remove from the heat and add the ouzo. Using a long kitchen match, carefully ignite the alcohol and then let the flames subside. Return to medium-high heat and cook for 2 minutes. Add the broth and ¹⁄₄ of the basil along with

the mussels, cover, and steam for 4 to 5 minutes, shaking the pan from time to time to allow the mussels to cook evenly. When all of the mussels have opened, transfer them to a large, flat, ovenproof serving dish, placing them, top shell toward the outside, in a concentric circle. Discard any mussels that have not opened.

3. Add the lemon zest and half of the feta cheese to the sauce. Season with salt and pepper and add the remaining basil. Spoon the sauce over the mussels. Sprinkle the mus-

sel meat with the remaining feta cheese. Drizzle extra virgin olive oil over all and place under the broiler for 2 minutes, or just until the cheese has softened.

4. Remove from the broiler and serve immediately.

Meat and Poultry

Meat has never been part of the daily diet in Greece. However, I would guess that anyone only slightly familiar with Greek cooking would know that lamb is the national favorite. For centuries, Greeks have celebrated almost every important occasion with a roasted baby lamb. Every Greek and Greek American can wax poetic on the succulence and flavor of an olive oil–lemon–rosemary–brushed roasted lamb. I know that I can! ✷ But, beyond the whole roasted baby lamb, every part of the animal is eaten. All of the innards are considered to be among the most delicious parts of the animal and are much loved, fried in olive oil, drizzled with lemon, sprinkled with Greek oregano, and eaten as a meze. Even the intestines are used in the traditional magiritsa, or Easter soup.

Other than lamb, Greek cuisine features kid (young goat), generally braised, as it tends to become dry when spit-roasted, and mature goat, which is often simmered in an aromatic broth to which pasta is added. Fresh pork and veal are also available, but beef is not common. ✽ Until recently, chickens were not raised for their meat but for their eggs. Hens would occasionally be featured on festive occasions or cooked for their nutritional value when feeding children or the infirm. During the last thirty years, chickens have become plentiful and quite inexpensive, so they are increasingly being used in everyday cooking. ✽ Game birds and small game such as hare are commonly used in traditional cooking. In fact, stifado (page 220) prepared with wild rabbit is a classic Greek dish. It is relished so much that, in Greece, rabbits are now raised to meet the demand for it.

SOUS-CHEF ADOLFO
VEGA CONCENTRATES
ON ASSEMBLY.

Cabbage Dolmades (Braised Cabbage Filled with Ground Lamb and Beef with Lemon-Dill Sauce)

Throughout the north of Greece you will find vats of whole heads of pickled cabbage, which cooks keep on hand to make all types of traditional dishes. I wanted to do something that would be a play on the flavor but not require the long brining session. The version that I came up with works for all cabbages—even Chinese cabbage—and offers a quick brining that simply picks up the flavors of the traditional Greek method.

2 medium heads of green cabbage

3 cups white vinegar

10 peppercorns

3 bay leaves

2 tablespoons sugar

2 tablespoons coarse salt plus more to taste

³/₄ cup Arborio rice, soaked, rinsed until the water runs clear, and drained

5 tablespoons extra virgin olive oil

1¹/₄ cups finely diced onion

3 slices white bread

¹/₂ cup milk

10 ounces lean ground lamb

10 ounces lean ground beef

4 ounces lean ground pork

2 garlic cloves, finely minced

¹/₂ cup grated kefalotyri cheese

4 tablespoons finely chopped fresh dill, divided

1 tablespoon finely chopped fresh flat-leaf parsley

1 large egg

2 tablespoons Fresh Bread Crumbs (page 57; optional)

Freshly ground pepper

3 cups well-seasoned Chicken Stock (page 281)

2 tablespoons fresh lemon juice

3 scallions, sliced diagonally

1¹/₂ cups Avgolemono Sauce (page 127)

1. Line a baking sheet with parchment paper. Set aside.

2. Remove and discard any damaged outer leaves from the cabbage. Using a small sharp knife, remove the core from each cabbage and separate all of the leaves. Set aside.

3. Combine the vinegar with the peppercorns, bay leaves, sugar, and 2 tablespoons salt in a large nonreactive pot. Stir in 3 quarts water and place over high heat. Bring to a boil and simmer for 5 minutes. Add the cabbage 5 to 6 leaves at a time, and blanch for 2 to 3 minutes. Using tongs, transfer the leaves to the baking sheet to cool. Continue blanching and cooling leaves until all leaves are done.

4. Remove most of the rib from the large leaves by laying the leaf flat and then carefully running a small sharp knife over the rib to make it even with the leaf. You do not want to completely remove the rib; you just want a nice, flat leaf that is pliable and easy to roll. Cabbage leaves can be refrigerated covered in brine for up to three days.

5. Place the rice in a heatproof bowl and cover with hot water.

6. Use the larger outer cabbage leaves for the dolmades and the smaller leaves to line the bottom of a large baking dish.

7. Line the bottom of a large baking dish with some of the reserved small cabbage leaves. You will need the remainder to cover the dolmades while baking. Set aside.

8. Heat 2 tablespoons of the olive oil in a large sauté pan over medium heat. Add the onion along with a pinch of salt. Cover and cook, stirring frequently, for 10 to 12 minutes, or until soft and translucent. Remove from the heat and spread out on a cookie sheet to cool.

9. Place the bread in the milk in a shallow bowl. Soak for a couple of minutes. Using your hands, break up the wet bread. Set aside.

10. Drain the rice well. Combine the lamb, beef, and pork in a large mixing bowl. Add the reserved onion and soaked bread along with the rice, garlic, cheese, 2 tablespoons of the dill, and parsley, using your hands to blend the mixture. Add the egg and again use your hands to blend. You want a moist but not sticky mix. If necessary, add no more than 2 tablespoons of bread crumbs to tighten the mix. Season with salt and pepper to taste. Cover and refrigerate for 30 minutes.

11. Preheat the oven to 375°F.

12. Combine the stock, lemon juice, and remaining 3 tablespoons olive oil in a medium nonreactive saucepan over medium heat. Bring to a simmer. Remove from the heat, season with salt and pepper to taste, and keep warm.

13. Lay the large cabbage leaves out on a clean surface. Working with one leaf at a time, form about 1/4 cup of the meat mixture into a cylinder shape. Place the cylinder near the bottom of the leaf. Fold the bottom up

and over the meat and then fold in both sides of the cabbage completely. Roll the cabbage leaf up and over the filling to make a nice neat packet. Place each packet, seam side down, in the leaf-lined dish. Place the packets tightly together so that they can't unroll while cooking.

14. When all of the dolmades have been made and placed in the baking dish, cover with the remaining small cabbage leaves. You should have about 24 dolmates. Pour the hot stock mixture over the stuffed leaves. Cover with aluminum foil. Place in the preheated oven and bake for about 45 minutes, or until the filling is cooked.

15. Remove from the oven and drain off all liquid.

16. Fold the scallions and the remaining dill into the Avgolemono Sauce. Place 4 dolmades on each of 6 plates and spoon about $1/4$ cup of the Avgolemono Sauce over the top.

Grilled Lamb Chops with Ionian Garlic Sauce

At Molyvos, I am constantly changing the menu according to the season and to what strikes me. I usually serve chops family style when entertaining at home— especially when grilling outdoors in the summer. Ionian Garlic Sauce is a great accent and, since it can be made in advance, a terrific boon to the home cook. Perfect accompaniments would be Chickpea Rice (page 236) and some grilled vegetables.

1½ cups extra virgin olive oil

Juice of 1 lemon

2 tablespoons chopped garlic

1 tablespoon dried Greek oregano

1½ teaspoons dried Greek savory

Coarse salt and freshly ground pepper

4 racks of lamb, trimmed of excess fat

Ionian Garlic Sauce (recipe follows)

1. Combine 1¼ cups of the olive oil with the lemon juice, garlic, oregano, savory, and salt and pepper to taste in a small mixing bowl.

2. Place the lamb in a glass baking dish and pour the marinade over the lamb, turning to coat all sides. Then lay each rack meat side down, cover the dish with plastic wrap, and refrigerate for 12 hours.

3. Preheat and oil the grill.

4. Remove the lamb from the refrigerator. Using your fingertips, remove excess marinade from the racks, allowing the mixture to drip back into the dish.

5. Season the racks with salt and pepper to taste and place them, meat side down, on the hot grill. Grill for 3 minutes and then turn and grill the remaining side for 3 minutes. Transfer to a platter and let rest for a few minutes. The lamb will still be cold and raw in the center.

6. Cut the lamb racks into individual chops. (You may save the end chops, which are sometimes not as nice as the center, for a salad or snack.) Using a pastry brush, lightly coat each chop with some of the remaining ¼ cup olive oil. Season with salt and pepper to taste.

(continued)

7. Return the grill to medium-high heat. When hot, add the chops, in batches of 4 to 5, and grill for about 2 minutes, or just long enough to mark the meat with the grill. Turn slightly and grill for another 2 minutes, or just long enough to burn a crosshatch into the meat. Continue to grill for another 2 minutes for rare, or until the chops are nicely browned and cooked to your desired degree of doneness.

8. Arrange the grilled chops on a serving platter and serve with Ionian Garlic Sauce on the side.

Ionian Garlic Sauce

Makes about 1½ cups

½ cup roughly chopped fresh flat-leaf parsley leaves

½ cup roughly chopped fresh dill

½ cup roughly chopped fresh mint

½ cup roughly chopped watercress leaves

¼ cup roughly chopped fresh oregano leaves

About 1 teaspoon coarse salt

1 lemon

2 garlic cloves, peeled

¼ cup red wine vinegar

1½ tablespoons sugar

About ½ cup extra virgin olive oil

1. Place the parsley, dill, mint, watercress, and oregano on a cutting board. Evenly sprinkle the salt over the mixture. The salt will cause the herbs and watercress to begin to "weep" their liquid.

2. Pull the herbs and watercress together in the center of the board and sprinkle with the juice of ½ lemon. Using a sharp knife, begin chopping the herbs and watercress until a very fine, moist mixture has formed. Set aside.

3. Place the garlic on a clean cutting board along with a pinch of salt and, using a sharp knife, work the garlic into a paste.

4. Combine the juice of the remaining lemon half with the vinegar and sugar in a small mixing bowl. Add the reserved herbs and garlic and season with salt to taste. Add just enough olive oil to make a vinaigrette. Reserve, covered, at room temperature until ready to use.

STEAMED MEDITERRANEAN MUSSELS WITH CINNAMON BASIL, OUZO, AND FETA CHEESE, PAGE 184

ROASTED LEG OF LAMB WITH MARINATED TOMATOES, PAGE 195

LAMB YOUVETSI, PAGE 198

GRILLED FREE-RANGE VEAL CHOP WITH CREAMY POLENTA AND
WARM WILD MUSHROOM AND WATERCRESS SALAD, PAGE 211

ORECCHIETTE WITH OCTOPUS, PAGE 228

VEGETABLES STUFFED WITH RICE, BULGUR, PINE NUTS, AND CURRANTS, PAGE 242

BAKLAVA, PAGE 254

SPOON SWEETS, LEFT TO RIGHT: SOUR CHERRY, PAGE 274; ORANGE, PAGE 272; LEMON, PAGE 272

Roasted Leg of Lamb with Marinated Tomatoes

For my entire life, every celebration—birthdays, Easter, whatever—will find some type of lamb on the table. This is my interpretation of a dish that both my mother and my grandmother made. At Molyvos, with twenty-four hours' notice, we will serve this dish family-style. We present the whole leg to the table, and then it is carved to order in the kitchen. At home we serve it with simply roasted potatoes and vegetables.

Ask the butcher to prepare the lamb. Although it's a simple process, it can be accomplished very quickly by a trained butcher.

One 7- to 8-pound leg of lamb, main bone
    removed, shank bone intact
Coarse salt and freshly ground pepper
1 garlic clove, quartered
2 tablespoons olive oil

1 1/2 teaspoons dried Greek oregano
1/2 cup dry white wine
2 1/2 cups Chicken Stock (page 281)
Marinated Tomatoes (recipe follows)
Herbed Bread Crumbs (recipe follows)

1. Lay the lamb out flat on a clean work surface. Season the top with salt and pepper. Starting at a narrow end, roll the lamb up, cigar-fashion. Using kitchen string, tie the meat in place so that it will hold its shape and cook evenly.

2. Make 4 small slits in the lamb. Insert a garlic sliver into each slit. Lightly coat the lamb with olive oil. Sprinkle the oregano over the lamb and again season with salt and pepper. Wrap in plastic wrap and refrigerate for at least 3 and up to 12 hours.

3. When ready to roast, preheat the oven to 450°F.

4. Remove the lamb from the refrigerator, unwrap, and place it in a large roasting pan. Place in the preheated oven and roast for 25 minutes.

5. Remove the lamb from the oven and pour the wine into the pan. Add the stock, reduce the oven temperature to 400°F and return the pan to the oven. Roast, basting frequently with the pan juices, for 40 to 50 minutes. If the pan juices dry up, add stock or water as needed.

(continued)

6. Remove the lamb from the oven. Spoon a thin layer of Marinated Tomatoes over the lamb, pressing down slightly to make them adhere. Return the lamb to the oven and roast, basting every 5 minutes, for 10 minutes. Sprinkle on the Herbed Bread Crumbs, lightly pressing to make them adhere. Roast for 5 minutes longer.

7. Remove the lamb from the oven and allow it to rest for 15 minutes before cutting the strings and slicing for serving.

JAVIER ASSEMBLING PLATES FOR THE DAILY SUMMER DISH, MADE FROM FRESH LOCAL PRODUCE.

Marinated Tomatoes

Makes about 2 cups

2 beefsteak tomatoes, peeled (see page 113)

2 garlic cloves, minced

2 tablespoons chopped fresh flat-leaf parsley

$1/2$ teaspoon dried Greek oregano

2 tablespoons extra virgin olive oil

Coarse salt and freshly ground pepper

Cut the tomatoes into quarters. Using a small sharp knife, carefully remove and discard the core, pulp, and seeds. Cut the tomatoes into small dice and place in a small mixing bowl. Add the garlic, parsley, and oregano, tossing to blend. Drizzle with the olive oil and season with salt and pepper to taste. Set aside to marinate at room temperature for at least 1 hour before using.

Herbed Bread Crumbs

Makes about 1 cup

1 cup Fresh Bread Crumbs (page 57)

1 garlic clove, minced

1 teaspoon dried Greek oregano

Juice of 1 lemon

$1/4$ cup extra virgin olive oil

Coarse salt and freshly ground pepper

Combine the bread crumbs, garlic, and oregano in a small mixing bowl. Squeeze the lemon juice over the mixture, tossing to blend. Drizzle with the olive oil and season with a pinch of salt and pepper. The crumbs should stick together when pinched; if not, add a bit more olive oil.

Lamb Youvetsi

One of the first times I experienced this dish in Greece I was struck by the fact that there seemed to be no way to guarantee that each diner received a fair share of meat and bone. When I decided to add it to the Molyvos menu, I, of course, had to do something that would give us perfect control over each portion. I came up with the idea of using very large lamb shanks that we could then cut crosswise into thick osso buco–like pieces. However, since most butchers don't carry large shanks, I have gone back to individual shanks for this recipe.

Greek cooks would not use stock as the cooking liquid. Traditionally the lamb meat would infuse the sauce, but I think the stock adds another layer of richness to the final dish.

Six 1-pound lamb shanks cut crosswise into
 twelve 2-inch-thick pieces (small end pieces
 reserved)
About 1¹/₂ cups extra virgin olive oil
Juice of 1 lemon
3 tablespoons sliced garlic
2¹/₂ tablespoons dried savory
Freshly ground pepper and coarse salt
1 quart Chicken Stock (page 281)
4 fresh parsley stems
3 bay leaves

2 garlic cloves, peeled and smashed
6¹/₄ cups diced onion
1 quart dry red wine, such as Aghiorghitiko,
 Cabernet Sauvignon, or Sangiovese
¹/₂ teaspoon Aleppo pepper (see page 9)
One 32-ounce can whole tomatoes packed in
 puree, drained and crushed by hand
2 cinnamon sticks
2¹/₂ cups orzo
¹/₂ cup coarsely grated kefalotyri cheese
2 tablespoons chopped fresh flat-leaf parsley

1. Set the small end pieces of lamb aside.

2. Combine 1 cup of the olive oil with the lemon juice, sliced garlic, 2 tablespoons of the savory, and 1 teaspoon pepper in a small mixing bowl.

3. Place the twelve 2-inch pieces of lamb in a large resealable plastic bag. Add the marinade and press lightly on the bag to release all the air. Seal and refrigerate for 12 hours.

4. Preheat the oven to 375°F.

5. Heat 2 tablespoons of the remaining olive oil in a large heavy saucepan over medium heat. Add the reserved small end pieces of lamb, stirring to coat. Place in the preheated oven. Sear, turning occasionally, for about 15 minutes, or until nicely browned. Remove from the oven and set aside to cool just slightly.

6. Place the cooled lamb pieces in a large saucepan. Add the stock, bring to a boil, lower to a simmer, skim off any impurities, add parsley stems, 1 bay leaf, the smashed garlic, and ¼ cup of the onion. Place over medium heat and simmer for about 30 minutes, or until the stock is well flavored with the lamb. Remove from the heat and let stand for 5 minutes. Strain through a fine sieve, discarding the solids, and set aside.

7. Raise the oven temperature to 425°F.

8. Remove the lamb shanks from the plastic bag and, using your hands, push all of the excess marinade from the lamb. Place the lamb on a platter lined with paper towels to drain off any excess marinade. Set aside.

9. Transfer the marinade to a small bowl and, using a slotted spoon, remove all of the sliced garlic. Discard the marinade. Place the garlic on a cutting board and, using a sharp knife, finely chop it. Set the garlic aside.

10. Heat 2 tablespoons of the remaining oil in a large straight-sided sauté pan over medium-high heat. Season 6 pieces of lamb shank with salt and pepper to taste and add to the hot pan. Sear, turning frequently, for about 10 minutes, or until all sides are nicely

browned. Transfer the seared lamb to a platter to rest and allow the juices to collect. Repeat this process to sear the remaining 6 pieces of lamb.

11. Drain the excess oil from the sauté pan. Return the pan to medium-low heat and add the wine. Using a wooden spoon, stir to loosen the browned bits on the bottom of the pan. Cook for about 15 minutes, or until the wine has reduced by three quarters. Remove from the heat and strain the reduced wine through a fine sieve into a clean container. Set aside.

12. Place a heavy Dutch oven over medium heat. Add 3 tablespoons of the remaining oil. When warm, add the remaining 6 cups onion along with a pinch of salt. Stir to coat lightly, cover, and reduce the heat to low. Cook, stirring occasionally, for about 15 minutes, or until the onion is quite soft and translucent.

13. Raise the heat to medium and stir in the reserved chopped garlic. Cook for 1 minute. Add the Aleppo pepper along with the remaining savory and stir to blend well. Add the reserved reduced wine. Raise the heat and bring to a boil. Immediately lower the heat to a simmer and cook, stirring occasionally, for about 20 minutes, or until the pan is almost dry. Stir in the tomatoes and bring to a boil. Immediately stir in the reserved stock and bring to a boil. Lower the heat to a simmer and, using a metal spoon, skim off any foam or fatty bits that rise to the surface. Add the 2 remaining bay leaves along with the cinnamon sticks. When well

combined, simmer for 5 minutes to infuse the flavors. Remove the pan from the heat.

14. Add the reserved shanks to the tomato mixture. Cover and transfer to the preheated oven. Braise, turning the lamb occasionally, for about 2½ hours, or until the lamb is very tender and nearly falling off the bone.

15. While the lamb is braising, blanch the orzo in a large pot of boiling salted water for 2 minutes. Drain well and transfer to an ice-water bath to stop the cooking. Drain well again. Add the remaining tablespoon of olive oil and toss to coat, to remove the excess starch from the pasta. Set aside.

16. Remove the lamb from the oven, leaving the oven on. Uncover and, using a slotted spoon, transfer the shanks to a platter. Tent lightly with aluminum foil to keep warm. Measure out and reserve 1½ cups of the cooking liquid.

17. Stir the blanched orzo into the liquid remaining in the Dutch oven. Return the pan to the oven and cook, uncovered, for about 15 minutes, or until most of the liquid has been absorbed and the orzo is almost cooked through. Check from time to time to ensure that the liquid has not evaporated. If the pan seems to be getting too dry, add some of the reserved cooking liquid, no more than ¼ cup at a time as you do not want the orzo to be soupy. Do not turn off the oven.

18. Remove the pan from the oven and place the reserved shanks on top of the orzo. Cover, return the pan to the oven, and cook for 10 minutes.

19. Remove the pan from the oven and either serve family-style—straight from the braising pan—or stir the mixture and then place an equal portion of the orzo on each of 6 dinner plates, top with 2 pieces of lamb shank, and spoon a bit of the reserved sauce over all. Either way, sprinkle the top with the grated cheese and chopped parsley before serving.

Aglaia's Moussaka

I didn't much like moussaka growing up—too much spice, too much béchamel. When I first visited Aglaia Kremezi in her kitchen, I told her of my childhood dislike, and she said, "I have a recipe that is much lighter than the usual, and I'll bet you will like it." She made it for me, and although I did like hers, we both agreed that the béchamel was still too heavy. We tried adding some yogurt, which did the trick. I've tweaked the recipe a bit for the restaurant, but I still follow the Greek adage "Make today, cook and eat tomorrow," which I advise home cooks to do also. Make sure all the components are fully cooked before assembly or the texture of the finished dish will be off.

$^1/_4$ cup dried currants

One 28-ounce can whole plum tomatoes

$2^1/_4$ cups olive oil

1 pound 90-percent-lean ground beef

1 pound lean ground lamb

Coarse salt and freshly ground pepper

2 tablespoons ras el hanout, or more to taste

1 teaspoon Aleppo pepper, or more to taste (see page 9)

About $1^1/_2$ teaspoons ground cinnamon, or more to taste

4 cups finely diced onion

6 garlic cloves, sliced

2 cups dry red wine, such as Aghiorghitiko, Cabernet Sauvignon, or Sangiovese

Eighteen $^1/_4$-inch-thick slices (from about 1 pound) Idaho potatoes

2 medium yellow or red bell peppers, diced

Eighteen $^1/_4$-inch-thick slices (from about 2 pounds) eggplant

3 cups Yogurt Béchamel Sauce (page 103)

1 cup freshly grated kefalotyri or Parmesan cheese (about $^1/_4$ pound)

1. Place the currants in hot water to cover and set aside to soak for 30 minutes.

2. Drain the tomatoes, reserving the juice. Using your hands, crush the tomatoes. Measure out $2^1/_2$ cups and combine them with the juice. (You will probably have about $^1/_2$ cup tomatoes left over.) Set the tomatoes aside.

3. Place a large skillet over medium heat. When very hot but not smoking, add 2 tablespoons of the olive oil, swirling to coat the pan. Add about a quarter each of the beef

and lamb and cook, stirring to break up the meat, for 5 minutes, or until the meat has browned lightly. Season with a generous pinch of salt and pepper and then with ¼ teaspoon each of ras el hanout and Aleppo pepper and a pinch of cinnamon. Using a slotted spoon, transfer the mixture to a colander placed in a mixing bowl.

4. Return the pan to medium heat and repeat three times to brown and season all the meat. Discard the oil.

5. Return the skillet to medium heat. Add ¼ cup of the remaining olive oil and, when hot, add the onion along with a pinch of salt. Cover and cook, stirring occasionally, for about 10 minutes, or until the onion is soft and translucent. Add the garlic, stirring to just combine and cook for another minute. Add the wine and cook, stirring occasionally, for about 25 minutes, or until the pan is almost dry. Add the reserved tomatoes along with their juice, stirring to combine. Bring to a simmer. Add the reserved meat mixture, stirring to combine well. (Take care as the pan will be quite full.) Taste and, if necessary, season with additional ras el hanout, Aleppo pepper, and cinnamon. Lower the heat, and cook at a bare simmer for 6 to 8 minutes.

6. Drain the currants and stir them into the meat mixture. Taste and, if necessary, season with salt and pepper to taste. Cook for another 30 minutes. Transfer the meat mixture to a mixing bowl set over an ice bath to cool. When cool, set aside.

7. Place a large sauté pan over medium heat. When hot, add ½ cup of the remaining olive oil, swirling to coat the pan. When very hot, add the potato slices, 6 at a time, and fry, turning occasionally, for about 15 minutes, or until blond. Transfer to a double layer of paper towel to drain. Repeat the process with the remaining potatoes, adding more oil as needed. When all of the potatoes have been fried, drain off half of the oil in the pan.

8. Return the pan to medium heat. When hot, add ¼ cup of the remaining olive oil, swirling to coat the pan. When very hot, add the peppers and sauté for about 5 minutes, or until just wilted. Season with salt and pepper to taste and remove from the heat. Transfer to a plate to cool.

9. Preheat the oven to 500°F.

10. Combine ½ cup of the remaining olive oil with salt and pepper to taste in a small bowl. Using a pastry brush, lightly coat both sides of the eggplant slices with the seasoned oil. Then season the slices with additional salt and pepper to taste. Place half of the slices on a baking sheet. Do not crowd the pan. Place in the preheated oven and roast for 6 to 8 minutes, or until lightly charred. Turn and roast for another 8 minutes, or until both sides are equally charred. Transfer to a platter to cool and continue broiling until all the eggplant is well cooked and charred.

11. If baking the moussaka immediately, lower the oven temperature to 350°F.

12. Place the potato slices in one even layer over the bottom of a 13 × 8 × 2-inch deep rectangular baking dish. Place the eggplant slices, slightly overlapping, in one even layer over the potatoes. Follow the eggplant with an even layer of the peppers. Spoon the meat mixture over the peppers, spreading it out with a spatula to make an even layer. Top with a thin layer of béchamel and sprinkle with cheese. At this point, the moussaka may be covered with plastic wrap and refrigerated for up to 2 days before baking.

13. Place the moussaka on a baking sheet in the preheated oven and bake for 25 minutes, or until bubbling around the edges.

14. Remove from the oven and let stand for about 10 minutes before serving.

Lamb Casserole

Inspired by the traditional Greek *kreas kokinisto* (meat cooked in tomato sauce), I came up with this dish that resembles the classic French stew beef bourguignonne. The sauce gets reduced so that it almost resembles a dark chocolate mole. The sweet squash is a perfect accompaniment, and the nuttiness of the bulgur adds just the right accent to the rich sauce. In Greece, a similar dish would usually be made with veal.

³/₄ cup Mavrodaphne wine

1 cup halved pitted dried plums (prunes)

3¹/₂ pounds lamb stew meat from the leg or
    shoulder, cut into 1-inch cubes, patted dry

Coarse salt and freshly ground pepper

6 tablespoons olive oil

3¹/₂ cups diced onions

2 garlic cloves, chopped

One 14-ounce can chopped tomatoes with juice

One 750-ml bottle dry red wine, such as
    Aghiorghitiko, Cabernet Sauvignon, or
    Sangiovese

4¹/₂ cups Lamb Stock (page 284)

2 bay leaves

1 cinnamon stick

1 teaspoon Kalamata or balsamic vinegar

Grated zest of 1 orange, plus more for garnish if
    desired

1 tablespoon chopped fresh flat-leaf parsley

Toasted Bulgur Wheat (recipe follows)

Roasted Squash (recipe follows)

1 tablespoon chopped fresh chives, for garnish
    (optional)

I. Place the Mavrodaphne wine in a small saucepan over low heat and bring to a boil. The wine will ignite. Once the flames subside, add the prunes and set aside to soak for 10 minutes.

2. Season the lamb with salt and pepper to taste and drizzle with 1 tablespoon of the olive oil.

3. Heat 1 tablespoon of the remaining oil in a heavy Dutch oven over medium heat. Add a third of the meat in a single layer and sear, turning occasionally, for about 5 minutes, or until nicely browned on all sides. As it browns, transfer the meat to a heatproof bowl to catch all the juices. Set aside. Repeat two times with the rest of the lamb.

4. Add the remaining 2 tablespoons oil to the Dutch oven. Stir in the onions and a pinch of salt. Cover and cook, stirring occasionally, for 8 to 10 minutes, or until the onions have begun to caramelize. Uncover, raise the heat to medium, and cook, stirring occasionally, for 5 minutes, or until they are a rich brown color. Stir in the garlic and cook for 1 minute. Add the tomatoes and cook for 2 minutes. Add the red wine and bring to a boil. Lower the heat and simmer for about 45 minutes, or until the liquid has reduced by half.

5. Add the stock and bring to a simmer, skimming off any impurities that rise to the top. Add the bay leaves and cinnamon stick. Strain the prunes through a fine sieve and add the liquid to the pan. Reserve the prunes. Stir in the lamb, cover, lower the heat to a bare simmer, and cook, checking occasionally, for 60 to 80 minutes, or until the lamb is very tender. During the last 15 minutes of cooking, add the prunes. The liquid should barely simmer throughout the cooking process. (The stew may be cooked up to this point and held, refrigerated, for up to 3 days. Do not finish until ready to serve.)

6. Remove from the heat and stir in the vinegar.

7. When ready to serve, gently fold in the orange zest and parsley. Place the Toasted Bulgur Wheat in the center of a large serving platter. Make a well in the center and place the Roasted Squash in it. Cover with the stew and serve immediately, garnished with orange zest and chives, if desired.

Toasted Bulgur Wheat

Serves 6

1 cup bulgur wheat

2¹/₂ tablespoons plus 1 teaspoon extra virgin olive oil

1 medium onion, finely diced

Coarse salt

1¹/₂ cups Herb Tea (page 289)

1. Preheat the oven to 325°F.

2. Place the bulgur in a mixing bowl and drizzle with 1 teaspoon of the olive oil, tossing to coat. Transfer to a baking pan, spreading out in an even layer. Place in the preheated oven and bake for 15 minutes, or until very aromatic and golden brown. Remove from the oven and set aside.

3. Heat the remaining 2¹/₂ tablespoons olive oil in a medium saucepan over medium heat. Add the onion along with a pinch of salt, cover, and cook, stirring occasionally, for 8 to 10 minutes, or until soft and translucent. Stir in the reserved bulgur and another pinch of salt, stirring to combine. Stir in the Herb Tea, cover, and bring to a simmer. Reduce the heat and cook, covered, for about 10 minutes, or until the liquid has evaporated. Remove from the heat and set aside for 5 minutes. Remove the lid and, using a kitchen fork, fluff the grains to separate. Cover again and set aside for 8 minutes, or until the grains are very light and fluffy. Serve hot.

Roasted Squash

Serves 6

1 small calabaza, butternut, or acorn squash, peeled, seeded, and quartered

Coarse salt and freshly ground pepper

2 tablespoons extra virgin olive oil

1 teaspoon sugar

$^1/_2$ teaspoon ground cinnamon

$^1/_2$ teaspoon ground cumin

1. Preheat the oven to 450°F.

2. Place the squash in a mixing bowl. Add a pinch of salt and pepper, followed by the olive oil, sugar, cinnamon, and cumin, tossing to coat well.

3. Place the seasoned squash in a baking dish in the preheated oven. Bake for about 30 minutes, or until crisp-tender and slightly browned.

4. Remove from the oven. Cut the squash into cubes and serve hot.

Souvlaki with Yogurt-Garlic Sauce

This is a classic Greek souvlaki that tastes best grilled. At the opening of Molyvos, I served it with a very aromatic Bulgur Wheat and Couscous Pilaf that turns the dish into a complete meal. You will need twelve metal or bamboo skewers to make the souvlaki. If you use bamboo, be sure to soak them for an hour or two so that they don't ignite over the fire. If you grow fresh herbs, large, heavy rosemary branches also make great skewers and add a nice herby scent to the finished dish.

1 cup wood chips, preferably cherry or pecan

1¼ cups extra virgin olive oil

2 tablespoons finely chopped garlic

1 tablespoon dried Greek oregano

Coarse salt and freshly ground pepper

2 pounds very lean boneless lamb from the leg or filet of beef, cut into 1½ inch cubes

3 yellow bell peppers, cut into 1-inch squares

36 red pearl onions, peeled and blanched

36 cherry tomatoes

Yogurt-Garlic Sauce (page 37)

Bulgur Wheat and Couscous Pilaf (optional; page 233)

1. Combine the olive oil with the garlic, oregano, and salt and pepper to taste in a small mixing bowl. Remove ¼ cup, reserving the remainder. Place the meat in a medium mixing bowl, add the ¼ cup marinade, tossing to coat. Cover with plastic wrap and refrigerate for 1 hour.

2. Remove the meat from the refrigerator. Working with one skewer at a time, thread one piece of pepper onto it. Follow the pepper with an onion, then a piece of meat, and finally a tomato. Repeat this process 2 more times until you have a total of 3 pieces of each on one skewer. Continue threading skewers until you have 12.

3. Place the filled skewers in a shallow nonreactive pan large enough to hold them in a single layer. Pour on the reserved marinade, cover tightly with plastic wrap, and refrigerate for 8 hours.

4. When ready to serve, soak the wood chips and preheat and oil the grill. Place the wood chips in cold water to cover while the grill is heating.

5. When the grill is hot, place the soaked wood chips on top of the coals (the chips should ignite and emit a flavorful smoke).

6. Remove the souvlaki from the refrigerator. Using your fingertips, carefully push the excess marinade from the souvlaki. Season with salt and pepper to taste. Place the skewers on the grill and grill, turning occasionally, for about 8 minutes, or until the meat is lightly charred and is medium-rare. The time will depend on the desired degree of doneness for the meat.

7. Remove the skewers from the grill and place on a serving platter. Serve with Yogurt-Garlic Sauce on the side along with Bulgur Wheat and Couscous Pilaf, if desired.

Pan-Roasted Sirloin Steak

Pan-roasted steak is easy to do at home. I also make this at the restaurant with the garnishes changing with the seasons. It's particularly delicious in the summer, when the sweetly acidic tomato juices mingle with the pan juices. I've given the basic recipe for two steaks, but I generally put a couple of pans on the stove and cook at least four steaks at a time so that everyone gets a taste as I continue to make more.

Two 16-ounce sirloin steaks with about ¹/₈ inch
    fat remaining around the edge
3 tablespoons extra virgin olive oil
¹/₂ teaspoon granulated garlic
¹/₂ teaspoon dried Greek oregano

Coarse salt and freshly ground pepper
Eight ¹/₂-inch-thick slices ripe beefsteak tomato
2 small bunches of watercress, tough stems
    removed
2 tablespoons Kalamata Vinaigrette (page 140)

1. Lightly drizzle each side of the steak with a total of 1 tablespoon of the oil. Season with granulated garlic, oregano, and salt and pepper to taste.

2. Place a heavy skillet (cast iron is terrific) over medium-high heat. When hot, add 1 tablespoon of the remaining olive oil to the pan and, when very hot but not smoking, add the seasoned steak. Sear, without moving the meat, for about 5 minutes, or until a crust has formed on the bottom. Turn the steak, lower the heat to medium, and continue to cook, basting continually with the pan juices, for about 8 minutes, or until medium-rare (135°F on an instant-read thermometer).

3. Transfer the steak to a cutting board and let rest for 5 minutes. Reserve the pan juices. Using a sharp knife, cut off the fat and then cut the steak diagonally into ¹/₂-inch-thick slices.

4. Place 2 slices of tomato on each plate. Drizzle with the remaining tablespoon of olive oil and season with salt and pepper to taste. Place the watercress in a medium mixing bowl. Add the Kalamata Vinaigrette and salt and pepper to taste, tossing to coat well. Make a small mound of watercress salad next to the tomatoes. Layer an equal portion of the sliced steak in front of the salad, drizzle the meat and plate with pan juices, and serve.

Grilled Free-Range Veal Chops with Creamy Polenta and Warm Wild Mushroom and Watercress Salad

I always use free-range, grain-fed veal in the restaurant as it is most true to the color, texture, and flavor of the Mediterranean-style veal served in Greece. Since the island of Corfu is just across the Ionian Sea from Italy, it is not a big stretch to combine elements of both cuisines. In this recipe I add a taste of Greece to the traditional Italian polenta with kefalotyri and feta cheese.

1¹/₂ cups extra virgin olive oil

3 garlic cloves, peeled and smashed

3 tablespoons roughly chopped fresh rosemary

1 tablespoon roughly chopped fresh flat-leaf parsley

1 teaspoon dried Greek oregano

Coarse salt and freshly ground pepper

Six 16-ounce free-range, grain-fed veal chops

6 large heavy fresh rosemary branches

1 hot green chile, such as Fresno, cut in half lengthwise

Creamy Polenta (recipe follows)

Warm Wild Mushroom and Watercress Salad (recipe follows)

1. Combine 1 cup of the olive oil with 2 cloves of the garlic, 2 tablespoons of the chopped rosemary, the parsley, the oregano, and a pinch of salt.

2. Place the chops in a single layer in a large baking dish. Pour the olive oil mixture over the chops, cover with plastic wrap, and allow to marinate for at least 3 hours or overnight.

3. When ready to cook, preheat and oil the grill.

4. Using kitchen twine, tie the rosemary branches together to make a brush. Set aside.

5. Combine the remaining ¹/₂ cup olive oil with the chile in a small saucepan over medium heat. When just a bit over room temperature, add the remaining chopped rosemary and garlic clove. Season with salt and pepper to taste and cook for a couple of minutes, or just until warm. Remove from the heat and set aside to cool slightly.

(continued)

6. Remove the chops from the marinade and, using your hands, push off as much of the marinade as possible. Season with salt and pepper to taste.

7. Using the rosemary brush, lightly coat each chop with the warm oil mixture. Place on the hot grill and grill, occasionally brushing with the warm oil, for 10 minutes. Turn and grill the other side, brushing with the warm oil, for 11 minutes, or until the meat is medium (140°F on an instant-read thermometer).

8. Remove the meat from the grill. Place an equal portion of the Creamy Polenta in the center of each of 6 dinner plates. Place an equal portion of the salad on the opposite side of the plate and nestle a chop into the polenta on each one. Serve immediately.

Creamy Polenta

2¹/₂ cups whole milk
4 tablespoons (¹/₂ stick) unsalted butter
Coarse salt and freshly ground pepper
1³/₄ cups coarsely ground cornmeal
³/₄ cup crumbled feta cheese
¹/₂ cup grated kefalotyri cheese
1 tablespoon chopped fresh chives

Combine the milk, 1 cup water, and 2 tablespoons of the butter in a large saucepan over medium heat. Bring to a simmer. Season with 1 teaspoon salt and a touch of pepper and begin whisking in the cornmeal. Once all the cornmeal has been whisked in and no lumps appear, lower the heat, switch to a rubber spatula, and cook, occasionally mixing and stirring, for about 15 minutes, or until the cornmeal has softened. Fold in the cheeses along with the remaining 2 tablespoons butter. The texture should resemble soft mashed potatoes. If too thick, beat in hot milk or water a bit at a time. Fold in the chives. Taste and, if necessary, season with additional salt and pepper.

Warm Wild Mushroom and Watercress Salad

Serves 6

3 to 4 tablespoons extra virgin olive oil

$^1/_2$ pound oyster or chanterelle mushrooms

$^1/_2$ pound cremini mushrooms, stems removed and caps quartered

$^1/_2$ pound shiitake mushrooms, stems removed and caps sliced

Coarse salt and freshly ground pepper

3 garlic cloves, chopped

1 teaspoon minced fresh thyme

3 cups watercress, tough stems removed

3 to 4 tablespoons Kalamata Vinaigrette (page 140)

1. Heat the olive oil in a large sauté pan over medium heat. Working in batches, add the mushrooms, season with salt and pepper to taste, and sauté for about 5 minutes, or until the mushrooms have softened and exuded their liquid and the pan is almost dry. Remove from the heat and stir in the garlic and thyme. Taste and, if necessary, season with additional salt and pepper. Using a slotted spoon, transfer the mushrooms to a colander placed in a mixing bowl to drain. There should be no juices left if the mushrooms have been cooked properly.

2. Place the watercress in a large mixing bowl. Add the warm mushrooms and drizzle with just enough Kalamata Vinaigrette to season lightly. Season with salt and pepper to taste and toss to blend. Serve immediately.

Roasted Lemon-Garlic Chicken

This is a simple but delicious roast chicken. You can have the butcher bone the chickens for ease of preparation. I leave the large wing bone intact because I think it makes a nicer presentation. The marinated roast chicken is terrific without the sauce, but since it takes so little time to make, the sauce does add the extra restaurant-style touch. It would be extra delicious served with Potato-Olive Stew (page 238).

$^1/_2$ cup extra virgin olive oil plus 1 tablespoon, divided

2 lemons

2 garlic cloves, sliced

1 tablespoon dried Greek oregano

Coarse salt and freshly ground pepper

One $3^1/_2$- to 4-pound chicken, skin on, halved and boned but with first wing bone intact

$^1/_2$ teaspoon minced garlic

$^1/_4$ cup dry white wine

2 cups Fortified Chicken Stock (page 282)

2 tablespoons unsalted butter at room temperature

1. Combine $^1/_4$ cup of the olive oil with the peel of both lemons and the juice of 1 lemon, the sliced garlic, oregano, and a pinch of salt and pepper in a small mixing bowl. Set aside.

2. Place one half of the chicken, skin side down, in a nonreactive baking dish. Drizzle with some of the olive oil mixture; then top with the other half, flesh side down. Drizzle with the remaining olive oil mixture. Cover with plastic wrap and refrigerate for at least 3 hours or overnight.

3. When ready to cook, preheat the oven to 425°F.

4. Remove the chicken from the refrigerator. Using your fingertips, push off all excess marinade. Season with salt and pepper to taste.

5. Place two 10-inch ovenproof, preferably non-stick, sauté pans over medium-high heat. Add 2 tablespoons of the remaining olive oil to each pan. When hot, add the chicken halves, skin side down. Cook for

about 8 minutes, or until golden and crisp and the edge of the flesh is opaque. Transfer the pan to the preheated oven and bake for 8 minutes, or until the flesh is white and just a bit resistant when touched. Turn and bake for another 3 minutes, or until very crisp.

6. Remove the pan from the oven. Transfer the chicken to a large platter and tent lightly with aluminum foil to keep warm.

7. Strain the cooking juices from the pan through a fine sieve and set aside.

8. Place the pan over medium heat. Add a tablespoon of oil and the minced garlic and cook for 30 seconds. Remove the pan from the heat and add the wine and the juice of the remaining lemon. Return to medium heat and bring to a simmer. Add the stock along with any juices that have accumulated on the platter and the reserved cooking juices and bring to a boil. Lower the heat and simmer for about 6 minutes, or until reduced by one half. Whisk in the butter and continue to cook for 5 minutes, or until the sauce coats the back of a metal spoon. Remove from the heat and season with salt and pepper to taste. Cut the meat into slices and serve family-style.

Baby Chicken Fricassee Avgolemono

This is a rather elegant version of an old-fashioned chicken fricassee. The Greek flavors add an interesting depth and the mustard greens a hint of spiciness. It can be made in advance and re-heated just before serving, so it makes a great dish for entertaining. Since the chickens are small, you'll want to allow one per person.

2 cups plus 2 tablespoons extra virgin olive oil

2 lemons

1 teaspoon chopped garlic

1 tablespoon dried Greek oregano

1 tablespoon roughly chopped fresh flat-leaf parsley

6 baby chickens, cut into quarters, breast and thigh bones removed, leg bone intact

Coarse salt and freshly ground pepper

4 garlic cloves, sliced

1 cup dry white wine

3 cups Chicken Stock (page 281)

4 bunches of mustard greens, stems removed, blanched (see page 11), and cut into ¼-inch-thick strips (about 8 cups)

24 baby carrots, peeled with a bit of the stem left on, blanched

6 tablespoons Avgolemono Sauce (page 127)

3 tablespoons chopped fresh dill

2 scallions, sliced diagonally

1. Combine 1 cup of the olive oil with the juice and grated zest of one of the lemons. Add the chopped garlic, oregano, and parsley. Set aside.

2. Place the chicken pieces in a single layer in a nonreactive baking dish. Pour the reserved marinade over the chicken. Cover with plastic wrap and refrigerate for at least 3 hours or overnight.

3. When ready to cook, remove the chicken from the refrigerator. Using your fingertips, push off excess marinade. Using a clean kitchen towel, pat the chicken dry.

4. Place a large, ovenproof sauté pan over medium-high heat. Add about ¼ cup of the remaining olive oil. Working with 6 pieces of leg and/or thigh at a time, when the oil is very hot but not smoking, season the chicken pieces with salt and pepper to taste and place them, skin side down, in the hot pan. Sear for 2 to 3 minutes, or until golden and the flesh is beginning to cook around the edges. Turn and cook for an additional 2 to 3 minutes, or just until the meat is beginning to cook. Pour off the oil and start with fresh oil as you continue to cook the remaining legs and thighs. Continue searing in the same manner but when cooking the breast, sear the skin side for 2 to 3 minutes and then turn and sear for only 1 minute. Watch this process carefully as you want all of the pieces to be cooked to about the same degree of doneness. They should be cooked about halfway. Transfer the chicken to a platter.

5. Prcheat the oven to 450°F.

6. After the last sear, leave about half of the remaining oil in the pan. Place over low heat and add the sliced garlic. Cook, stirring constantly, for 1 minute.

7. Remove the pan from the heat, add the wine, and return to medium heat. Add the juice of the remaining lemon and cook for about 5 minutes, or until the pan is almost dry. Add the stock, raise the heat to medium-high, and bring to a simmer. Pour any juices that have accumulated from the resting chicken into the pan, stirring to combine. Taste and, if necessary, add salt and pepper.

8. Place the reserved chicken into the sauce in a slightly overlapping pattern and bring to a simmer. Cover and place in the preheated oven. Bake for 12 to 15 minutes, or just until the chicken is cooked through. While the chicken is cooking, make the Avgolemono Sauce.

9. Remove the pan from the oven. Do not turn off the oven. Uncover and transfer the chicken to a serving platter, reserving the pan and sauce. Tent lightly with aluminum foil to keep warm.

10. Place a medium sauté pan over medium heat. Add the remaining 2 tablespoons of olive oil along with the greens. Cook, tossing occasionally, for about 4 minutes, or until hot. Remove from the heat and set aside.

11. Repeat this process to heat the carrots.

12. Remove 1 cup of the chicken braising liquid and whisk it into the Avgolemono Sauce to temper it. Return the pan to medium heat and pour the mixture back into the pan. Add the chicken, basting it with some of the sauce. Cook at a bare simmer for 1 to 2 minutes or until thickened. Fold in the dill. Taste and, if necessary, season with salt and pepper.

13. Place a mound of the greens in the center of a large serving platter. Place the chicken on top of the greens. Ladle the sauce over the chicken and place the carrots around the edge of the plate. Sprinkle with scallions and serve.

Rabbit Stifado (Rabbit Stew with Red Wine and Pearl Onions)

The first time that I prepared this dish was in Greece, cooking with Aglaia Kremezi. It seemed so much the essence of Greek cooking, I wanted to feature it at Molyvos. It was one of the stars of the original menu—so much so that it remains a constant at the restaurant today.

In the traditional Greek kitchen, no stock would be used. Water would be the braising liquid, and the cooking meat would add the flavor. My version gives a bit more depth to the finished dish.

3 rabbit loins, rib bones and fat removed

4 rabbit legs and thighs

Coarse salt and freshly ground pepper

$^1/_2$ cup olive oil

3 whole cloves

1 bay leaf

1 cinnamon stick, broken into pieces

1 whole allspice

2 medium red onions, peeled, trimmed, and thinly sliced crosswise

2 garlic cloves, sliced

2 cups dry red wine, such as Aghiorghitiko, Cabernet Sauvignon, or Sangiovese

1 cup Mavrodaphne wine

One 28-ounce can whole tomatoes in juice, chopped

2$^1/_2$ cups Rabbit Stock (page 285)

Caramelized Pearl Onions (page 160)

1 tablespoon unsalted butter at room temperature

1 tablespoon chopped fresh flat-leaf parsley, plus more for garnish

I. Preheat the oven to 425°F.

2. Season the rabbit with salt and pepper to taste.

3. Heat the olive oil in a heavy Dutch oven over medium heat. Add the rabbit loins and sear, turning frequently, for 8 to 10 minutes, or until nicely browned on all sides. Sear the legs and thighs in the same fashion. Sear in batches if necessary to keep from crowding the pan.

4. Transfer the rabbit to a plate and discard half of the oil in the pan.

5. Combine the cloves, bay leaf, cinnamon stick, and allspice in a piece of cheesecloth about 6 inches square. Gather up the ends and, using kitchen twine, tie the bag closed. Set the sachet aside.

6. Return the pan to low heat. When hot, add the onions and a pinch of salt. Cover and cook, stirring occasionally, for about 10 minutes, or until lightly colored and wilted. The onions will take on the color of the browned bits in the pan. Add the garlic, stir to combine, and cook for 1 minute. Add the wines, raise the heat, and bring to a boil, stirring with a wooden spoon to scrape all of the browned bits from the bottom of the pan. Lower the heat and simmer for 10 to 15 minutes, or until the liquid has reduced and the pan is almost dry. Add the tomatoes, raise the heat to medium-high, and stir to combine. Cover and cook for 5 minutes.

7. Add the stock and bring to a boil. Add the reserved sachet and return the rabbit to the pan along with any juices that have accumulated on the plate. Taste and, if necessary, add salt and pepper. (Season carefully because the salt from the stock will concentrate as the liquid reduces.) Cover and transfer the pan to the preheated oven. Braise for 35 minutes.

8. Remove the pan from the oven. Add the Caramelized Pearl Onions, cover again, and return to the oven. Braise for another 25 minutes, or until the rabbit is easily pierced with the point of a small sharp knife.

9. Remove from the oven. Using tongs, carefully remove the rabbit from the pan and place it on a warm serving platter.

10. Place the pan on the stovetop over medium heat and bring to a boil. Whisk in the butter. Fold in the parsley, taste, and, if necessary, season with salt and pepper. Spoon the sauce over the rabbit, sprinkle with parsley, and serve.

Pastas, Grains, and Vegetables

Like the cuisines of many countries with a history of rural, peasant populations, Greek cooking has a large repertoire of filling dishes made from pastas and grains and dried legumes combined with seasonal or wild vegetables or greens. These are the staple foods throughout the country. Arid, rocky conditions have made it difficult to cultivate a wide variety of vegetables in Greece, so Greek cooks have become quite adept at using wild greens (horta). Many familiar vegetable dishes evolved from the Lenten prohibition of meat but are now consumed throughout the year.

Makaronia tou Spartoksylo
with Tomato, Kalamata Olives, and Feta

Makaronia tou spartoksylo is a type of Greek pasta that is hand-rolled on a branch of Spanish broom *(spartoksylo)*. It is not generally available in America but is easily replaced with the Italian pasta strozzapreti (priest chokers). I recommend using the Rustichella d'Abruzzo brand because of its high quality and artisanal rustic character. This dish is terrific for a quick pasta fix. The sauce takes no time to prepare; it finishes in the time it takes for the water to boil and the pasta to cook. As long as you have the ingredients on hand—they really are simple Greek staples—this is the perfect meal for unexpected guests.

Coarse salt and freshly ground pepper

About 4 tablespoons extra virgin olive oil

6 garlic cloves, sliced lengthwise

1 teaspoon dried Greek oregano

One 28-ounce can crushed tomatoes, preferably California Redpack or Italian San Marzano

1 tablespoon sugar

1 pound dried makaronia tou spartoksylo or strozzapreti pasta

¼ cup sliced pitted Kalamata olives

2 tablespoons chopped fresh flat-leaf parsley

½ cup crumbled feta cheese

1. Bring a large pot of salted water to a boil over medium-high heat.

2. Meanwhile, heat 2 tablespoons of the olive oil in a heavy saucepan over medium heat until hot. Add the garlic and sauté for about 3 minutes, or until the edges begin to turn light gold. Add the oregano and a pinch of salt and pepper and stir to combine. Add the tomatoes and cook, stirring constantly, for about 5 minutes, or until the mixture comes to a boil. Lower the heat to a bare simmer and skim off any impurities that rise

to the top. Add the sugar and simmer until the flavors have blended and the sauce has thickened slightly. Do not cook for longer than 25 minutes.

3. Meanwhile cook the pasta according to the package directions until al dente. Remove from the heat and drain well. Always cook the pasta to 1 minute less than your desired degree of doneness as it will continue to cook in the sauce.

4. Remove the tomato sauce from the heat and fold in the olives and parsley. Season

with salt and pepper to taste. Ladle about 1½ cups of the sauce into the pasta pot. Add the drained pasta, toss to coat lightly, and drizzle with extra virgin olive oil. Return to low heat for 1 minute to allow the pasta to absorb the flavors of the sauce.

5. Divide the pasta among 6 shallow pasta bowls and, if desired, ladle some of the remaining sauce over each. Sprinkle each bowl with an equal portion of the feta, drizzle with extra virgin olive oil, and serve.

Makaronia with Walnut Pesto

Greeks call all dried pasta *makaronia*. A simpler version of the traditional Genoese basil-scented pesto, this is one of my favorite quick meals. Just take care when processing the pesto mix that you don't puree it—you want a coarse texture that will just cling to the warm pasta.

About ³/₄ cup milk

2 slices white bread

1 garlic clove, chopped

1¹/₄ cups walnuts

¹/₄ cup grated kefalotyri cheese

¹/₄ cup fresh flat-leaf parsley leaves with some stems attached, coarsely chopped

2 tablespoons extra virgin olive oil

Coarse salt and freshly ground pepper

1 pound dried pasta, such as spartoksylou or trofie

Freshly grated myzithra cheese to taste

1. Place the milk in a shallow bowl. Tear each slice of bread in half and place them in the milk for about 2 minutes. Using your fingertips, break up the bread so that it can absorb all of the milk. Transfer the soaked bread along with the milk to a food processor fitted with the metal blade.

2. Add the garlic, walnuts, kefalotyri cheese, parsley, and olive oil to the processor and process to a coarse paste. Do not overprocess. Scrape it from the processor bowl into a mixing bowl large enough to hold the pasta. If the mixture seems too thick, add more milk, but no more than ¹/₄ cup. Season with salt and pepper to taste. Set aside.

3. Cook the pasta according to the package directions. Drain well, reserving about 1 cup of the cooking water.

4. Add ¹/₄ cup of the pasta water to the pesto, stirring to blend. Add the pasta, tossing to coat. If necessary, add some or all of the remaining water to create a slightly thick coating. Season with a generous helping of pepper. Sprinkle with the myzithra cheese and serve immediately with additional cheese passed on the side.

Orecchiette with Octopus

What pasta dish could be more Greek than one with octopus? This recipe has become a favorite of our customers. It's a perfect combination, with the slight spiciness of the Aleppo and the coolness of mint at the finish.

$^1/_4$ cup plus 2 tablespoons olive oil

1 large onion, finely diced

Coarse salt and freshly ground pepper

4 garlic cloves, minced

2 teaspoons dried Greek oregano

$^1/_2$ teaspoon Aleppo pepper (see page 9)

$^1/_2$ cup dry white wine

One 28-ounce can whole tomatoes in juice, chopped

3 Poached Octopus (page 55), cut into $^1/_4$-inch pieces

1 pound dry orecchiette pasta

Grated zest of 2 lemons

$^1/_4$ cup torn fresh mint leaves

I. Heat $^1/_4$ cup of the oil in a large saucepan over medium heat. Add the onion and a pinch of salt, cover, and cook, stirring occasionally, for about 8 minutes, or until the onion is quite soft. Add the garlic and cook for 1 minute. Stir in the oregano and Aleppo pepper and cook for a couple of minutes, or until very fragrant. Add the wine and simmer for about 10 minutes, or until the liquid has reduced by half.

2. Raise the heat, add the tomatoes along with their juice, and bring to a boil. Lower the heat to a simmer, add the octopus, and season with salt and pepper to taste. Cover and simmer, stirring occasionally, for about 30 minutes, or until very tender.

3. Cook the pasta in rapidly boiling salted water according to the package directions until al dente. Drain well and add to the sauce, tossing to coat. Stir in the remaining olive oil along with the lemon zest and mint and serve immediately.

Didima (Short Pasta Twists), Gulf Shrimp, Zucchini, and Marinated Tomatoes

More Italian in origin, this is a version of a dish I make at home when tomatoes are at their peak and small, garden-fresh zucchini is plentiful. *Didima* means "twins" in Greek as does its counterpart *gemelli* in the Italian pasta lexicon. This small twisted pasta shape holds up to a rich sauce very well, but if you prefer you can try any other small, hearty pasta such as penne or shells.

The sauce is just barely cooked—you should be able to taste the freshness of the tomatoes.

3 medium very ripe beefsteak tomatoes, peeled

10 large fresh basil leaves, torn, plus leaves for garnish

2 garlic cloves, sliced

About $^3/_4$ cup extra virgin olive oil

Coarse salt and freshly ground pepper

1 pound dry didima or gemelli pasta

4 small ($^1/_2$-inch-diameter) zucchini, sliced crosswise almost paper-thin

24 small shrimp, peeled

Pinch of Aleppo pepper (see page 9)

1. Cut the tomatoes in half crosswise. Using your hands, squeeze out and reserve the seeds, membrane, and juices.

2. Press the seeds, membrane, and juices through a very fine sieve into a clean container. Discard the solids and reserve the strained juices. Set aside.

3. Place the tomato halves, cut side down, on a flat surface. Using a sharp knife, cut each half crosswise into 3 slices of equal width. Roughly chop the slices into small pieces. You should have about 2 cups.

(Do not use more than $2^1/_4$ cups or the sauce will be runny.) Place in a nonreactive container. Add the strained juices along with the torn basil leaves and garlic, tossing to coat well. Drizzle with $^1/_4$ cup of the oil and season lightly with salt and pepper. Cover and set aside to marinate for at least 3 hours at room temperature. (This can be done the day before with the tomatoes allowed to marinate in the refrigerator. If so, bring them to room temperature before using.)

(continued)

4. Cook the pasta according to the package directions, removing it about 90 seconds before the suggested cooking time is up.

5. Lightly coat a 10-inch sauté pan with 2 tablespoons olive oil. Add the zucchini, season with salt and pepper, and cook, stirring, for 2 to 3 minutes. Add 2 cups of the marinated tomatoes. When hot, stir in the shrimp and Aleppo pepper and cook, stirring frequently, for about 2 minutes, or until the shrimp are light pink and just cooked. Drain the pasta and add it to the shrimp mixture. Cook, stirring constantly, for 1 to 2 minutes to combine. Drizzle with 2 tablespoons of olive oil. Taste and, if necessary, season with salt and pepper. Do not overcook the sauce—the flavors should be fresh.

6. Transfer to a serving platter or bowl, drizzle with the remaining 2 tablespoons extra virgin olive oil, garnish with basil leaves, and serve.

Braised Horta with Barley

When in Greece, I was always amazed to see people stop their cars at the side of the road, jump out, and pick whatever greens (horta) they found along the roadside—even in urban Athens! Most wild greens have a very assertive flavor, like arugula or dandelion. You can use chicory, escarole, mustard greens, black kale, or even chard—or a combination of a few—to make this dish. The greens just have to be strongly flavored to stay true to the original.

At Molyvos, I often fold in some raw greens such as pea shoots, arugula, or baby spinach just before serving for a hint of freshness.

3 large leeks

Coarse salt and freshly ground pepper

12 cups lightly packed greens

1¼ cups unspiced Herb Tea (page 289)

6 tablespoons plus 1 teaspoon extra virgin olive oil

½ cup pearl barley, rinsed well under cold running water

2 cups diced onion

Juice of 2 lemons

2 tablespoons chopped fresh dill

1. Wash the leeks well. Trim off the root end and almost all of the green. Cut in half lengthwise. Then, cut crosswise into half-moon shapes. Set aside.

2. Bring a large pot of salted water to a boil over high heat. Add the greens, one third at a time, and blanch for 2 to 3 minutes. Using tongs, remove the greens from the water and drain well. Separately reserve the cooking liquid. Set aside.

3. Place the unspiced Herb Tea along with 1 teaspoon of the olive oil in a medium saucepan over medium-high heat and bring to a simmer. Add the barley and cover. Lower the heat and cook, stirring occasionally, for 20 to 25 minutes, or until the barley is tender. Remove from the heat and set aside.

4. Heat ¼ cup of the olive oil in a large saucepan over medium heat. Add the onion along with a pinch of salt. Cover and cook, stirring occasionally, for 8 minutes, or until the onion is soft. Add the leeks along with another pinch of salt, cover, and cook, stir-

ring occasionally, for 10 minutes longer, or until the onion and leeks are very soft but have not taken on any color.

5. Stir in 1 quart of the greens-cooking liquid along with the juice of 1 lemon. Bring to a boil; then lower the heat to a simmer. Stir in the blanched greens and season with salt and pepper to taste. Simmer, stirring occasionally, for 10 to 12 minutes, or until the greens are tender and well flavored. Fold in the barley and cook for 2 minutes. Fold in the remaining 2 tablespoons olive oil, the juice of the remaining lemon, and the dill. Taste and, if necessary, season with salt and pepper. Serve immediately.

Bulgur Wheat and Couscous Pilaf

This can be either a light lunch salad or a terrific side dish with all types of roasts and grilled meats. It can be served either warm or at room temperature, which makes it a perfect buffet item. A drizzle of Yogurt-Garlic Sauce (page 37) makes a marvelous addition.

3/4 cup golden raisins

1 cup bulgur wheat

3 tablespoons plus 1 teaspoon olive oil

1 cup finely diced onion

Coarse salt and freshly ground pepper

2 cups Herb Tea (page 289)

1/2 cup couscous

2 scallions, including some of the green part, finely sliced

3/4 cup almonds, toasted (see page 77)

1 tablespoon chopped fresh flat-leaf parsley

2 tablespoons chopped fresh mint

1. Place the raisins in boiling water to cover. Set aside to soak for about 15 minutes, or until nicely plumped. Drain well and set aside.

2. Preheat the oven to 375°F.

3. Place the bulgur wheat in a medium mixing bowl. Drizzle with 2 teaspoons of the olive oil, tossing to coat lightly. Transfer the bulgur to a baking pan, spreading it out in an even layer. Place in the preheated oven and bake for 15 to 20 minutes, or until aromatic and golden brown. Remove from the oven and set aside.

4. Heat 2½ tablespoons of the remaining oil in a medium saucepan over medium heat.

Add the onion along with a pinch of salt. Cover and cook, stirring occasionally, for about 10 minutes, or until the onion is soft. Add the bulgur wheat, stirring to coat with the oil. Add 1½ cups of the Herb Tea, stir, and season with salt to taste. Cover and cook for about 10 minutes, or until the liquid has reduced to just below the level of the wheat. Remove from the heat and allow to bloom for 10 minutes, or until all of the liquid is absorbed and the bulgur is tender. Using a fork, fluff the grains to separate. Cover again and set aside.

5. While the bulgur is cooking, bring the remaining ½ cup Herb Tea to a boil over high heat. Place the couscous in a heatproof

dish. Add the remaining ½ teaspoon oil, stirring to blend. Add the hot Herb Tea, cover, and let rest for about 10 minutes, or until the grains have absorbed the liquid. Using a fork, fluff the grains to separate.

6. Fold the couscous into the cooked bulgur. Fold in the reserved plumped raisins along with the scallions, almonds, parsley, and mint, tossing to just blend. Taste and, if necessary, season with salt and pepper. Serve immediately.

Lentils and Rice

This combination is a staple in the Greek kitchen. It is used as an accompaniment for fish and meat. In our house, this dish was always served along with souvlaki in the summer. For additional richness, you can use stock in place of the water to cook the rice.

1 cup dried lentils

2 garlic cloves, peeled and smashed

2 bay leaves

Coarse salt and freshly ground pepper

2 tablespoons extra virgin olive oil

1 cup finely diced onion

1 teaspoon dried Greek oregano

$^1/_2$ teaspoon ground cumin

1 cup chopped canned plum tomatoes with juice

2 cups converted long-grain white rice

Pinch of Aleppo pepper (see page 9)

$3^1/_2$ cups Vegetable Stock (page 280)

$^1/_2$ cup chopped fresh cilantro leaves

1. Preheat the oven to 350°F.

2. Place the lentils in a saucepan with cold water to cover by 2 inches. Add the garlic, 1 bay leaf, and a pinch of salt. Bring to a simmer over medium-high heat. Simmer, stirring occasionally, for about 15 minutes, or until almost tender. Remove from the heat and drain well. Set aside.

3. Heat the olive oil in a medium saucepan over medium heat. Add the onion along with a pinch of salt. Cover and cook, stirring occasionally, for about 8 minutes, or until the onion is quite soft. Add the oregano, cumin, and remaining bay leaf and cook for 1 minute.

4. Stir in the tomatoes and bring to a simmer. Simmer for 3 minutes. Add the reserved lentils and season with salt and pepper to taste.

5. Stir in the rice along with the Aleppo pepper. Add the stock. It should cover the mixture by 1 inch. Season with salt and pepper and bring to a bare simmer. Immediately cover and transfer to the preheated oven. Bake for about 20 minutes, or until the rice is cooked.

6. Remove from the oven and let rest for 5 minutes. Uncover and fluff with a fork. Fold in the cilantro and serve immediately.

Chickpea Rice

This is one of the original rice pilafs from the Molyvos menu, and it remains a much-requested dish. Although we use it as a side dish, it also makes a delicious main course for vegetarians if you replace the chicken stock with a vegetable stock or broth. If you prefer, you can substitute cranberry beans or black-eyed peas for the chickpeas.

$^1/_4$ cup olive oil

2 cups finely diced onion

Coarse salt and freshly ground pepper

$^1/_2$ cup cooked chickpeas (recipe follows)

2 cups converted long-grain white rice

$3^1/_2$ cups Chicken Stock (page 281)

1 bay leaf

1 cinnamon stick

Pinch of Aleppo pepper (see page 9)

3 tablespoons chopped fresh flat-leaf parsley

1. Preheat the oven to 350°F.

2. Heat the olive oil in a medium saucepan over medium heat until very hot but not smoking. Add the onion along with a pinch of salt. Cover and cook, stirring occasionally, for about 10 minutes, or until very soft and translucent. Add the chickpeas along with another pinch of salt and cook, stirring, for 2 minutes longer. Add the rice and stir to coat with the oil. Add the stock, bay leaf, cinnamon stick, and Aleppo pepper. Raise the heat to high and bring to a boil.

3. Immediately lower the heat to a bare simmer. Season with salt to taste and a hint of pepper. Cover and place in the preheated oven. Bake for about 20 minutes, or until the liquid has been absorbed and the rice is al dente.

4. Remove from the oven and let rest, covered, for 5 minutes. Stir in the parsley and serve immediately.

Chickpeas

Makes about 4 cups

1 pound dried chickpeas
6 garlic cloves, peeled
4 black peppercorns
4 parsley stems
1 bay leaf
$\frac{1}{2}$ small white onion
About 1 tablespoon coarse salt, or to taste

1. Sort through the chickpeas to remove any gravel or debris. Place in a large mixing bowl and add enough cold water to cover by 2 inches. Place in the refrigerator to soak overnight.

2. Drain the chickpeas and place in a large heavy saucepan with water to cover by 2 inches. Place over high heat and bring to a boil. Lower the heat and cook at a bare simmer, frequently skimming off any foam that rises to the top.

3. Combine the garlic, peppercorns, parsley, bay leaf, and onion in a piece of cheesecloth about 6 inches square. Gather up the ends and, using kitchen twine, tie the bag closed. Add the sachet to the chickpeas and simmer for 30 to 40 minutes, or until the chickpeas are tender. About 15 minutes before the chickpeas are done, add the salt.

4. Remove from the heat and set aside to cool in the cooking liquid. When cool, the chickpeas may be stored in their cooking liquid, covered and refrigerated, for up to 4 days.

Potato-Olive Stew

This dish is very simple to put together and adds a lot of zest to a meal of grilled or roasted meat, poultry, or fish. If you can't find fingerling potatoes, use any small, firm-fleshed new potato. This is a perfect accompaniment to the Roasted Lemon-Garlic Chicken on page 214.

2½ pounds fingerling potatoes

6 tablespoons extra virgin olive oil

1 teaspoon dried Greek oregano

Coarse salt and freshly ground pepper

3 garlic cloves, sliced

2 cups crushed Italian plum tomatoes

1½ cups mixed Greek olives, pitted (see Note)

1 teaspoon chopped fresh rosemary

1. Preheat the oven to 450°F.

2. Cut the potatoes crosswise into ¼-inch-thick slices. Place the potatoes in cold water to prevent discoloration. When all have been cut, drain well and pat dry.

3. Place the potatoes in a mixing bowl. Drizzle with about 2 tablespoons of the olive oil. Add the oregano and season with just a pinch of salt and pepper. Toss to coat. Set aside.

4. Place a heavy medium roasting pan in the preheated oven for about 5 minutes, or until very hot. Remove the pan from the oven and, using 2 tablespoons of olive oil, lightly coat the bottom of the pan.

5. Place the potatoes in the hot pan, stirring to ensure that they don't stick to the bottom of the pan. Return the pan to the oven. Roast the potatoes for about 20 minutes, or until golden brown but still firm to the touch.

6. Remove the pan from the oven. Stir in the garlic. Return the pan to the oven for 1 minute.

7. Remove the pan from the oven and stir in the tomatoes and olives. Return to the oven and cook for 5 minutes, stir, and continue to cook for an additional 5 minutes, or until the potatoes are very tender.

8. Remove from the oven. Drizzle with the remaining olive oil and season with salt and pepper to taste. Fold in rosemary and serve.

NOTE: I use a combination of Kalamata, cracked green, and Thassos olives. To remove the pits, I lightly smash the olive so the pit can be pushed out without mangling the olive.

Patatokeftedes

These savory Greek-style potato cakes make a terrific accompaniment for grilled meats or poultry. They also make a great vegetarian dish served with Ionian Garlic Sauce (page 194). The potato mixture can be formed into cakes and frozen for up to three months prior to breading. When ready to cook, remove the cakes from the freezer and thaw slightly, then proceed with the breading and frying.

3 medium Idaho potatoes

Coarse salt and freshly ground pepper

$^1/_2$ cup plus 2 tablespoons olive oil, plus more if needed

$1^1/_2$ cups finely diced onion

$2^1/_2$ cups finely diced leek

2 large eggs

$1^1/_2$ ounces feta cheese, crumbled

$1^1/_2$ ounces manouri cheese

$^1/_4$ cup Greek yogurt (see page 13)

1 tablespoon minced fresh flat-leaf parsley

1 tablespoon chopped fresh chives

$^1/_2$ teaspoon minced garlic

$2^1/_4$ cups Fresh Bread Crumbs (page 57)

2 cups milk

1 cup all-purpose flour

$^1/_2$ cup cornstarch

1. Place the unpeeled potatoes in cold salted water to cover by 1 inch in a large saucepan over high heat. Bring to a boil. Lower the heat and simmer for about 20 minutes, or until the potatoes are tender when pierced with the point of a small sharp knife. Remove from the heat, drain well, and set aside to cool.

2. Heat 2 tablespoons of the oil in a medium sauté pan over medium heat. Add the onion along with a pinch of salt. Cover and cook, stirring occasionally, for about 8 minutes, or until the onion is soft but has not taken on any color. Add the leek along with a pinch of salt. Cover and cook, stirring occasionally, for another 8 minutes, or until the leek is very soft. Remove from the heat and set aside to cool.

3. When the potatoes are cool, peel and grate them through the large holes of a box grater. Place in a large mixing bowl and add the reserved onion-leek mixture. Stir in one

of the eggs along with the feta and manouri cheeses, yogurt, parsley, chives, and garlic, stirring to blend well. Using about $\frac{1}{4}$ cup of the bread crumbs, add just enough to firm the mix—you do not want it to be dry.

4. Line a baking pan with parchment paper. Set aside.

5. Using an ice cream scoop, portion out the mixture to make 6 scoops. Using your hands, form the scoops into cakes about $2\frac{1}{2}$ inches in diameter and $\frac{1}{4}$ inch high. Place the cakes on the prepared baking sheet. Cover with plastic wrap and place in the freezer for about 30 minutes, or until almost frozen. Remove the cakes from the freezer.

6. Place 4 shallow dishes side by side on the countertop. Place the milk in the first dish. Combine the flour and cornstarch with salt and pepper to taste in the second dish. Place the remaining egg in the third dish and whisk until well blended. Combine the remaining 2 cups of Fresh Bread Crumbs in the fourth and final dish.

7. Working with one piece at a time, dip a potato cake into the milk first, then the flour mixture, then the egg, and finally the bread crumbs, pressing lightly so that the bread crumbs adhere to the potato cake. Place the coated potato cakes on another baking pan lined with parchment paper and set aside.

8. Heat $\frac{1}{4}$ cup of the remaining olive oil in a large sauté pan over medium-high heat. When a couple of bread crumbs dropped into the oil sizzle and crisp immediately, begin adding the potato cakes to the oil, 3 at a time. Fry for 3 minutes, or until golden; then turn and fry the other side for 3 minutes, or until golden. Add more oil if necessary to keep the cakes from sticking. Using a slotted spatula, transfer the browned cakes to a double layer of paper towel to drain. Continue to fry the remaining cakes, adding the remaining $\frac{1}{4}$ cup oil to the pan, as necessary. Keep warm until ready to serve or, if making in advance, reheat, uncovered, in a preheated 350°F oven.

Okra, Onion, and Tomato Stew

This is a classic Greek combination. Okra is extremely popular in Greece and is served in many different ways. This stew, combined with a bulgur wheat pilaf, makes a superb vegetarian main course. It also is a very tasty accompaniment to a slow-roasted leg of lamb or grilled chicken.

$1/4$ cup plus 2 tablespoons olive oil

1 pound small fresh okra, trimmed

Coarse salt and freshly ground pepper

$2^{1}/_{2}$ cups onion julienne

3 garlic cloves, sliced

$1/2$ teaspoon dried Greek oregano

$1/4$ teaspoon Aleppo pepper (see page 9)

2 cups canned crushed tomatoes with juice

1 cup Vegetable Stock (page 280)

$1/2$ cup sliced pitted Kalamata olives

2 tablespoons chopped fresh flat-leaf parsley

1 tablespoon extra virgin olive oil

1. Heat 1 tablespoon of the olive oil in a large saucepan over medium heat. Add half of the okra and sauté for about 3 minutes, or until lightly colored. Season with salt and pepper and transfer to a baking dish. Repeat with the remaining okra. Set the okra aside.

2. Heat the remaining $1/4$ cup olive oil in a large heavy saucepan over medium heat. Add the onion julienne along with a pinch of salt. Cover and cook, stirring occasionally, for about 10 minutes, or until very soft. Stir in the garlic and continue cooking for 3 minutes, or until the onion begins to caramelize lightly. Add the oregano and Aleppo pepper, stirring to blend. Cook for 1 minute. Add the tomatoes and bring to a simmer. Lower the

heat and cook at a bare simmer for 6 minutes. Add the stock and bring to a boil. Then add the okra and simmer for 20 minutes, or until the okra is almost tender. Fold in the olives, parsley, and extra virgin olive oil.

3. Remove from the heat. Taste and, if necessary, season with salt and pepper. Serve immediately.

SERVES 6

Vegetables Stuffed with Rice, Bulgur, Pine Nuts, and Currants

Stuffed vegetables are very common in Greece during the summer months. I, too, serve this dish only during summer, when local tomatoes, zucchini, and peppers are at their very best. Simple but great!

The tomatoes should be about the size of tennis balls.

6 medium beefsteak tomatoes

Coarse salt and freshly ground pepper

1 zucchini, at least 11 inches long

7 yellow bell peppers, 6 roasted (see page 145) and left whole, 1 finely diced

1 cup Herb Tea (page 289)

1 cup bulgur wheat

3 tablespoons plus 1 teaspoon extra virgin olive oil, plus oil for seasoning and drizzling

$^1/_2$ cup dried currants

$2^1/_2$ cups finely diced onion

2 garlic cloves, finely chopped

1 cup long-grain white rice

5 cups hot Vegetable Stock (page 280)

1 cup grated manouri cheese

$^1/_2$ cup pine nuts, toasted (see page 77)

2 tablespoons fresh mint chiffonade (see page 46)

2 tablespoons chopped fresh dill

1 tablespoon chopped fresh flat-leaf parsley

1. Using a sharp knife, carefully cut the tops off each tomato to make a lid. Reserve the tops. Using a spoon, carefully remove and discard the seeds. Scoop out and reserve the flesh, leaving just a thin shell. Season the interior with salt and then place the tomatoes upside down on a triple layer of paper towel to drain.

2. Chop the tomato flesh and set it aside.

3. Trim the ends of the zucchini, then cut the zucchini crosswise into 3 pieces, each about $3^1/_2$ inches long. Cut each piece in half lengthwise and carefully remove the flesh, leaving a thin shell. Chop the flesh and set aside.

4. Using a sharp knife, carefully slit one side of each roasted yellow pepper. Taking care not to tear the peppers, using a small sharp knife, carefully remove the seeds and

membranes from each one. You want to have 6 whole, hollow peppers, complete with stem. Set aside.

5. Place the Herb Tea in a medium saucepan over medium heat and bring to a simmer. Add the bulgur along with 1 teaspoon of the extra virgin olive oil and salt to taste. Cover and bring to a boil. Lower the heat and simmer for a couple of minutes, or just until you can see the grains begin to absorb the liquid. Remove from the heat and let rest, covered, for 15 minutes, or until the bulgur has absorbed the liquid and can be fluffed with a fork. Set aside.

6. Place the currants in a small heatproof bowl. Cover with hot water and set aside to plump for about 15 minutes.

7. Place a large saucepan over medium heat. Add the remaining 3 tablespoons olive oil and, when hot, add the onion and a pinch of salt. Cover and cook, stirring frequently, for about 10 minutes, or until translucent. Add the garlic and cook, stirring, for another minute. Add the reserved zucchini flesh, cover, and cook, stirring occasionally, for 5 minutes. Uncover and stir in the finely diced yellow pepper. Cover and cook for 2 minutes. Uncover, add the reserved tomato pulp, and cook, stirring frequently, for 2 minutes. Add the rice, stirring to blend well. Add 1½ cups of the hot stock and bring to a boil.

Lower the heat, cover, and cook at a bare simmer for 12 to 15 minutes, or until the rice has absorbed the liquid but is still slightly al dente. Remove from the heat and set aside to cool.

8. Preheat the oven to 425°F.

9. Transfer the rice to a heatproof mixing bowl. Add the bulgur; drain the currants and add them along with the cheese, pine nuts, mint, dill, and parsley. Season with salt and pepper to taste and toss to blend well.

10. Season the inside of the tomato and zucchini shells with extra virgin olive oil and salt and pepper to taste.

11. Spoon some of the rice mixture into the tomato and zucchini shells, mounding it slightly. Carefully open the slit in the peppers and spoon the remaining rice mixture into the peppers. Place the tomatoes and zucchini in a baking dish stuffed side up. Place the peppers in the pan slit down. Place a lid on each tomato. Pour the remaining hot stock over all. Drizzle the tops with extra virgin olive oil. Cover with aluminum foil and place in the preheated oven. Bake the tomatoes and peppers for about 20 minutes and the zucchini for about 30 minutes, or until the stuffing is hot and the vegetables are heated through.

12. Remove from the oven, uncover, and serve.

Briam

Briam is a classic mix of summer vegetables and beans that can be eaten warm or at room temperature. Wonderful as a side dish, it can also be served on its own with some feta cheese, olives, and crusty bread.

1 medium eggplant, cut into ¹/₄-inch dice

³/₄ cup extra virgin olive oil

Coarse salt and freshly ground pepper

Pinch of Aleppo pepper, plus more to taste (see page 9)

Pinch of dried Greek oregano, plus more to taste

1 medium white onion, finely diced

3 garlic cloves, sliced

¹/₄ cup dry white wine

1 beefsteak tomato, peeled, seeded, and finely diced (see page 113)

1¹/₄ cups Vegetable Stock (page 280)

2 medium zucchini, trimmed, quartered lengthwise, and sliced crosswise ¹/₂ inch thick

1 red bell pepper, roasted, peeled, seeded, membrane removed, and cut into ³/₄-inch pieces (see page 145)

1 yellow bell pepper, roasted, peeled, seeded, membrane removed, and cut into ³/₄-inch pieces (see page 145)

2 cups cooked or canned gigantes or cannellini beans (see Note)

10 fresh basil leaves, chopped

1 cup Fresh Bread Crumbs (page 57)

I. Preheat the oven to 400°F.

2. Combine the eggplant with ¹/₄ cup of the olive oil in a mixing bowl. Season with salt, pepper, Aleppo pepper, and oregano, tossing to coat well. Transfer the seasoned eggplant to a nonstick baking pan in a single layer. Place in the preheated oven and bake for 20 minutes, or until golden brown. Remove from the oven and set aside.

3. Reduce the oven temperature to 375°F.

4. Heat ¹/₄ cup of the remaining olive oil in a deep skillet over medium heat. Add the onion along with a pinch of salt. Cover and cook, stirring occasionally, for about 5 minutes, or until soft and translucent.

5. Stir in the garlic and cook for another minute. Season with salt, pepper, Aleppo pepper, and oregano to taste and cook, stirring, for a minute. Stir in the wine, followed by the tomato and stock. Bring to a boil, lower the

heat, and simmer for about 15 minutes, or until the flavors have blended and the sauce has reduced somewhat.

6. Add the zucchini and return to a simmer. Simmer for about 7 minutes, or until the zucchini is cooked but not falling apart.

7. Add the red and yellow bell peppers and the beans along with the eggplant. Bring to a simmer and cook for 5 minutes. Stir in the basil.

8. Transfer the mixture to a 2-quart baking dish. Sprinkle the bread crumbs in an even layer over the top. Drizzle the remaining $\frac{1}{4}$ cup olive oil over all. Place in the preheated oven and bake for 25 minutes, or until golden brown and bubbling. Remove from the oven and serve.

NOTE: If using canned beans, rinse well under cool running water to eliminate excess salt.

Vegetable Moussaka

This is my take on the most classic of all Greek dishes. With the potato-skordalia topping, it's a complete vegetarian dish. Please note that all of the components of the dish should be prepped as far in advance as possible—even if the dish is not going to be cooked straightaway. Greek cooks follow this advice so that the final dish has the most flavor possible.

1½ cups plus 2 tablespoons olive oil

5 cups finely diced onion

Coarse salt and freshly ground pepper

4 garlic cloves, sliced

2 tablespoons ras el hanout

1 teaspoon Aleppo pepper (see page 9)

1 teaspoon ground cinnamon

3 cups (about 2 pounds) peeled, seeded, chopped ripe tomatoes (see page 113)

2 cups dry red wine, such as Aghiorghitiko, Cabernet Sauvignon, or Sangiovese

1 cup diced Oven-Dried Tomatoes (page 168)

3 medium eggplants, cut crosswise into eighteen ¼-inch-thick slices

3 medium zucchini (about ½ pound), cut crosswise into eighteen ¼-inch-thick slices

4 to 5 medium potatoes, peeled and cut crosswise into ¼-inch-thick slices (40 to 45 slices)

2 medium red or yellow bell peppers, cut lengthwise into 8 pieces

1 medium potato, cooked, peeled, and riced

About 2 cups Skordalia (page 94)

1 cup Fresh Bread Crumbs (page 57)

2 tablespoons grated kefalotyri cheese

I. Preheat a large saucepan over medium-high heat. When hot but not smoking, add 5 tablespoons of the oil, swirling to coat the bottom of the pan. Add the onion and a pinch of salt. Stir, lower the heat, cover, and cook, stirring occasionally, for 20 to 25 minutes, or until the onion is quite soft. Add the garlic and cook for another minute. Stir in the ras el hanout, Aleppo pepper, and cinnamon and cook for a couple of minutes, or until very fragrant. Add the fresh tomatoes, raise the heat to medium, cover, and cook for 6 to 8 minutes. Stir in the wine and simmer for 10 minutes. Fold in the Oven-Dried

Tomatoes and cook for an additional 10 minutes, or until the liquid has reduced by three quarters. Taste and, if necessary, season with salt and pepper.

2.   Remove from the heat and set aside to cool. (This can be done up to 1 day in advance and stored in the refrigerator, tightly covered with plastic wrap.)

3.   Preheat the oven to 500°F.

4.   Season ½ cup of the remaining olive oil with salt and pepper to taste. Using a pastry brush, lightly coat each side of the eggplant slices with the seasoned oil. Then season both sides with additional salt and pepper to taste. Place the seasoned eggplant slices in a single layer on a baking sheet. Place in the oven and roast for 8 to 10 minutes, or until nicely charred and tender. Turn and roast the remaining side for 8 to 10 minutes, brushing with additional oil if necessary to keep the eggplant moist. The eggplant must be soft and tender. Remove from the oven and set aside to cool.

5.   Repeat with the zucchini slices, using another ¼ cup olive oil, salt, and pepper, roasting for 4 to 6 minutes on each side. Set aside to cool.

6.   Heat ½ cup of the remaining olive oil in a large sauté pan over medium heat, swirling to coat the bottom of the pan. When very hot but not smoking, add 6 potato slices and fry, turning once, for about 12 minutes, or until golden on both sides. Place on a double layer of paper towel to drain. Continue fry-

ing until all of the potato slices have been cooked. Set aside.

7.   When all of the potato slices have been fried, drain half of the oil from the pan. Return the pan to medium heat. When very hot, add the bell peppers and sauté for 5 to 6 minutes, or until just wilted. Season with salt and pepper to taste and remove from the heat. Transfer to a plate to cool.

8.   When all of the components are cool, lower the oven to 350°F.

9.   Place a layer of slightly overlapping potato slices in the bottom of a 9 × 13 × 2-inch baking dish. Add a layer of slightly overlapping eggplant slices, followed by a layer of slightly overlapping zucchini slices. Sprinkle the zucchini with a layer of peppers. Spoon a generous portion of the tomato mixture over the vegetables, spreading it out in an even layer. Repeat this process to make another layer. Fold the riced potato into the Skordalia. When blended, spoon over the moussaka to make a thin layer. (The moussaka can be made up to this point, tightly covered with plastic wrap and refrigerated, up to 2 days ahead.)

10.   Combine the bread crumbs with the remaining 1 tablespoon olive oil. Season with salt and pepper to taste. Sprinkle over the top of the casserole. Top with the grated cheese. Place in the preheated oven and bake for 50 to 60 minutes, or until heated through and golden brown on top. Remove from the oven and serve immediately.

Sweets

Throughout Greece, dessert is most frequently some yogurt or fresh cheese, honey, spoon sweets, and/or fresh fruit. Desserts, as we know them, are usually reserved for festive occasions such as holidays and saint's days. Spoon sweets or jams (pages 272–275) are extremely important, and a few jars are always found in the Greek kitchen—homemade when possible. I have chosen just a few traditional desserts. Each one will make a wonderful ending to any meal.

Ravani with Caramelized Pears, Vanilla-Scented Syrup, and Almond Cream

This is a contemporary version of a very traditional Greek cake. I now often fold in about ½ cup each of diced candied orange and lemon peel to add a little zip. If you don't want to bother with individual servings, make the cake in a 9-inch square baking pan and cut it into squares to serve. Although it has a number of components, all of them can be made in advance. Served as suggested, this ravani makes a very special dessert.

6 tablespoons unsalted butter at room
    temperature

¼ cup all-purpose flour

¼ teaspoon baking powder

¼ teaspoon baking soda

¼ teaspoon salt

¼ cup sugar

2 large eggs at room temperature, separated

¼ teaspoon pure vanilla extract

2½ tablespoons coarsely chopped almonds

½ cup fine semolina flour (see page 13)

¼ cup coarse semolina flour

Vanilla Syrup (recipe follows)

Caramelized Pears (recipe follows)

2 cups Almond Cream (recipe follows)

8 fresh mint sprigs (optional)

¼ cup slivered almonds, toasted (see page 77; optional)

1. Preheat the oven to 325°F. Lightly coat six 4-ounce ramekins with nonstick spray. Set aside.

2. Combine the all-purpose flour, baking powder, baking soda, and salt in a medium mixing bowl. Set aside.

3. Place the butter in the bowl of an electric mixer fitted with the paddle and beat until light. Add the sugar and continue beat-

ing until pale yellow and creamy, scraping down the sides of the bowl from time to time.

4. Add the egg yolks one at a time, beating to incorporate after each addition. Stir in the vanilla.

5. Add the chopped almonds and, when incorporated, the flour mixture, beating to incorporate, scraping down the sides of the

bowl from time to time. Slowly add the semolina and continue mixing for 1 to 2 minutes until well combined.

6. Using an electric mixer fitted with the whip attachment, beat the egg whites until stiff peaks form. Then fold the egg white mixture into the batter, taking care that the mixtures are well blended.

7. Spoon enough of the batter into each prepared ramekin to fill it by half. Place in the preheated oven and bake for 15 minutes. Turn the ramekins and bake for another 10 minutes, or until a cake tester inserted in the center comes out clean.

8. Remove from the oven. Spoon 2 tablespoons of the Vanilla Syrup over each warm cake and let rest for 15 minutes before serving.

9. Invert a cake in the center of each of 6 dessert plates. Drizzle a little Vanilla Syrup over the cake and around the plate. Place about 1 tablespoon of the Caramelized Pears to the side and garnish with a dollop of Almond Cream. If using, place a mint sprig on top and sprinkle toasted almonds around the plate. Serve immediately.

Vanilla Syrup

Makes about 2 1/2 cups

3¹/₄ cups sugar
1¹/₄ cups honey
1 tablespoon grated orange zest
Pinch of coarse salt
¹/₂ vanilla bean, split

1. Combine all the ingredients except the orange zest with 2 cups water in a medium saucepan. Stir in the zest. Bring to a boil over medium-high heat. Lower the heat and simmer for 15 minutes.

2. Remove from the heat and set aside to cool. When cool, strain through a fine sieve into a clean container. Use immediately or store, covered and refrigerated, for up to 2 weeks.

Caramelized Pears

Serves 6

4 tablespoons (¹/₂ stick) unsalted butter
¹/₂ cup sugar
¹/₄ vanilla bean, split
4 Bosc pears, peeled, cored, and thinly sliced lengthwise
Pinch of ground cinnamon
¹/₄ cup orange liqueur
1 tablespoon lemon juice
Pinch of coarse salt

1. Place the butter in a large heavy sauté pan over medium heat. When the butter begins to brown, add the sugar, stirring to blend. Cook, stirring constantly, for about 5 minutes, or until the sugar begins to caramelize. Scrape the vanilla seeds from the pod into the sugar mixture and then add the bean.

2. Add the pears and cinnamon and continue to sauté for about 4 minutes, or until the pears begin to caramelize. Stir in the liqueur and simmer for 2 minutes. Add the lemon juice and salt and sauté for about 5 minutes longer, or until the pears are very tender and well caramelized.

3. Remove from the heat and set aside to cool. Serve or store, covered and refrigerated, for up to 3 days.

Almond Cream

Makes about 2 cups

1 cup heavy cream, well chilled
¹/₄ cup confectioners' sugar
¹/₄ teaspoon almond extract

Place the cream in the chilled bowl of an electric mixer fitted with the whip. Begin whipping on medium and then slowly add the sugar, beating until almost firm. Add the almond extract and continue beating until firm. Use immediately.

Baklava

When we were in the process of organizing the menu for Molyvos, all of the chefs were agonizing over an innovative way to prepare baklava, because we didn't just want to rely on tradition. As we were standing in the kitchen working with phyllo dough, Mrs. Livanos came in. She watched us for a moment and then said, "All I do is roll it up." We looked at each other and said "That's it." And that is how our nontraditional baklava came to be! We still laugh about it.

1³/₄ cups coarsely ground walnuts

³/₄ cup coarsely ground pistachios

¹/₄ cup sugar

1 teaspoon ground cinnamon

1 package frozen #7 phyllo dough, thawed as directed on package

1 cup clarified butter (see page 9)

2¹/₂ cups Baklava Syrup (recipe follows)

1. Combine the walnuts, pistachios, sugar, and cinnamon in a mixing bowl, stirring to blend well. Set aside.

2. Preheat the oven to 350°F. Line a baking pan with parchment paper.

3. Hold the phyllo as directed on page 12.

4. Lay one sheet of phyllo out on a clean work surface. Using a pastry brush, lightly coat it with clarified butter. Lay another sheet of phyllo on the buttered sheet, extending the dough 3 inches beyond the top edge. Lightly coat this sheet with clarified butter without coating the 3-inch extension. Lay another sheet of phyllo down as before and lightly coat with clarified butter, again leaving the extension unbuttered. Leaving the 3-inch extension uncovered, sprinkle the rest of the dough with ¹/₂ cup of the nut mixture. (It's helpful to cover the extension with a piece of parchment paper or aluminum foil.)

5. Place a sheet of phyllo over the nut mixture. Lightly brush with clarified butter again, leaving the 3-inch extension unbuttered. Lay another sheet of phyllo on the buttered sheet. Lightly coat this sheet with clarified butter, followed by ¹/₂ cup of the nut mixture. Repeat this process 3 more times, ending with the nut mixture. You will have used 11 sheets of phyllo.

6. Starting at the bottom of the layered phyllo, roll the dough up, cigar fashion, toward the top, brushing with clarified butter as you go. You should now have a firm log.

7. Lay one sheet of phyllo on a clean work surface. Place the log at the bottom of the phyllo and roll, brushing lightly with clarified butter as you go, to enclose the log completely with the phyllo. Repeat this process to firmly enclose the log.

8. Using a sharp knife, trim off any ragged ends of phyllo dough. Cut the log crosswise into 6 to 8 equal pieces.

9. Place the baklava in the prepared baking pan, cut side down. Place in the preheated oven and bake for 15 minutes. Rotate the pan 180 degrees and bake for another 15 minutes, or until all of the surfaces are golden brown. Remove from the oven and set aside to cool slightly.

10. While still warm, drizzle each piece of baklava with 2 tablespoons of the warm Baklava Syrup. Let stand for 10 minutes and then turn them over and repeat the drizzling. Let stand for 20–30 minutes (or longer). Place on a serving platter and drizzle each piece with a tablespoon of syrup.

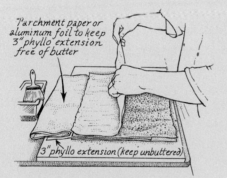

1. PLACE A SHEET OF PHYLLO OVER THE NUT MIXTURE.

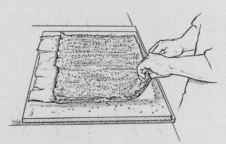

2. STARTING AT THE BOTTOM OF THE LAYERED PHYLLO, ROLL THE DOUGH UP, CIGAR FASHION.

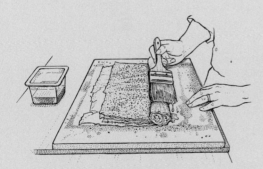

3. BRUSH WITH CLARIFIED BUTTER AS YOU GO.

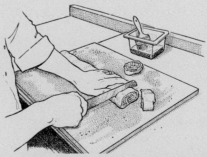

4. USING A SHARP KNIFE, TRIM OFF ANY RAGGED ENDS OF PHYLLO DOUGH.

Baklava Syrup

Makes about 1 quart

3 cups sugar
¹/₂ cup honey
Zest of 1 orange in large strips
Zest of 1 lemon in large strips
1 cinnamon stick
1 tablespoon fresh lemon juice

1. Place 1 quart water in a medium heavy saucepan. Stir in the sugar, honey, orange zest, lemon zest, cinnamon stick, and lemon juice and bring to a boil over medium heat. Lower the heat and simmer, skimming occasionally to remove any foam that rises to the top, for 25 to 30 minutes, or until the liquid has become syrupy. Do not reduce the liquid too much as it has to be thin enough to drizzle easily.

2. Remove from the heat. When cool, strain through a fine sieve and set aside until ready to use. (The syrup can be made in advance and stored, covered and refrigerated, for up to 2 weeks.)

SERVES 6

Bougatsa

This sweetened semolina custard baked in phyllo is one of the most common desserts in a Greek home, mainly because it's made with ingredients always on hand. The first time I experienced it, the dessert was made in the traditional way, baked in one large cake pan. At Molyvos we need to make individual desserts, so I devised the following recipe using strudel dough, which is easier to work with than the very thinnest phyllo. If you want to make a traditional bougatsa, see the variation.

3 cups milk

1 cup granulated sugar

Grated zest of 2 lemons

³/₄ cup fine semolina flour

2 large eggs plus 1 large egg yolk, beaten, at
    room temperature

4 tablespoons (¹/₂ stick) unsalted butter at room
    temperature

8 tablespoons (1 stick) unsalted butter, melted

2 tablespoons olive oil

5 teaspoons ground cinnamon

20 frozen strudel dough sheets, thawed as
    directed on package (see Note)

3 tablespoons confectioners' sugar

1. Line an 8-inch square glass baking dish with plastic wrap. Set aside.

2. Combine the milk, ³/₄ cup of the granulated sugar, and the lemon zest in a medium saucepan over medium heat. Bring to a simmer and immediately whisk in the semolina. Simmer, whisking constantly, for about 3 minutes, or until thick.

3. Remove from the heat and immediately beat in the eggs. Return the saucepan to medium heat and cook, stirring constantly, for 1 minute.

4. Remove from the heat and beat in the 4 tablespoons butter. Pour the custard into the prepared dish, spreading out evenly with a rubber spatula. Cover the entire dish with plastic wrap, pushing down and pressing so that the film is directly on the custard and the custard top is very smooth. Refrigerate for 3 hours. It should look like firm polenta.

5. Preheat the oven to 375°F.

6. Combine the melted butter and olive oil in a small bowl. Set aside.

(continued)

7. Combine the remaining ¼ cup granulated sugar with 4 teaspoons of the cinnamon in another small bowl. Set aside.

8. Line a baking sheet with parchment paper. Place a wire rack on the lined baking sheet and set aside.

9. Hold the strudel dough as directed for phyllo on page 12.

10. Remove the chilled custard from the refrigerator. Unwrap and invert onto a cutting board. Using a sharp knife, cut the custard lengthwise into 3 equal pieces.

11. Lay one sheet of strudel dough out on a clean work surface. Using a pastry brush, lightly coat it with the butter/oil mixture. Lay another sheet of strudel dough on top, lightly coat it with the butter/oil mixture, and sprinkle with cinnamon sugar. Repeat this with another piece of dough, butter/oil, and sugar. Finally, lay another sheet of strudel dough on top and lightly coat it with the butter/oil mixture.

12. Lay one strip of custard across the bottom of the layered strudel. Carefully roll the custard to the other end, wrapping it in strudel dough, leaving the ends exposed. Continue this process until all of the custard pieces are wrapped in this fashion. Cut each log in half crosswise. Set aside.

13. Repeat the layering of 4 pieces of strudel dough as step 11 using the same butter/oil and cinnamon sugar ratio.

14. Place 3 wrapped custards across the bottom of the layered dough with the exposed ends facing toward the top and bottom of the dough. Using a sharp knife, cut as straight a line as possible to make 3 strips of dough equal in size to the width of the custards so that they will be completely enclosed when wrapped.

15. Working with one at a time, roll the strudel-wrapped custards end over end, wrapping to cover the exposed sides. You should now have 3 completely strudel-wrapped custards. Lightly coat the exterior of each with the butter/oil mixture.

16. Repeat this process (steps 13–15) to enclose the remaining 3 pieces.

17. Place the strudel-wrapped custards on the prepared baking sheet. Place the sheet in the preheated oven and bake for 30 minutes, or until golden brown and crisp.

18. While the custards are baking, make the topping. Combine the remaining teaspoon of cinnamon with the confectioners' sugar in a small bowl. Set aside.

19. Remove the custards from the oven and immediately sprinkle with the cinnamon topping. Serve warm or at room temperature.

NOTE: The very thin strudel sheets are best for this recipe. If you can't find them, #4 phyllo dough will work well. However, you will need 3 more sheets (for steps 13–15), as each sheet of phyllo is only wide enough to enclose 2 custards.

TRADITIONAL BOUGATSA: Add an additional cup of milk to the custard, as you want it to be slightly loose. Lightly butter a 9-inch round cake pan. Using a pastry brush, thoroughly coat the inside of an 8-inch round cake pan with the butter/olive oil. Working with one sheet of phyllo at a time, place a corner in the center of the pan, and gently press the dough against the inside of the pan so that the dough adheres to every space (the phyllo corner should be centered in the pan so that the 3 remaining edges overhang on all sides). Lay the corner of a second sheet into the center of the pan, slightly overlapping phyllo leaves so that much of the pan's surface is covered by dough. Press into the pan. Lay the third sheet in the same manner, covering the remainder of the pan's surface while overlapping slightly. Press dough into pan. Now you have one layer of dough. Using a pastry brush, coat the dough with a generous amount of the butter/olive oil. Lightly sprinkle with the cinnamon and granulated sugar mixture. Lay three more sheets of phyllo into the cake pan in the same manner, and brush thoroughly with butter/oil. Sprinkle with sugar/cinnamon blend. Repeat one more time. The point is to have 9 layers that can be brought up and over to cover the filling. Pour in the custard, then bring the phyllo up and over to enclose it completely. Brush the top with melted butter and bake as directed.

GEORGINA, WHO CREATES PASTRIES AND
SWEETS, PREPARES THE BOUGATSA.

Loukoumades with Thyme Honey Syrup

Both sides of my family have a version of fried dough—the Italians have their zeppole, and the Greeks have loukoumades. They are both delicious, so I take no sides in the "Which is better?" debate.

1¹/₄ cups warm (70–80°F) water

3 tablespoons fresh yeast, or 1¹/₂ (¹/₄-ounce) envelopes active dry yeast

4¹/₂ teaspoons granulated sugar

3¹/₄ cups all-purpose flour

¹/₂ teaspoon sea salt

1¹/₂ teaspoons mastic

1 large egg, lightly beaten

1¹/₄ cups milk

3 tablespoons ouzo

Thyme Honey Syrup (recipe follows)

About 6 cups vegetable oil for frying

About ¹/₄ cup confectioners' sugar

About ¹/₄ cup ground walnuts

About 1 teaspoon ground cinnamon

I. Combine the warm water, yeast, and 1 teaspoon of the granulated sugar in a small bowl, stirring to blend. Set aside for 10 minutes.

2. Combine 3 cups of the flour with the salt and 2¹/₂ teaspoons of the granulated sugar and set aside.

3. Combine the remaining teaspoon of the granulated sugar and mastic in a spice grinder and process until finely ground. Combine with the flour mixture, stirring to blend, and then sift the flour mixture into a large mixing bowl.

4. Make a well in the center of the flour mixture and add the egg. Pour the milk and ouzo, into the yeast mixture. Stir the wet ingredients into the flour with a wooden spoon, stirring gently to make a wet dough. The batter should be thick but still pourable. If too wet, add the remaining ¹/₂ cup flour. Cover with plastic wrap and set aside for 1¹/₂ hours, or until doubled in volume. The batter should be active, somewhat like a sticky bread dough.

5. Place the Thyme Honey Syrup in a shallow container and set aside.

6. Place the oil in a deep-fat fryer with a basket over medium-high heat. Bring to 325°F on an instant-read thermometer.

7. Scoop up a handful of the dough and, pressing your fingers to your palm, allow the dough to form a bubble at the point where your fingers meet your thumb. Using a teaspoon dipped in cold water, carefully scrape the bubble of dough into the hot oil. Working quickly, continue making balls until you have 6 to 8 in the hot oil. Using a metal spoon, gently lift the hot oil up and over to bathe the dough balls, making sure they are browning evenly. Check the temperature of the oil from time to time. You do not want it to get any hotter than 350°F, or the dough will darken too quickly. If the batter sinks and stays on the bottom of the pot when put into the oil, the oil is not hot enough. If it doesn't sink and immediately returns to the top, the oil is too hot. When golden brown, using a slotted spoon, transfer the fried dough to a double layer of paper towel to drain and continue making and frying dough.

8. Just before serving, refry the balls for about 30 seconds to crisp and heat them. Drain well and then place the hot drained dough balls in the Thyme Honey Syrup, turning to coat.

9. Place the coated balls in a large shallow container. When all of the dough has been fried and coated, pour any remaining Thyme Honey Syrup over all.

10. When ready to serve, place the Loukoumades on a serving platter or individual dessert plates. Sprinkle with confectioners' sugar, ground walnuts, and ground cinnamon, and serve.

GEORGINA BRINGS THE LOUKOUMADES TO ME TO TASTE EVERY DAY.

Thyme Honey Syrup

Makes about 2¼ cups

2 cups thyme honey
½ cup sugar
1 cinnamon stick
Zest of 1 lemon in strips
Zest of 1 orange in strips

1. Combine the honey with ½ cup water, the sugar, cinnamon, and citrus zests in a medium saucepan over medium heat. Cook, skimming frequently to remove any impurities that rise to the top, for 10 minutes.

2. Remove from the heat and strain through a fine sieve into a clean container.

3. Use immediately or cover and refrigerate until ready to use. Bring to room temperature before using. Covered and refrigerated, the honey will keep indefinitely.

Karydopita with Greek Yogurt and Orange Spoon Sweets

In Greece, this cake is traditionally served during the Lenten season, because it doesn't require the use of any dairy products, which are not eaten during this period of fasting. During the rest of the year the yogurt garnish is a nice touch. I have adapted this from a traditional recipe given to me by Aglaia Kremezi.

$\frac{1}{3}$ cup Frangelico liqueur (see Note)

1 teaspoon baking soda

1 cup fine semolina flour

1 cup coarsely chopped walnuts

$\frac{1}{3}$ cup sugar

1 teaspoon baking powder

1 teaspoon ground cinnamon

$\frac{1}{4}$ teaspoon ground cloves

Grated zest of 2 oranges

$\frac{1}{2}$ cup fresh orange juice

$\frac{1}{4}$ cup olive oil

Baklava Syrup (page 256)

$\frac{1}{4}$ cup plus 2 tablespoons Greek yogurt (see page 13)

$\frac{1}{4}$ cup plus 2 tablespoons Orange Spoon Sweets (page 272)

1. Preheat the oven to 325°F. Spray the interior of six $\frac{1}{2}$-cup soufflé dishes with nonstick vegetable spray. Place the dishes on a parchment paper–lined baking sheet. Set aside.

2. Place the Frangelico in a small mixing bowl. Stir in the baking soda and set aside.

3. Combine the semolina, walnuts, sugar, baking powder, cinnamon, and cloves in a mixing bowl. Make a well in the center and set aside.

4. Stir the orange zest and juice into the Frangelico mixture. When well blended, pour the liquid into the well in the dry ingredients and stir to combine. Fold in 2 tablespoons of the olive oil and, when blended, fold in the remaining 2 tablespoons.

5. Ladle about $\frac{3}{4}$ cup of the batter into each of the prepared soufflé dishes. Place in the preheated oven and bake for 20 minutes, or until a cake tester inserted in the center comes out clean. Remove from the oven and set aside to cool slightly.

(continued)

6. When slightly cool, using half of the Baklava Syrup, immediately drizzle an equal portion of syrup over each cake.

7. When ready to serve, drizzle with the remaining syrup and serve with a tablespoon each of Greek yogurt and Orange Spoon Sweets in the center of each cake.

NOTE: Frangelico is a hazelnut-flavored liqueur scented with berries and flowers. It is available at most liquor stores.

JESÚS TORCHING GREEK COFFEE CRÈME BRÛLÉE,

Rice Pudding with Sour Cherry Spoon Sweets

My grandmother made rice pudding with the familiar long-grain rice, but I love the creaminess that Arborio rice provides. No matter what rice is used, this is a dessert that always transports me right back to childhood.

3¹/₂ cups milk

3 cups heavy cream

1 cup sugar

Grated zest of 1 lemon

1 cinnamon stick

1 vanilla bean

1 cup plus 3 tablespoons Arborio rice

5 large egg yolks at room temperature

Ground cinnamon for garnish

Candied Lemon Zest (optional; recipe follows)

Sour Cherry Spoon Sweets (page 274)

1. Combine the milk, cream, sugar, zest, and cinnamon stick in a medium heavy saucepan over medium heat. Split the vanilla bean lengthwise and scrape the seeds into the mixture. Add the scraped bean, bring to a boil, reduce the heat, and simmer for 25 minutes, or until reduced by half.

2. While the milk mixture is cooking, prepare the rice. Place 1 cup water in a large heavy saucepan over medium heat and bring to a boil. Stir in the rice, cover, and remove from the heat. Let stand for 3 minutes. Pour the rice into a fine sieve and drain well.

3. Slowly sprinkle the rice into the simmering milk mixture, whisking constantly to keep the rice from sticking. Lower the heat and cook at a bare simmer for 15 minutes.

4. Place the egg yolks in a bowl and whisk to blend well.

5. Remove the rice from the heat and, whisking constantly, beat about 1 cup of the rice mixture into the eggs to temper them. Whisking constantly, transfer the egg mixture to the rice in the saucepan. Return the mixture to medium heat and cook, stirring constantly, for about 3 minutes, or until thick and creamy.

6. Pour the rice pudding into a shallow container. Place the container in an ice bath to cool.

(continued)

7. When the rice pudding is cool, remove and discard the vanilla bean and cinnamon stick. (At this point the pudding may be transferred to a nonreactive container, covered, and refrigerated for up to 3 days.)

8. Spoon the pudding into individual serving dishes. Sprinkle a bit of cinnamon on top, garnish with a piece of Candied Lemon Zest if desired, and serve with Sour Cherry Spoon Sweets on the side.

Candied Lemon Zest

3 whole unblemished lemons, preferably organic
1¼ cups sugar

1. Remove the zest from each lemon, trying to produce one long ribbon. Set aside.

2. Combine ¼ cup of the sugar and ¼ cup cold water in a medium heavy saucepan over high heat. Add the lemon zest and insert a candy thermometer into the pot. Cook, without stirring, for about 3 minutes, or until the mixture reaches 115°F on the thermometer.

3. Remove from the heat and, using a slotted spoon, transfer the zest to a mixing bowl. Add the remaining cup of sugar and toss to coat. Set aside to dry for at least 12 hours.

4. When dry, cut the zest into the desired shapes and serve as a garnish or as a treat with coffee. It will keep, tightly covered, for 1 month.

Baked Quince with Samos Syrup

This is a seasonal dish, as quince can usually be found only in late fall. In fact, in the restaurant it's one of our signature fall dishes. It's very important to save any peelings, cores, and pits from the quince since they contain lots of pectin, which is necessary to prepare the dish properly. This is one dessert that must be served at room temperature, as chilling will cause the liquid to solidify and make the finished dish much less appetizing.

2 cups Samos wine

2 cups Mavrodaphne wine

1½ cups sugar

3 medium fresh quince, halved with the core and
    pits removed and reserved

6 whole cloves

3 cinnamon sticks

2 tablespoons fresh lemon juice

Greek yogurt (see page 13) or Mastic Ice Cream
    (page 270) (optional)

1. Preheat the oven to 400°F.

2. Combine the wines with 1 cup of the sugar, 1 cup water, and the reserved quince cores in a large heavy saucepan over high heat. Bring to a boil, then lower the heat and simmer for 10 minutes. Remove from the heat and strain through a fine sieve, discarding the solids. Reserve the liquid.

3. Pierce each quince half with a clove. Place the quince in a bowl, add the cinnamon sticks and lemon juice, and toss to coat. Place the quince cut side up in a baking dish. Pour the reserved wine mixture over the quince and bake in the preheated oven for 20 minutes, or until the cut sides of the quince have begun to caramelize.

4. Lower the oven temperature to 350°F.

5. Sprinkle the remaining ½ cup sugar over the quince. Bake for 10 minutes, or until the quince are tender when pierced with the point of a small sharp knife.

6. Remove from the oven and allow to rest in the baking dish until the quince reach room temperature. Do not refrigerate.

7. Serve at room temperature, drizzled with some of the cooking syrup as well as with a dollop of Greek yogurt or Mastic Ice Cream if desired.

Roasted Black Mission Figs with Yogurt and Almond Praline

Figs are one of my favorite foods. Although I often use them raw, this recipe came about when I wanted to do something more than just pop them into my mouth. It went on to become an extremely popular dessert at Molyvos, although we do it only when figs are in season. If time is short, you don't have to add the praline, but it certainly provides the finishing touch!

³/₄ cup sugar

³/₄ cup Samos wine

1 cinnamon stick

24 fresh Black Mission figs

3 cups Greek yogurt (see page 13)

Almond Praline (recipe follows)

6 fresh mint sprigs (optional)

1. Preheat the oven to 350°F.

2. Combine ¹/₂ cup of the sugar with the wine, ³/₄ cup water, and the cinnamon stick in a small saucepan over medium-high heat. Bring to a boil, then lower the heat and simmer for 25 minutes, or until the syrup is slightly thick (similar to maple syrup). Remove from the heat and set aside. When the syrup is cool, remove the cinnamon stick.

3. Remove the stems from the figs and, using a small paring knife, score the stem end, taking care not to cut deeply into the flesh.

4. Place the figs in a glass baking dish, stem end up. Pour the reserved syrup over the figs

and sprinkle with the remaining ¹/₄ cup sugar. Place in the preheated oven and roast for 20 minutes, or until the figs are quite soft.

5. Remove from the oven and carefully transfer the figs to a serving platter, reserving the syrup.

6. Place ¹/₂ cup yogurt in the bottom of each of 6 large red wine goblets or other glass dishes. Place 4 figs on top of the yogurt in each glass. Drizzle with the reserved syrup and garnish with a sprinkle of Almond Praline and a sprig of mint if desired. Serve immediately.

Almond Praline

Makes about ¹/₂ cup

¹/₂ **cup sliced almonds**
2 teaspoons unsalted butter at room temperature
2 teaspoons sugar
Pinch of coarse salt

1. Preheat the oven to 350°F. Line a baking pan with parchment paper.

2. Place the almonds in a small mixing bowl and, using a wooden spoon, press on them to crush them slightly. Stir in the butter, sugar, and salt.

3. Spread the almond mixture in the prepared baking pan. Place in the preheated oven and bake for 6 minutes, or just until melted. Remove from the oven and, when cool enough to handle, break the praline into small pieces and toss the pieces gently around the pan.

4. Return the pan to the oven and bake for 2 minutes longer, or until the praline is golden brown. Remove from the oven and set aside to cool.

5. When cool, place in an airtight container, cover, and store at room temperature for up to 1 month.

FAYEZ PREPARING GREEK COFFEE
FOR A TABLE.

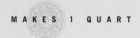

Mastic Ice Cream

Unless you grew up on it, the flavor of mastic, the crystallized sap of the mastic tree, takes some time to get used to, but once you do, you're hooked. At Molyvos, we always have Mastic Ice Cream in the freezer as it is such a terrific accompaniment to baked fruits and other desserts. My favorite combination is roasted figs, Mastic Ice Cream, and Sour Cherry Spoon Sweets (page 274).

1¼ cups plus 2½ teaspoons sugar

2¼ teaspoons mastic

2 cups heavy cream

2 cups milk

15 large egg yolks at room temperature

1. Combine the 2½ teaspoons sugar with the mastic in a spice grinder and process to a fine powder. Set aside.

2. Combine the cream and milk with the remaining 1¼ cups sugar in a medium heavy saucepan over medium heat. Bring to a boil and immediately turn off the heat.

3. Place the egg yolks in a large mixing bowl. Add the mastic mixture and, using a wire whisk, beat until frothy. Whisking constantly, slowly pour about 1 cup of the hot cream mixture into the egg yolks to temper them.

4. Return the heat under the saucepan to medium. Whisking constantly, add the tempered yolks to the hot cream mixture. Cook, stirring constantly with a wooden spoon, for

about 10 minutes, or until thickened. Do not boil, or the mixture will curdle. To test for consistency, run your finger across the back of the spoon after lifting it from the custard. The line will hold if the custard is of the correct consistency. Continue cooking if it does not, taking care not to boil.

5. Remove the custard from the heat and strain through a fine sieve into a clean container. Place the container in a larger bowl of ice and, stirring frequently, cool the custard quickly. When cool, cover and refrigerate for 1 hour.

6. Transfer the custard to an ice cream maker and freeze according to the manufacturer's directions.

Spoon Sweets

In Greece, almost any fruit or vegetable (including such diverse products as young green pistachios and baby eggplants) finds its way into a spoon sweet. Just as in other countries where traditions are fading, many of these recipes are being lost to convenience. At Molyvos, in an attempt to keep to these artisanal ways, we still make our own spoon sweets all year long with whatever fruit or vegetable seems to be ripe and willing. Spoon sweets are a perfect light ending to a rich meal with just a couple of cookies, and they also make great toppings for thick and creamy Greek yogurt. They are always served as an almost ceremonial gift at the end of a meal.

While in Athens on our trip to document the foods that we would be serving at Molyvos, Nick Livanos's uncle Taki decided that he wanted to make a spoon sweet for us. He went downstairs and out into the street, where he picked bitter oranges off the tree in front of his house. He brought them into the kitchen, scrubbed all of the city's pollution off them, and proceeded to make his own orange spoon sweet for us to taste. It was an unforgettable experience.

In addition, for me personally, I will never forget the pride in Nick Livanos's cousin's voice as she urged us to have "just a bite" of her cherry spoon sweet before we left the table. She presented a beautiful tray with a silver spoon for each of us holding just one cherry. The flavor was extraordinary!

Of all the four spoon sweets given here, the Lemon Spoon Sweets are the most time consuming to make, but because it is such a traditional recipe, I wanted to share it. You will need three days as well as a scale to make them. Believe me, the taste is well worth the time that it takes to create this marvelous old-fashioned treat.

For all spoon sweets you should taste the fruit before adding the sugar. If the fruit is very sweet, you might need to add only about half of the sugar called for in the recipe.

You can purchase larding needles and unwaxed kitchen thread at kitchen supply stores as well as most specialty food stores.

For the Lemon Spoon Sweets, you can add cinnamon, clove, $1/2$ split vanilla bean, or, in fact, any herb or spice that you like to add interest. However, I prefer the unadulterated lemon flavor.

Orange Spoon Sweets

4 juice oranges, preferably organic, well scrubbed and dried

2 cups sugar (see page 271)

¹/₄ cup white wine

1. Place the oranges in a medium saucepan of cold water over high heat. Bring to a boil and boil for 1 minute. Drain well. Repeat this blanching process 3 times. Drain well and cool.

2. When the oranges are cool enough to handle, cut them in half crosswise. Remove and discard the seeds. Place the orange halves, cut side down, on a cutting board. Using a sharp knife, cut each half vertically into very thin slices.

3. Place the orange slices in a large mixing bowl. Add the sugar and toss to coat evenly.

4. Place 1¹/₂ cups water and the wine in a nonreactive saucepan over high heat and bring to a boil. Add the orange slices and again bring to a boil. Lower the heat and simmer for 1¹/₂ hours, or until quite thick.

5. Remove from the heat and allow to cool. Serve immediately or transfer to a nonreactive container, cover, and refrigerate for up to 2 weeks.

Lemon Spoon Sweets

12 medium thick-skinned lemons, preferably organic

Sugar to equal ³/₄ of the weight of the fruit, about 1 cup plus 2 tablespoons

1. Begin this preparation in the morning. Using a kitchen scrub pad (such as a Dobie pad), scrub the lemons under warm running water until the skin is bright yellow. Do not remove the skin.

2. Using the fine side of a box grater, zest off just the very exterior yellow peel of each lemon; you do not want to grate any white pith. Reserve the zest for another use. You should be left with whole lemons that are completely white with just a faint yellow tint.

3. Using a small sharp knife, lightly score the pith from top to bottom 4 or 5 times at equal intervals. Carefully remove each segment of the pith and discard the lemon pulp. One at a time, place the petal-shaped pieces of pith, outside surface down, on a cutting board. Using a paring knife, horizontally slice across to remove most of the fibrous tissue from the inside.

4. Thread a large larding needle (see page 271) with unwaxed thread about 12 inches long. Set aside.

5. Roll each lemon petal into a tight cigar-like roll. Insert the needle through the center of the roll to hold it tightly in place. Continue stringing lemon petals until all the petals are on a string. You will need to make a few strings.

6. Place the threaded lemon petal rolls in a large bowl with cold water to cover by about 2 inches. Place in the refrigerator. At noon, drain and cover again with fresh cold water. In the early evening, repeat the draining and covering with water. Just before bedtime, again drain and cover with cold water. Refrigerate until the next morning. As they soak, the lemon rolls will become more pliable.

7. In the morning, drain the lemon rolls. Transfer to a large saucepan and add cold water to cover by 2 inches. Place over high heat and bring to a boil. Boil for 1 minute. Remove from the heat and drain well. Repeat this process 3 times. After the final time, taste for bitterness. The lemon rolls should have a little bite but not be bitter. If still bitter, repeat the process until bitterness disappears. Set aside to cool.

8. Remove the lemon rolls from the string. The rolls should hold their shape.

9. Weigh the rolls. You should have about 12 ounces.

10. Measure out sugar to equal the weight of the rolls.

11. Place the sugar in a nonreactive 2-quart saucepan. Add 2 cups water. The mixture should resemble wet sand. Place over medium heat and cook, stirring constantly, for about 1 minute, or until the sugar dissolves.

12. Stir in the lemon rolls. Add water, if necessary, to cover the rolls by 2 inches. Bring to a boil, then lower to a simmer and cover, with the lid slightly ajar. Simmer, stirring and skimming occasionally, for about 1½ hours, or until the liquid is clear and syrupy. Periodically taste the syrup for sweetness, allowing it to cool first—it should be neither too sweet nor too tart.

13. To test for doneness, lift some of the syrup up by a metal spoon. When it runs off the spoon and holds a stream, it is done. The liquid will solidify further as it cools.

14. Remove from the heat and transfer to a nonreactive container. Set aside to cool. When cool, cover and refrigerate for 8 hours or overnight.

15. Remove from the refrigerator and check for texture, consistency, and flavor. Even if it is perfect—and I'll almost guarantee that it won't be—add ½ cup water and place in a nonreactive saucepan over medium heat. Bring to a simmer and simmer for 15 minutes. Remove from the heat and set aside to cool.

16. When cool, check the consistency. It should be quite thick. Serve or transfer to a glass container, cover, and refrigerate for up to 3 months.

Sour Cherry Spoon Sweets

$^{1}/_{2}$ **pound dried sour cherries**

1 cup sugar (see page 271)

Pinch of coarse salt

2 teaspoons fresh lemon juice

$^{1}/_{4}$ **cup kirschwasser**

1 teaspoon pure vanilla extract

1.   Place the cherries in a colander under cold running water to rinse well. Transfer to a small mixing bowl and add 2 cups cold water. (The water should cover the cherries by about 1 inch.) Set aside to soak for 2 hours. Drain well, separately reserving the cherries and the soaking liquid.

2.   Place the cherries in a small heavy saucepan. Sprinkle the sugar over the top to cover the cherries. Add a pinch of salt along with the reserved soaking liquid. Place over high heat and bring to a boil. Lower the heat and simmer, without stirring, for 20 minutes. Brush the sides of the pan with a wet pastry brush from time to time to keep the sugars from crystallizing around the edges.

3.   Remove from the heat and set aside for at least 2 hours.

4.   Return the saucepan to high heat and bring to a boil, using a metal spoon to skim off any foam that rises to the top. Insert a candy thermometer into the pot and boil for about 20 minutes, or until the mixture reaches 230°F to 240°F on the thermometer. Stir in the lemon juice and boil for 1 minute.

5.   Remove the saucepan from the heat. Stir in the kirschwasser and vanilla and set aside to cool. When cool, serve or transfer to a nonreactive container, cover, and refrigerate for up to 3 months.

Quince Spoon Sweets

3 quince

1 cup Samos wine

2 cinnamon sticks

12 cups sugar

1. Peel and core the quince, reserving both. Using a very sharp knife, cut the quince into thin matchsticks. Set aside.

2. Combine the quince cores and peels in a medium heavy saucepan. Add 2 cups cold water, the wine, and 1 cinnamon stick. Place over medium-high heat and bring to a boil. Lower the heat to a simmer and simmer for 30 minutes. Remove from the heat and strain through a fine sieve, discarding the solids.

3. Place the liquid in a large heavy saucepan. Add the reserved quince along with the sugar and remaining cinnamon stick. Place over medium heat and bring to a boil. Lower the heat and simmer, stirring and skimming frequently, for about 2 hours, or until the liquid has become syrupy and the fruit has turned a deep amber color. Remove from the heat and set aside to cool.

4. When cool, serve or transfer to a nonreactive container, cover, and refrigerate for up to 3 months.

Stocks and Broths

Some of the most basic preparations found in a restaurant kitchen are stocks, intensely flavored liquids that are the foundation of many classic dishes and sauces. They are made by gently simmering a specific group of ingredients in liquid to extract deep flavor, aroma, color, and body. Broths are generally made by simmering meat, poultry, or fish in liquid and aromatics and are used as the base for soups, stews, or braised dishes. At Molyvos, we keep a variety of stocks and broths on hand at all times.

All stocks have certain essential components—a flavoring agent such as meat or fish bones; a vegetable mixture called *mirepoix* in French, which contains onions or leeks, carrot, and celery; and a liquid, usually water. An herb sachet may also be added. When preparing white stocks, the bones (and, if using, meat) are cooked in their raw state, resulting in a liquid that is relatively clear and lightly flavored. Deeply colored brown stocks are formed by first roasting the bones until nicely caramelized to achieve full-bodied flavor in the final stage. The following stock recipes are the standards in the Molyvos kitchen.

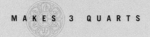

Vegetable Stock

Using water to cook rice and grains results in a flat, almost flavorless dish. Starches obtain much of their flavor from the cooking liquid, so this stock is the perfect medium to inject great flavor into the finished dish.

$^1/_2$ bunch of fresh parsley stems

6 garlic cloves, peeled

5 black peppercorns

2 bay leaves

3 celery ribs, peeled and cut into medium dice

2 large carrots, cut into medium dice

2 large onions, cut into medium dice

2 tablespoons olive oil

Coarse salt

1 tablespoon tomato paste

1. Preheat the oven to 425°F.

2. Combine the parsley, garlic, peppercorns, and bay leaves in a piece of cheesecloth about 6 inches square. Gather up the ends and, using kitchen twine, tie the bag closed. Set the sachet aside.

3. Combine the celery, carrots, and onions in a mixing bowl.

4. Place a medium roasting pan in the preheated oven for a couple of minutes, or until very hot. Remove from the oven and add the oil, moving the pan around to lightly coat the bottom with oil. Add the celery, carrots, and onions in a single layer. Place the pan in the oven and roast, stirring occasionally, for 15 to 20 minutes, or until the vegetables are well

caramelized. Remove from the oven and drain off any oil remaining in the pan.

5. Transfer the vegetables to a stockpot. Add a gallon of water along with a pinch of salt and place over medium-high heat. Bring to a boil, skimming frequently to remove any impurities that rise to the surface. Immediately lower the heat, add the reserved sachet, and simmer for 15 minutes. Stir in the tomato paste and continue to simmer for 15 to 20 minutes.

6. Remove from the heat and season lightly with salt. Let rest for about 10 minutes, then strain through a fine sieve into a clean container. Use immediately or store, tightly covered and refrigerated, for up to 3 days or frozen for up to 3 months.

Chicken Stock

10 white peppercorns

4 garlic cloves, crushed

3 fresh parsley stems

3 fresh thyme sprigs

1 bay leaf

8 pounds chicken bones

Coarse salt

1 onion, halved

1 carrot, trimmed and cut into chunks

1 celery rib, trimmed and cut into chunks

1 leek, trimmed, split in half lengthwise, and
    well washed

1. Combine the peppercorns, garlic, parsley, thyme, and bay leaf in a piece of cheesecloth about 6 inches square. Gather up the ends and, using kitchen twine, tie the bag closed. Set the sachet aside.

2. Place the chicken bones and 6 quarts cold water in a medium stockpot. Place over medium-high heat and bring to a slow boil. Remove from the heat and drain well through a colander, discarding the liquid. Leaving the bones in the colander, place under cold running water to rinse off any impurities that cling to the bones.

3. Place the chicken bones back in the stockpot with cold water to cover by 1 inch. Place over medium-high heat and bring to a slow boil. Boil for 3 minutes, constantly skimming off the foam and particles that rise to the top.

4. Lower the heat to a gentle simmer and add a pinch of salt. Simmer, skimming constantly, for about 1 hour, or until the liquid is quite clear.

5. Add the onion, carrot, celery, and leek along with the sachet and bring to a simmer. Cook at a bare simmer, skimming constantly, for about 6 hours, or until the stock is rich and flavorful.

6. Remove from the heat. Place a cone-shaped sieve into a container and carefully ladle the broth through the sieve into the container, one ladle at a time, taking care not to push on the solids. This step is very important as you do not want to upset the stock and reintroduce solid matter into the clear liquid. Discard the solids.

(continued)

7. Place the clear liquid into an ice bath to cool quickly and allow any remaining fat to solidify on top. Place the stock in a nonreactive container, cover, and refrigerate for 8 hours or overnight. The fat will solidify over the top and form a protective seal, which can be removed easily when the stock is used.

8. Store in a nonreactive container, covered and refrigerated, for up to 2 days or frozen for up to 3 months.

FORTIFIED CHICKEN STOCK: Heat 2 tablespoons olive oil in a medium stockpot over medium heat. Add 3 sliced shallots and sauté for about 5 minutes, or until nicely caramelized but not burned. Add 1 cup dry white wine and bring to a simmer. Simmer for about 30 minutes, or until the pan is almost dry. Stir in 4 pounds roasted chicken bones. Add 1 gallon chicken stock and bring to a simmer, skimming frequently to remove any impurities that rise to the top. Add the sachet (as for basic Chicken Stock) and simmer for about 1 hour, or until you have a rich, flavorful stock. Strain and store as directed.

Veal Stock

10 white peppercorns

3 fresh parsley stems

3 fresh thyme sprigs

1 bay leaf

8 pounds veal leg bones, cut crosswise into
   3-inch pieces

2 tablespoons canola oil

3 celery ribs, cut crosswise into chunks

2 carrots, cut crosswise into chunks

2 onions, cut into chunks with skin

$1/2$ cup tomato paste

Pinch of coarse salt

1. Combine the peppercorns, parsley, thyme, and bay leaf in a piece of cheesecloth about 6 inches square. Gather up the ends and, using kitchen twine, tie the bag closed. Set the sachet aside.

2. Place the bones in a colander and rinse under cold running water. Pat dry.

3. Preheat the oven to 400°F.

4. Place a medium roasting pan in the preheated oven for a couple of minutes, or until very hot. Remove from the oven and add the oil, moving the pan around to lightly coat the bottom with oil. Place the bones in the roasting pan in a single layer. Return to the oven and roast, stirring and turning occasionally, for about 35 minutes, or until golden brown. Remove from the oven and transfer the bones to a medium stockpot. Set aside. Do not turn off the oven.

5. Place the celery, carrots, and onions in the roasting pan, stirring to coat lightly with the fat in the pan. Place in the preheated oven and roast, stirring occasionally, for about 20 minutes, or until nicely caramelized. Remove from the oven and transfer the vegetables to a bowl. Set aside.

6. Place the roasting pan over 2 burners on the stovetop over medium heat. Add 1 cup water and stir constantly to deglaze the pan. Remove from the heat and strain the liquid in the pan through a fine sieve, discarding the solids and reserving the liquid.

7. Add 2 gallons of cold water to the bones. Place over medium heat and bring to a slow boil. Lower the heat to a gentle simmer and cook, frequently skimming off the foam and particles that rise to the top, for 2 hours.

(continued)

8. Add the tomato paste along with the re-served caramelized vegetables, pan liquid, and sachet and bring to a simmer. Add a pinch of salt and cook at a bare simmer, skimming constantly, for about 6 hours, or until the stock is rich and flavorful.

9. Remove from the heat. Place a cone-shaped sieve into a container and carefully ladle the broth through the sieve into the container, one ladle at a time, taking care not to push on the solids. This step is very important as you do not want to upset the stock and reintroduce solid matter into the liquid. Discard the solids.

10. Place the stock into an ice bath to cool quickly and allow any remaining fat to solid-ify on top. Place the stock in a nonreactive container, cover, and refrigerate for 8 hours or overnight. The fat will solidify over the top and form a protective seal, which can be removed easily when the stock is used.

11. Store in a nonreactive container, cov-ered and refrigerated, for up to 2 days or frozen for up to 3 months.

LAMB STOCK: Follow the directions for Veal Stock, replacing the veal bones with the same amount of lamb leg bones and eliminating the celery. Add another onion.

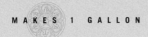

Rabbit Stock

10 fresh flat-leaf parsley stems

3 garlic cloves, crushed

2 bay leaves

2 whole cloves

1 cinnamon stick

8 pounds rabbit bones, cut into 3-inch pieces

2 tablespoons extra virgin olive oil

2 tablespoons tomato paste

2 onions, chopped

1 carrot, chopped

1 celery rib, chopped

$^1/_2$ cup Cabernet Sauvignon

$^1/_2$ cup Mavrodaphne wine

1 quart Chicken Stock (page 281)

1 quart Veal Stock (page 283)

1. Combine the parsley, garlic, bay leaves, cloves, and cinnamon stick in a piece of cheesecloth about 6 inches square. Gather up the ends and, using kitchen twine, tie the bag closed. Set the sachet aside.

2. Place the bones in a colander and rinse under cold running water. Pat dry.

3. Preheat the oven to 400°F.

4. Place a medium roasting pan in the preheated oven for a couple of minutes, or until very hot. Remove from the oven and add the oil, moving the pan around to lightly coat the bottom with oil. Place the bones in the roasting pan in a single layer and roast for 20 minutes. Rub the tomato paste into the bones and return to the oven. Roast, stirring and turning occasionally, for about 25 minutes, or until golden brown. Remove from

the oven and transfer the bones to a medium stockpot. Set aside. Do not turn off the oven.

5. Place the onions, carrot, and celery in the roasting pan, stirring to coat lightly with the fat in the pan. Place in the preheated oven and roast, stirring occasionally, for about 20 minutes, or until nicely caramelized. Remove from the oven and transfer the vegetables to a bowl. Set aside.

6. Place the roasting pan over 2 burners on the stovetop over medium heat. Add the wines to the pan and, using a wooden spoon, scrape the browned bits from the bottom to deglaze it. Cook for about 10 minutes, or until the liquid has reduced by half. Remove from the heat and strain through a fine sieve, discarding the solids. Pour the liquid into the stockpot.

7. Add the stocks to the stockpot along with 1 gallon cold water and place over medium-high heat. Bring to a slow boil, skimming off any impurities that rise to the top. Reduce the heat to a simmer and simmer, skimming frequently, for 1 hour. Add the reserved vegetables and sachet and continue to simmer for another 4 to 6 hours, or until the stock is well flavored.

8. Remove from the heat and strain through a fine sieve into a clean container. Place the container in a larger bowl of ice to bring the temperature down quickly. When cool, cover and refrigerate for up to 3 days or freeze for up to 3 weeks.

Clam Broth

12 large chowder clams

2 garlic cloves, sliced

2 fresh parsley stems

1 bay leaf

½ cup dry white wine

1. Using a kitchen scrub pad (such as a Dobie pad), vigorously wash the clams under cold running water. Place in a large bowl of cold water and swish the water to dislodge any remaining debris. Pour off the water and rinse the clams 2 or 3 more times, or until the water is perfectly clear.

2. Combine the garlic, parsley, and bay leaf in a large shallow nonreactive saucepan over medium heat. Add the wine and bring to a boil. Boil for about 5 minutes, or until reduced by half. Add 2 quarts water and bring to a simmer. Put the clams into the broth, cover, and raise the heat. Bring to a low simmer and cook for about 15 minutes, or until the clams have opened and a fragrant broth has formed. Turn off the heat and steep for 5 minutes.

3. Remove from the heat and drain well through a fine sieve, discarding the solids. Taste the broth. If too strongly flavored for your taste, add water, ¼ cup at a time. Place in an ice bath to cool quickly.

4. Store, covered and refrigerated, for up to 1 week or frozen for up to 3 weeks.

Molyvos Demi-Glace

1 gallon Veal Stock (see page 283)
¹/₂ cup dry red wine, such as Aghiorghitiko,
     Cabernet Sauvignon, or Sangiovese

I. Combine the stock with the red wine in a heavy saucepan over medium-low heat. Bring to a slow boil. Lower the heat and simmer, skimming off any impurities that rise to the surface, for about 40 minutes, or until reduced by half and the sauce coats the back of a metal spoon.

2. Remove from the heat and let rest for a few minutes. Skim off any impurities that rise to the surface. Strain through a fine sieve into a clean container. Place in an ice bath to quickly cool.

3. Store, covered and refrigerated, for up to 3 days. Demi-glace can also be frozen in an ice cube tray and then transferred from the tray to a resealable plastic bag and kept frozen for up to 3 weeks. Individual cubes can be used to enrich pan sauces.

Herb Tea

1 large carrot, cut into chunks

$^1/_2$ cup chopped onion

10 fresh flat-leaf parsley sprigs

5 peppercorns

3 allspice berries

3 whole cloves

3 garlic cloves, smashed

2 bay leaves

2 fresh mint sprigs

1 fresh thyme sprig

1 cinnamon stick

1 teaspoon fennel seeds

1 lemon, cut in half crosswise

I. Place the carrot, onion, and $2^1/_2$ quarts cold water in a large saucepan.

2. Add the parsley with the peppercorns, allspice, cloves, garlic, bay leaves, mint, thyme, cinnamon stick, and fennel seeds.

3. Squeeze the lemon juice into the mixture and then add the lemon to the pan.

4. Place the mixture over medium-low heat and bring to a simmer. Cook at a bare simmer for 25 minutes. Remove from the heat and set aside to steep for 10 minutes. Strain through a fine sieve, discarding the solids. If not using immediately, place the liquid in a clean container and store, covered and refrigerated, for up to 3 days.

NOTE: For some recipes I use an unspiced Herb Tea, which is simply this recipe without the peppercorns, allspice, cloves, cinnamon, and fennel.

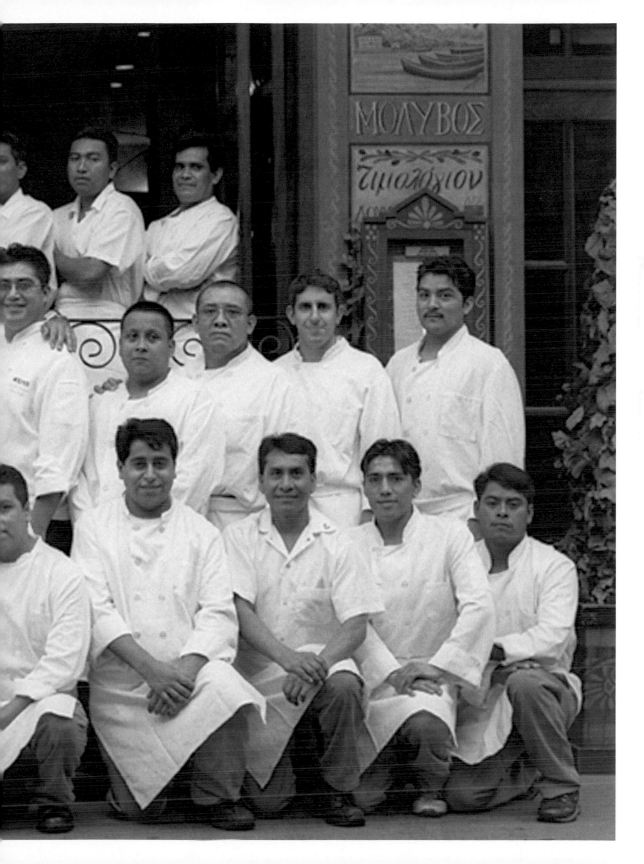

Sources

GREEK PRODUCTS

Athens Foods
13600 Snow Road
Cleveland, OH 44142
(216) 676–8500
Manufacturer of frozen Apollo
phyllo dough. Call for your
nearest retail outlet.

ethnicgrocer.com
Greek spices, olive oils, olives,
grains, and other Greek products.

Euro-USA
4 Hazel Drive
Pittsburgh, PA 15228
Fax: (412) 344–4599
Greek pastas including trahana,
Greek olives, and olive oils. Fax
for information on your nearest
retail outlet.

Hellas International, Inc.
35 Congress Street
Salem, MA 01970
(800) 274–1233
Greek olives, olive oils, vinegars,
and honeys. Call for your nearest
retail outlet.

**Kalustyan Oriental Export
Trading Company**
123 Lexington Avenue
New York, NY 10016
(212) 685–3451
kalustyans.com
Greek spices, Aleppo pepper,
grains, and beans.

Krinos Foods, Inc.
47–00 Northern Boulevard
Long Island City, NY 11101
(718) 729–9000
Frozen Krinos phyllo dough and
many other Greek products. Call
for your nearest retail outlet.

Mount Vikos
477 Laurel Avenue
St. Paul, MN 55102
(651) 298–0864
Greek olives, cheeses, and olive
oils. Call for your nearest retail
outlet.

Poseidon Bakery
629 Ninth Avenue
New York, NY 10036
(212) 757–6173
Fresh phyllo pastry.

Titan Foods
25–56 31st Street
Long Island City, NY
11102–1749
(718) 616–7771
titanfoods.com
Wide selection of Greek foods,
including barley rusks from Crete,
spices, mastic, olives, and frozen
prepared foods.

SPICES

Adriana's Caravan
404 Vanderbilt Avenue
Brooklyn, NY 11218
(800) 316–0820
adrianascaravan.com

The Spice Hunter
PO Box 8110
San Luis Obispo, CA
93403–8110
(800) 444–3061
spicehunter.com or e-mail at
consumerline@spicehunter.com

worldspice.com
Aleppo pepper and other
Greek spices.

GENERAL ETHNIC
AND SPECIALTY FOODS

Dean & Deluca
Mail Order Department
560 Broadway
New York, NY 10012
(800) 221–7714
deandeluca.com. Catalog available.

Zingerman's
620 Phoenix Avenue
Ann Arbor, MI 48108
(888) 636–8162
zingermans.com. Catalog available.

SEAFOOD

Browne Trading Corporation
260 Commercial Street
Portland, ME 04101
(800) 944–9848
browne-trading.com.

Citarella
2135 Broadway
New York, NY 10024
(212) 874–0383
citarella.com

GREEK CHEESES

Ideal Cheese
942 First Avenue
New York, NY 10012
(800) 382–0109
idealcheese.com

Murray's Cheese
254 Bleecker Street
New York, NY 10014
(212) 243–3289 or
(888) 692–4339
murrayscheese.com

Index

draining, 14
karydopita with orange spoon
    sweets and, 263–64
leek and cheese pie, 78–79
roasted Black Mission figs with
    almond praline and, 268–69
trahana, 13, 75; squash pie with
    rice, fennel, feta, and
    (kolokithopita), 73–74
tzatziki (Greek yogurt with
    cucumber, garlic, and
    mint), 34
yogurt béchamel sauce, 103
yogurt-garlic sauce, 37; bulgur

wheat and couscous pilaf
    with, 233–34; chilled baked
    gigantes with celery, onion,
    and tomatoes, 91–92;
    souvlaki with, 208–9;
    steamed salmon wrapped in
    grape leaves with bulgur
    salad, 170–72; vegetable
    dolmades with, 35–36
Youvetsi
    lamb, 198–200
    monkfish, with orzo and
    tomatoes, 175–76

Zucchini
    briam, 244–45
    didima, Gulf shrimp, zucchini,
    and marinated tomatoes,
    229–30
    octopus pie with rice,
    tomatoes, and, 85–86
    stuffed with rice, bulgur, pine
    nuts, and currants, 242–43
    vegetable moussaka, 246–47